When the going was rough

a Rhodesian story

JAMES MACBRUCE

When the going was rough
© Copyright Femina Publishers 1983
Forum Building, Struben Street, Pretoria, 0002

Cover design by Mariana Smuts
Photosetting in 10 on 12 pt Palatino
by Dieter Zimmermann (Pty) Ltd, Johannesburg
and printed and bound by National Book Printers, Goodwood, Cape
First edition, first impression 1983

ISBN 0 907996 68 x

Acknowledgements

The author's thanks goes to the artists and photographers, as well as the many voluntary organisations, clubs, associations and individuals throughout Manicaland who were kind enough to supply information, as well as to the photographers for permission to include their work in this book.

Dedication

To the memory of the men, women and children who died in Rhodesia during the bush war, 1972-1980.

Regard our Cross
Alive for more than 1900 years
And still the Man who died there
Hears.
Silent on a moonlit night
Mid stormy skies
He loves.
And sighs.
"Bemedalled city still beset with strife
Take heed. Love life,
But love Me more",
He seems to plead.
All those who died for what they thought was right
Are in His care.
He is not lonely there.

Umtali 1981

Cross Kopje – always lit at night before the terrorist war.

Contents

MCM Citation

Foreword – **General Du Toit**
  (*Former Chief Staff Officer, Military Intelligence*)

Introduction

Chapter:

1. Fireworks begin	1
2. All systems go	14
3. Children's war	20
4. Women's work	29
5. Influx of wounded	42
6. Shopper's nightmare	49
7. The brown jobs	58
8. The mushroom club	70
9. Pro rege, pro lege	78
10. Wind of change	93
11. Quo vadis?	101
12. Serving the nation	111
13. Angels of death	123
14. Spiritual war	129
15. The wheels keep turning	135
16. Why?	147
17. Stay at Rusape or not?	158
18. Attacks at Odzi	166
19. Bullets fly at Inyanga	178
20. Penhalonga hopes for the best	193
21. Vumba peace shattered	205
22. Shadows fall at Melsetter	214
23. The cost of survival	225
24. Evil comes to Chipinga	232
25. Aftermath	247

The Acting President of Rhodesia, Mr Jack Pithey, with the Mayor, Clr. Max Phillips, and the Meritorius Conduct Medal, awarded to the City of Umtali on March 2, 1979.

Citation

The award of the Meritorious Conduct Medal to the City of Umtali

The people of the City of Umtali have stood in the "front line" in the struggle against the forces of barbarism and tyranny since the closure of the Mozambique border in March 1976. Their steadfastness, courage and fortitude in the face of perpetual danger from terrorist attack both within and outside Rhodesia has been magnificent and deserving of the highest admiration.

While all Umtali residents have responded in splendid fashion to the needs of the hour, special mention is made of the devotion to duty of the members of the Civil Defence Organisation, Special Constabulary, the Red Cross and all other service organisations. In addition, the work of women's voluntary organisations in providing for the welfare of Security Force personnel has been quite outstanding. Hospitals and medical services have also played an outstanding role in the treatment of the many casualties, both civilian and Security Forces, from all parts of the Eastern Districts, which has been the scene of prolonged and intensive terrorist activity.

The business and industrial sectors of Umtali are also to be commended for the exemplary manner in which they have sustained the economic life of the City in the face of exceptional difficulties.

Because of the continuous threat to the City, those residents with a Security Force commitment have been called upon to undertake duties in excess of the normal commitment imposed on other Rhodesians and they have responded wholeheartedly to this call in defence of their City.

2nd March, 1979   Acting President of Rhodesia

Citation only reprinted from the original for Lions Club of Umtali

Gazetteer

Birchenough Bridge

A suspension-type bridge, 332 m long and 76,8 m high, spanning the Sabi River, 118 km from Umtali on the road to Fort Victoria. Completed in June 1935. The ashes of Sir Henry Birchenough, a British South Africa Company director, and his wife are in the eastern abutment.

Burma Valley

A low-lying (about 1 000 metres) farming area between the Vumba mountains and the Mozambique border, where cotton, burley tobacco, dessert nuts, bananas and tropical fruit are grown.

Cashel

92 km south of Umtali. Named after Sub-Inspector R. Cashel, BSA Police, who had a farm in the North Melsetter district. Area first known as Penkridge, the name of a farm where there was a postal agency. The district was inhabited by Steyn descendants, and Johannesrust post office was named in memory of one of them. It later became Tandaai and in 1957 Cashel. Produces vegetables, fruit, barley, wheat and cattle.

Chipinga

Part of a large area settled by Thomas Moodie and other trekkers and named Melsetter. South Melsetter became Chipinga in 1907, but was administered from Melsetter until 1920. It is hemmed in by mountains, has fertile soil and good rainfall. Area known as Gazaland. In 1924 tea was grown at New Year's Gift, expanding to other estates later. 183 km from Umtali. Dairying, coffee, wattle and mixed farming.

Inyanga

Area of mountains and streams, visited by Rhodes in 1897. He was so attracted that he bought a farm of 82 000 ha where he grew apples. The farm was bequeathed to the people of Rhodesia and has become a National Park containing the country's highest mountain, Mt Inyangani (2 594,8 m). Streams and dams have been stocked with trout, attracting fishermen in the season. Remains of ancient settlements cover a wide area. Four areas of development – Juliasdale (24 km from Inyanga on Rusape road), Rhodes Estate,

Inyanga village and Inyanga Downs (altitude 2 160 m). Produces tea, deciduous fruit, potatoes, timber and fish.

Inyazura

Important tobacco-growing area in Rusape district, 72 km from Umtali. Has produced outstanding rugby players. Railhead for Dorowa phosphate mine, 95 km south-west.

Melsetter

152 km south of Umtali in foothills of Chimanimani mountains, forming part of Mozambique boundary. Peaks rise to 2 450 m. Founded by Thomas Moodie in 1893, district was officially defined in 1895. Rhodes visited in 1897. Produces timber, fruit, coffee and cattle.

Mt Silinda

Site of American Board Mission established on land given by Rhodes in 1891, and the 2 500 ha Chirinda forest, one of the most interesting natural phenomena in the country with 45 m high trees, many centuries old. It is one of the last evergreen sub-tropical forests in the southern region.

Odzi

Tobacco-growing and mixed farming district 30 km from Umtali. Village started as postal agency in 1895. Railway siding in 1899. Region of rolling hills.

Penhalonga

Village in a valley 17 km from Umtali where three rivers meet. Nearby is ridge on Mozambique border where Rhodes first saw country that became Rhodesia. Name originally given to Penhalonga mine (opened February 1895) in honour of Count Penhalonga, founder, with Baron Rezende, of the Mozambique Company. J. H. Jeffreys discovered gold reefs that became Rezende Mine in 1889. More reefs were found and during 1920's Penhalonga was a boom town. Rezende finally closed in 1955. Site of first Umtali and place where country's nursing services started in 1891 when three nurses who had walked from Beira opened a camp hospital. Centre of a gold mining industry, forestry and mixed farming.

Rusape

93 km from Umtali. Established as administrative post by BSA Company in 1894. Developed when railway from Umtali to Salis-

bury went through. Centre for Makoni district which is tobacco, cattle and mixed farming area. Near the town is Lake Lesapi, built to store water for lowveld irrigation.

Umtali

Has had three sites. The first Umtali was a fort established in November 1890 near Penhalonga to protect Chief Mutasa from the Portuguese. Abandoned in 1891 when new township was established near Mutare River. Town moved again when it was found that Beira railway line could not be brought over the hills. New Umtali was laid out near railway route on same plan as old site with owners occupying same relative positions. Rhodes promised compensation to those who agreed to move. Many wood and iron buildings were carried over Christmas Pass to the new site. The town Sanitary Board held first meeting in new Umtali in September 1897. In 1899 a tramway was laid to connect the railway station to the town centre – the first and only tramway in Rhodesia. Old Umtali township was given to the American Methodist Church for a mission.

Proclaimed municipality June 1914. First municipal election August 5. On October 1, 1971, Umtali became a city and in November 1980 installed its first black Mayor.

A timber town, Umtali has timber industries, a cotton ginnery, food canning, milling concerns, grain depot, abattoir, coffee mill, nut process plant and a tea factory. There is also vehicle assembly, carpet, textile, rubber, glass, milk, leather, drink, foundry, engineering, processed food and service industries. The city is a major railway centre where a fleet of diesel electric locomotives and tank cars are repaired and maintained.

The city's northern boundary runs along a mountain range. To the east is Mozambique. There are hills to the south and a valley on the west, carrying the railway line to Salisbury.

Vumba

A mountainous area, 32 km from Umtali in the south-east, on the border with Mozambique. Was originally the home of Mbire tribe. White settlement began soon after a township was established at Old Umtali when Lionel Cripps acquired 1 800 ha which he called Cloudlands. The area produces coffee, timber and fruit.

Foreword

This narrative of the War in Rhodesia as experienced by civilians in Manicaland and especially Umtali, made a deep and lasting impression on me and I deem it a privilege to have been asked to contribute this Foreword.

The scenic Manicaland, bordering on Mozambique in which thousands of Zanu terrorists were based since 1975, was probably the most terrorist activated part of Rhodesia. Umtali, the capital right on the border, was also in the front line and an easy target for the heaviest weapons Zanu had at its disposal. The conduct of her citizens under the most trying conditions earned for Umtali the unique honour, very seldom bestowed, of a decoration, in this case the Meritorious Conduct Medal.

For the writing of this book, the author collected first-hand experiences of many persons involved, covering a wide diversity of events. This is skilfully blended into a most readable, comprehensive account. Although he is clearly and unashamedly emotionally involved as a white patriotic Rhodesian, his narrative is factual and professionally written. Posterity will be thankful to him for preserving this wealth of historical material.

The courage, grit and determination of Rhodesians to hold fast to values they held dear and the inventiveness and operational ability against overwhelming odds which emerge from this narrative, sets an inspiring example to all South Africans. It will also be a valuable source of study for students of revolutionary warfare.

The author does not claim to have given the complete picture. He does not deal with the terrorist side or with the purely military, political and strategic angles. These can only be included in a comprehensive history when the passing of time will bring respective.

Then perhaps it will also become more clear to us why the West tried so hard to destabilise Rhodesia or stood unconcernedly by whilst a highly developed country and civilisation with a vast potential for all its inhabitants was being destroyed. Perhaps then we shall also understand why the setting of Zimbabwe on the path of a bleak, unhappy Marxist future is regarded as such a pinnacle of achievement for Lord Carrington and the British Government.

H DE V DU TOIT
Lt Gen (ret) SSA SM

Introduction

On April 18, 1980, Rhodesia ceased to exist. At midnight the new, black-ruled state of Zimbabwe was born when the Prince of Wales handed over the Independence instrument to the President before a huge crowd in a Salisbury football stadium. The Union Jack was hauled down and the Zimbabwe flag, with its red star and Zimbabwe bird, was raised for the first time.

In the morning the British Governor, his bags already packed, departed. The 'Rhodesian problem' had been solved, an 'illegal regime' brought to its knees after 15 years in power and a majority-rule government installed in Britain's last African 'colony'. The sun of freedom had at last risen north of the Limpopo, and the world rejoiced.

Whites in the country were shocked and bewildered at the turn of events. Their enemies of only a few months before were now giving the orders, victorious not on the field of battle, but in a political take-over, planned far away, in a London conference room.

These same whites had lived under three Prime Ministers (Smith, Muzorewa and Mugabe) and four flags (those of Rhodesia, Zimbabwe-Rhodesia, Britain and Zimbabwe) in less than two years. Saddened and disillusioned, many of them packed up and left the country they loved. Thousands more have since followed. For them the changes that have taken place in socialist Zimbabwe have been unbearable. Denigrated as 'colonialist oppressors' by a 'progressive' people's government, harangued and abused by virtually every Government minister who speaks, and powerless to do anything to delay the headlong rush to an instant new order, the future, to many whites, has seemed hopeless. And so they have gone.

Under the new order all links with the past must be severed. The name Rhodesia and anything connected with it must be buried. No acknowledgment must be made of any achievements under white rule, nor of the development which, in a short 90 years, turned a primitive country and people into a viable 20th century state. It is obvious now that history in this part of Africa is going to begin in 1980.

The conviction that history cannot be ignored and the past just be swept under the carpet has produced this book. It is a part of the Rhodesian story. It tells how a handful of ordinary people stood up to years of violence, bloodshed and hate.

It is the story of the 'bush' war in Manicaland, the most easterly of Rhodesia's five provinces and bordered by Mozambique, with the attractive little city of Umtali, set in a basin surrounded by hills, as its hub.

The events described in the book are true, but they are by no means all that happened. To record everything would take several volumes.

The author lived among the people he has written about, sharing their sorrows and joys, the idealism and the effort, and feels it is his duty to tell other people now, before it is too late, how white Rhodesians reacted when the going was rough.

It has been humbling to listen to so many stories of courage, grit and determination that have come out of those troubled years. It is thrilling to realise how, under adversity, people will come together for the good of the community and serve others without counting the cost to themselves. It takes a crisis situation to get such 'togetherness'.

It is salutory, too, to realise the burden that was carried by so few for so many for so long. Umtali's population at the beginning of 1976 (the year the war hotted up in Manicaland) was 9 800 whites, 600 Asians, 600 Coloureds and 51 000 blacks. It was the whites, with a sprinkling of brown-skinned people, who kept the welfare organisations running, raised funds for every conceivable need, served their fellow countrymen in a number of voluntary capacities as canteen workers, special and reserve police, in civil defence, to name only some of the voluntary services, and kept the wheels of everyday life turning as well.

As a frontline city that came under direct enemy attack, Umtali had a unique role in the war. The fortitude of its people was honoured by the award of a Meritorious Conduct Medal in 1979.

But, as the Mayor of the day pointed out when he accepted the medal, Umtali is the capital of Manicaland and any honour presented to the city embraced all those living in the towns, villages and lonely farmhouses to the north, west and south who had borne the brunt of hostilities in the area.

"These people are our friends; they do their business with us, supply us with our food and the raw materials for our factories," he said. "Some have been forced to leave their homes and now live among us. Many have lost a husband, a wife or children. We mourn with them. No praise is too high for their steadfast endeavour."

That, in a nutshell, was the story of Manicaland at war, and that endeavour is the shining thread which the author has tried to weave into the tapestry of life that makes up this book.

No apologies are made for two omissions: politics and the 'chimurenga'* (revolution) fighters' view of the war in Manicaland. The world will have an endless supply of books on both topics in the years ahead: but the whites will be forgotten and their hopes, fears and sufferings ignored or derided as honour is paid to the new liberators – the 'freedom fighters', the 'boys in the bush', the 'guerillas' or 'comrades' of the 'hondo'* (war) – call them what you will.

I call these men terrorists. That is how they were known until 1980, and that is what they were, 'sicarii' – men of the dagger (in this case the gun) – waiting in ambush for unsuspecting families, killing people at work, attacking lonely farmhouses at night, murdering children, burning buses and, the most cowardly tactic of all, indiscriminately laying landmines.

Even more incomprehensible is the fact that they terrorised fellow blacks and destroyed many of the facilities, such as clinics, schools, dip tanks and bridges, painstakingly built up in the rural areas over the years, and now being replaced, at great cost, with overseas aid.

Since Independence, Prime Minister Mugabe has been preaching reconciliation. It is difficult for those who have suffered so much to adopt a conciliatory attitude, to turn the other cheek and forget all that has gone before. It is to the great credit of so many people, black and white, that they are trying to do just that. May God bless them for their sacrifice and courage. Their faith has inspired those who are left to go forward, God willing, into a brighter future.

*Shona words

1 Fireworks begin

"The people of the City of Umtali have stood in the front line in the struggle against the forces of barbarism and tyranny since the closure of the Mozambique border in March 1976."

– MCM CITATION

Anger, indignation, panic ... all of these filled the hearts and minds of thousands of bewildered people in a pretty little Rhodesian city very early one morning in 1976.

Rudely awakened from sleep by crashes and bangs at 04h00, it took a little while for realisation to dawn on them. Umtali was being attacked.

It was a new experience for the young. Older folk remembered cities being bombed in an earlier war in another continent. The date was Wednesday, August 11, 1976.

A somewhat terse report in that day's *Umtali Post* recorded the historic event. "Umtali came under rocket and mortar attack from Mozambique just after 04h00 today," the report said. "The spasmodic fire lasted for half an hour and bomb damage was inflicted on houses in Greenside and Darlington. There were no reported casualties."

It was the first attack made on a Rhodesian city from a neighbouring country. It came after news of the Army's 'hot pursuit' into Mozambique four days before.

A mother living in Circular Drive, Greenside, the Umtali street nearest to the international boundary, has a vivid recollection of that night.

"I was awakened by a noise in the distance, rather like rolling thunder. I got up and was standing by the window trying to place the sound when suddenly I saw several big red balls travelling in an arc through

1

the sky between me and Cross Kopje,* just across the road. Next there was a big bang and the street light opposite the house went out. I realised then what was happening and ran to call my son, asleep in the next room.

"He was in the Army, doing his National Service, and had just come home on leave. He wouldn't wake up and the banging went on. Eventually I managed to get through to him that we were being attacked and persuaded him to leave his bed and come into the passage.

"Then the telephone rang. I didn't really want to answer because it meant going into the living room where there are large windows looking onto the road where the bombs had fallen. The caller was another son, anxious to know if I was all right. 'Lie down on the floor!' he ordered, having just got me up from there.

"At dawn I joined the neighbours out in the street looking at the damage. Three bombs had dropped nearby, one in the middle of the tar outside my house. A number of windows had been shattered in the house next door, but mine was untouched. It was a miracle."

The city's civil defence system went into action, after months of practice, immediately after the first bang. Volunteers stood by until daylight, reassuring the public and waiting for further emergencies.

Some people panicked. They jumped into their cars while the bombs were still falling and drove up Christmas Pass (where the main road to Salisbury climbs over the mountain range on the western side of the city). Some took refuge in the Cecil Hotel, near the Police Station. Others packed their belongings in the morning and left for good.

The editor of *The Umtali Post* wrote in a leading article: "The war is now in our back yard. How we live with it is up to each and every one of us . . . We will win through this thing by keeping our heads cool, our wits sharp, our faith bright, and our powder very dry. God bless you all."

A mother of four sons, who were all to join the security forces in turn, said of that historic first attack:

"I woke up at about four in the morning to the sound of distant thumping. Then came the rattle of smallarms fire. I thought, 'They wouldn't dare! They wouldn't be so foolish as to launch a mortar attack on Umtali!'

"There was no time for further speculation. There was a devastating explosion, followed by several more. I sat bolt upright and shook my husband. 'Darling! They're bombing us!'

---

*A kopje topped with a large cross which was floodlit at night.

2

"'Yes, dear. I know. I heard!'

"Our three sons were home at the time – a lucky circumstance because usually two were in the Army, the youngest still at school. Our fourth son was married and living two blocks away.

"Ashley, who had a foot injury, swung past on his crutches issuing conflicting instructions. 'Get down on the floor! Get dressed. No lights. Draw the curtains.' There followed a scrabble for clothes. In the dark my husband, in his agitation and irritation, could find nothing suitable for the occasion, and he proceeded to lecture me on the size of my oft-proclaimed 'meagre wardrobe', my lack of system and general incompetence.

"I giggled and crawled into the passage feeling a prize idiot. It was 45 years since I'd been down on all fours. The boys were dumping a polythene mattress in the passage and peering through the windows to see where the firing was coming from.

"The front door was open as I moved in a crouching position to 'phone our eldest son. There was no answer. This could mean they'd been hit or were, incredibly, still asleep.

"'Those kids will sleep through anything', I muttered, just as their car pulled up outside. Les and his wife ran across the moonlit lawn. He was already in uniform, rifle and webbing at the ready.

"We were all together and that was all that mattered. Although the crumping and rattling continued for a short time, it seemed an age, while we expected the roof to cave in or broken glass to crash around us.

"Our family's reaction was mainly indignation – with a rousing cheer at first light for the sight and sound of our own jets sweeping across the morning sky, to wreak vengeance on the enemy – we hoped."

The noise of that first bombardment woke a couple on their farm at Odzi, 32 km from Umtali. They heard a sound like a roll of thunder away to the east.

"Thunder?" she asked sleepily.

"That's not thunder," her husband replied (he'd been in the Second World War), "that's the sound of mortars." He sprang out of bed. "They couldn't, surely, be attacking Umtali?"

They stood at the back door of their home and saw, on the horizon, huge splashes of light streaking the dark night sky with red. The noise accompanying each flash rolled over the hills and shook the window-panes in the farmhouse.

"My heart felt cold. Our daughter was living alone in a flat in Umtali. We had many friends there too. Each time the sky lit up and we heard the terrible boom of a mortar landing I wondered where the bombs were dropping.

"By now I was praying hard and sincerely," she said. "I remembered: 'Perfect love casteth out fear.'

'He that dwelleth in the secret place of the Most High shall abide under the shadow of the Almighty.'"

Next morning they drove to town to help where needed. Topping Christmas Pass and looking down on the little city lying in its basin between mountain ranges they were prepared to see broken buildings, crumbled walls, holes in the streets.

The pride and joy of a Darlington resident, this vintage car was damaged in the first rocket and mortar attack on Umtali in August 1976.

"It looks exactly the same," she cried out. "There's no damage to see."

Their daughter was fine and as they walked up Main Street they met friends and strangers who responded to their smiles and told of their experiences.

"If you didn't believe in God before and you were in Umtali last night, you believe in Him now!" a stranger said to them.

They heard of Jean, a young schoolgirl who suddenly decided to sleep in the spare room and not in her own bed.

4

"Just for fun!" she pleaded with her mother. A rocket cut her bed in half four hours later.

The Society for the Prevention of Cruelty to Animals collected 14 stray dogs after that first attack on Umtali. People had been drilled about taking shelter in passages, but forgot all about their animals. Terrified dogs and cats just ran away from the noise of bursting bombs. One dog, which lived in Greenside near Addams Barracks, was found a week later, cowering under a pile of wood near the SPCA kennels on the opposite side of the city. A Labrador was taken out of a swimming pool in Murambi.

Most of the animals were picked up with bleeding paws which had to be treated and bandaged. An Alsatian, missing for several days, was eventually found in another suburb with its feet torn to ribbons. A long time after the attack an injured dog was picked up in Sakubva, under an upturned wheelbarrow. It was found to have brain damage and was put down.

The next issue of *The Umtali Post* was on Friday, August 13. It presented an aptly gloomy front page – deaths, injuries, funerals, landmine victims, foresters fired on. The war was 'hotting up' all at once in Umtali and district.

But inside was a wonderfully heart-warming picture of one of Umtali's most respected citizens, the headmistress of Umtali Girls' High School. Smiling broadly, she was being driven down Main Street in style in a heavily-armoured car at the head of an impromptu schools' procession.

"Rhodesians Never Die" sang the pupils of Umtali Girls' High School as they marched down Main Street to show the world they were not scared by mortar bombs and rockets from Mozambique. Riding in the armoured car at the head of the procession is the headmistress.

It was the pupils' own idea. Undeterred by explosions near their boarding hostels the previous night, they marched through the streets singing 'Rhodesians Never Die', and hit the international headlines with their courage and high spirits.

Meanwhile the Manicaland Agricultural Show had opened as usual on Thursday, August 12. The showgrounds were full with a three-day programme of events which drew the crowds.

'What to Do When Mortars Fall', with full instructions for household safety, were issued by the Mayor, his Civil Defence Aide and the Police.

Plans were drawn for various types of bomb shelters and people started digging in their backyards or creating safe areas in their homes with sandbags and timber reinforcing. Windows and glass doors were 'taped' to cut down the danger of flying glass, and neighbours vied with one another in the patterns they produced on their street-facing windows.

Each night there was an additional bedtime chore – filling a flask with boiling water for coffee and putting aside clothes, torch and blankets where they could be easily found if a dash to the bunker was necessary.

Three months later, in November, the second attack on the city gave *The Umtali Post* the chance to say that Guy Fawkes Day had been celebrated a little earlier than usual.

Householders had been asked not to light fireworks on November 5, but those on the other side of the border decided to send over a few of their own brand, as a reminder, on November 3.

Wednesday is early closing day in Umtali and there were no shoppers and few cars about when the attack began at 17h15.

Two office workers, finishing off a job in a city centre building, stopped typing in midsentence when there was a loud bang nearby. The cleaner, who had been swabbing floors, dropped his bucket and fled. He joined the stream of Africans running down Main Street towards Sakubva.*

The two women, following official instructions, went into the basement of their building and huddled together waiting for the bombardment to continue. After waiting some time they decided they had better get home before darkness fell and the attack was renewed. They locked up, said goodbye and drove off in opposite directions, each thinking it was probably the last time she would see the other!

For the one, who lived in Greenside, it was to be an uncomfortable night spent in the new bomb shelter in the garden. For her companion,

---

*An African township on the outskirts of Umtali.

whose home was on the other side of Christmas Pass, it was a night of tension as she worked on Police Reserve duty, expecting to hear the noise of an attack on Umtali.

That Wednesday was an unforgettable one for two old age pensioners, George and May.

George (70) was in Salisbury visiting a sick son in hospital. He had every intention of spending the night there. But an intuition, "God's guidance, if you like", persuaded him to leave Salisbury and hurry home that afternoon.

As he drew up outside their home in Palmerston, his wife May (72) left the chair she habitually sat in to crochet and went out onto the verandah to greet him. Seconds later a rocket whistled overhead.

The couple, who had celebrated their golden wedding the week before, hugged each other. Then came a tremendous whistle and explosion as a second rocket hit a tree at the side of their house, burst into jagged fragments, gouged holes in the garden and road and shattered all the windows in the house.

"My wife's behaviour was fantastic. She was so brave. She just said that we had lived together for 50 years and we might as well die together," George said afterwards. "She wouldn't leave and spend the night elsewhere. We went out for a while to friends and then returned to clear up the glass and dig out the chunks of metal in the garden. We are lucky to be alive."

Four rockets landed in Umtali that evening, but life went on as usual. At the Courtauld Theatre sea horses and crabs, mermaids and ducks pirouetted about the stage as the Ballet Jeunesse danced on to entertain the city's senior citizens at the final rehearsal for the show.

One 122 mm rocket failed to explode. It was bedded in Fourth Avenue, opposite a motor showroom. After hours of digging, 'The Thing' was finally removed by Army engineers.

The *Umtali Post* had this to say: "Umtali has now endured its second missile attack from across the border. And for the second time, by the grace of God, no one was hurt. This is truly a matter for thanksgiving.

"The city can be very proud of its young people in particular. The ballet dancers carried on in the true tradition of the stage, while Umtali Girls' High pupils refused to let a few bangs put them off their studies.

"The spirit of a city under attack is summed up in the reaction of the elderly Palmerston couple whose home was damaged. They cleared up the mess and stayed put.

"From what happened on Wednesday it is clear that most people have learnt the lessons that Civil Defence hammered home after the

2nd/Lieut. Kobus Kirschner, of Engineer Squadron, with "The Thing", the unexploded 122 mm rocket, dug out of an Umtali street opposite a motor showroom in November 1976.

attack on the city in August. Remember them? Don't go outside to watch; move into the safest part of your house; draw the curtains; keep away from the windows; stay put; don't use the telephone except in case of real need. Simple advice, but it works.

"Those who dug shelters in their gardens after the first attack made use of them – and found ou⁺ the hard way what mistakes had been made in the design and construction.

"But there was one thing missing on the home front that night – communications.

"People were told through Civil Defence after the last attack that the broadcast band (old Radio Manica) would be used to keep them informed in any future incidents.

"On Wednesday those sheltering in bunkers or in their homes dutifully took their radios with them, switched on, and learnt precisely nothing about the one thing of vital concern to all in Umtali – the attack.

"There are little old ladies living on their own all over the city, as well as elderly men and young widows. It would help them all to keep calm on these occasions if they knew a bit more of what was going on – which bangs were ours, for example – and when the all clear had been given. Wardens passed on the message when they could, but not everyone has a telephone, and who can visit every house, flat and bunker in the city?

"Umtali can take it alright, but the powers-that-be must not forget that those who are not in the know need some reassurance when under fire."

Umtali had to go on 'taking it' for there were more attacks in 1978 and 1979.

On Thursday night, September 7, 1978, the city survived another pounding. Four people were injured and rushed to hospital. Several families had miraculous escapes. Hundreds of windows were shattered and the Mayor's garden was peppered with rockets, but it was 'business as usual' for all in the morning.

The following month there was a bombardment (and retaliation) which continued for 40 minutes. This was on Sunday night, October 15, and it was the longest and loudest of the attacks. 150 bombs and rockets were fired from three positions on Umtali Heights and Cecil Kop.* The outpatients' department and nurses' home at the Hospital were damaged. Two mortar bombs and 13 rockets landed in the grounds of

---

*Mountains overlooking Umtali.

Chancellor Junior School opposite the hospital, but the children sat it out in their safe places.

Again the hand of God was over the city and no one was killed, though there were several direct hits on houses. And once again people met together to praise and thank God for His deliverance.

In the first half of 1979 Dangamvura* was attacked twice. The first attack was light and abortive, but on April 8 the area was subjected to a heavy rocket, mortar and smallarms attack. Two pairs of semi-detached houses were destroyed and many others were holed by shrapnel and bullets. Remarkably, there was only one fatality.

Before the war officially ended, both Umtali and Dangamvura were attacked again.

On October 8, 1979, a group of between 20 and 25 armed men opened fire on the city from Cecil Kop with mortars and recoilless rifles. The shooting started at 12h20 and lasted about 40 minutes. Homes in the northern suburbs of Tiger's Kloof and Morningside bore the brunt of the attack.

In Vumba Avenue, where two bombs landed in the backyard, a housewife said: "When the missiles started coming over I tried to get under my bed for shelter, but got stuck. We saw the bombs flying over and when they were near we ducked. Five fell close to us."

A house in Arcadia Road received a direct hit, but the owners, awakened by the first explosions, were sheltering in the laundry downstairs.

Earlier that same night Aloe Park Motel, on the opposite side of the mountain from Umtali, had been mortared. Although many of the rooms were sprayed with shrapnel the guests escaped unhurt.

A house in the Umtali suburb of Fairbridge Park came under smallarms fire in November. The shooting was seen and heard at the Municipal Infectious Diseases Hospital nearby. The staff brought all the patients from their beds to the safe area, which happened to be a corridor, and gave them tea.

"We were all huddled together, typhoid next to measles, cracking jokes. No one seemed any the worse for the experience, nor the contact," said a patient afterwards.

Dangamvura was attacked for the third time in less than a year at 22h20 on August 27. Smallarms, rockets and recoilless rifles were used against a housing and school complex and one black man was injured.

---

*An African (home ownership) township on the southern outskirts of Umtali.

Apart from broken windows, holed houses and roofs, little damage was done.

In 1979 attacks were again made on Umtali peri-urban areas. A home in Weirmouth, not far from Dangamvura, was attacked twice, with stick grenades, mortars, rockets and smallarms. Terrorists also operated in Fern Valley, south of the city. A white woman was murdered in her home and houses were attacked. A bus was ambushed at the entrance to Dangamvura, and a black man killed in the incident.

*   *   *

It's no fun being called out of bed to sit in a corridor in the middle of the night, with your hair in curlers, cream on your face, your teeth in a glass beside the bed and your 80th birthday long behind you.

"But Strickland Lodge's old dears learnt to laugh about it," said the sister-in-charge of this Umtali home for the elderly.

During the first bombardment the older ones led the singing with First and Second World War songs, *Roll out the Barrel* and *We're Gonna Hang out the Washing on the Siegfried Line*, echoing through the corridors while the bombs thudded down.

"At Strickland Lodge, until the intensification of the rocket and mortar attacks in 1978, the war seemed to belong to another world," the sister said. "Those who had sons in the security forces nursed their private fears – like mothers throughout the country.

"Newspaper headlines, contact after contact, ambush after ambush, and the rising death toll in the locality had the same effect here as on all other citizens," she said.

Isolated from the grim side of war, however, the elderly were not much affected until the first bad attack, which took them by surprise and from which they emerged shocked and fearful. Later the sudden attacks, followed by a false alarm, told on their nerves.

There was never any panic, no outward sign of fear, only flinching as a door slammed shut. In the morning they would say: "Did you hear all those bangs last night? I was out of bed and into my dressing-gown before I realised it was only a landmine. Then I couldn't get back to sleep again."

As there was no 'safe place' in Strickland Lodge, the only thing to do in an attack was to attempt to get 37 old people, some with hearing aids switched off, out of bed and into the corridor under a single roof, to stick it out together, the sister-in-charge explained.

Residents of Strickland Lodge vividly recall one particularly dangerous rocket attack.

11

Mugs of hot, sweet tea cheer the old dears at Zororai, Sakubva.

The women apologised for curlers and face cream. Some were caught without their teeth. The explosions came thick and fast and each one was accompanied by a murmured prayer from the old folk. Suddenly, there was a tremendous blast close to the building. Next morning they found that a tree about 27 m away had been shredded by a rocket. This diverted the missile and prevented a direct hit on the Lodge.

Those residents who had been through the blitz on London or other cities were nonchalant. One man was almost reluctant to leave his bed. "The old people had complete faith in God's protection," the sister said.

After an attack it was 'sweet tea and Valium' all round. Umtali's senior citizens became blasé enough to laugh over the breakfast menu that appeared after one attack. It read:

Breakfast

(or: The Morning After)

Bombed banana
Oatmeal surprise
Screaming scrambled eggs
Terrorist tea and toast
Cuban coffee
Mao's Mortared marmalade

But the war continued and took an even more severe turn with bombs in shops. A Strickland Lodge resident was only centimetres away from the second of the devastating city bomb blasts. By a miracle she was not hurt.

At Zororai, a black old folks' home in Sakubva, local white benefactors did their best to improve the accommodation and standards of living for more than 50 old tribesmen and women, otherwise homeless, who had lived there for some years.

They, too, scrambled under their beds as fast as ageing limbs would allow when the rockets pounded down, trembling when the war moved close and the city's industrial area and Dangamvura were attacked.

2 All systems go

"While all Umtali residents have responded in splendid fashion to the needs of the hour, special mention is made of the devotion to duty of the members of the Civil Defence Organisation, Special Constabulary, the Red Cross and all other service organisations."

– MCM CITATION

After the first attack on Umtali from Mozambique the Mayor's Civil Defence Aide wrote: "No one was injured, by the grace of God. It was a blessing in disguise. Although we did not have to go into action, all the indications were that the system we have built up worked well."

Umtali had been preparing for trouble for some years. Officially it was called "taking measures to prepare for ... any natural disaster or major accident ... or an attack on the community."

The city and suburbs were divided into 12 wards, with an elected Warden, Deputy Warden and a few sub-wardens for each. Wardens' telephone numbers were given to everyone living in the ward and residents were encouraged to get to know their neighbours. There were regular wardens' meetings. First aid courses were organised, fire-fighting equipment was obtained and fire-drill held. Security of buildings was investigated and emergency and disaster plans drawn up. Realistic exercises were held and an intricate network of trained volunteers was built up throughout Umtali. The Mayor of the time directed this fine organisation which assumed a fully active role from late 1974.

With only their safety helmets, armbands and car stickers to identify them, Civil Defence members were responsible for preventing panic and maintaining the well-being of the community. Their most important role was probably that of panic prevention, and a system was effectively developed which enabled anyone to contact someone else in time of need.

During raids many people were comforted and reassured in this way. Then Radio Umtali was used to broadcast messages from the authorities. Many lonely and elderly folk switched on during a night attack to hear the brief reports. Residents were asked to switch off all the lights and remain in their houses or shelters.

How many of us remember *Edelweiss* being played endlessly during the small hours while families settled themselves beneath beds and in passages to wait out the storm of explosions and shattering glass?

Although a stream of cars was seen speeding over Christmas Pass when the first attack came, panic was averted. The public was reassured and found faith in the service provided by Civil Defence. Time and again the Chief of Police said: "We could not have managed without the assistance of Civil Defence." Other centres were impressed. They came to Umtali to learn how it was done. In the words of one Mayor: "It is difficult to be precise in providing the answer, but to generalise, the success achieved is due principally to all Civil Defence workers in Umtali who have given unstintingly of their spare time over the years, training for the event, and specifically to the devoted group of controllers and wardens who have responded to the challenge, encouraged others to take part, particularly in the training, and, in actual attacks, have responded to their duties in a manner far beyond that required of them in their briefings."

A great deal was learnt from the first attack and it is to the credit of those in control that Umtali benefited from this and was able to improve its Civil Defence organisation still further.

A siren was installed in October 1977 to warn people who had not heard the first bangs. There was no all clear, however. This could have been heard over the border.

Many exercises were held in each ward, as well as several combined ones which enabled the public to see that an efficient organisation had been built up. This had much to do with the high standard of morale, while the *esprit de corps* which developed from the meetings and exercises was truly encouraging.

Teams were trained in first aid, fire-fighting and the use of portable two-way radios. Each warden had a radio in his home, enabling the control room to make immediate contact and allowing wardens to speak to key personnel much more quickly. Before that there had been considerable jamming of the telephone system. *Friends of Rhodesia* in South Africa helped provide the radios, which cost thousands of dollars, following a visit of Civil Defence men to several centres in the Republic.

In 1977 the Umtali Ministers' Fraternal objected to mock Civil Defence exercises on Sundays. The Civil Defence Aide pointed out that he had only organised three in two years and that Sunday was the best, if not the only day when all could take part.

One Sunday morning a Greenside housewife was disturbed by a great commotion outside. Going out so see what was happening, she found 'casualties' all over her verandah and a fire blazing beside the house on the empty plot next door. As she appeared she was doused with water by a fire-fighting team, battling to put out the blaze. Rushing indoors she berated everyone until her husband sheepishly ad-

After the first attack on Umtali, bomb shelters were built in many suburban gardens.

mitted that the exercise had been arranged with him, but that he had forgotten to tell her!

Another Greenside team was putting out a fire during an exercise when the municipal fire engine arrived. Deciding to add realism to the scene the brigade turned on their hoses and sprayed everything with water, including the team. The Civil Defence volunteers were annoyed at the time, but could laugh about it afterwards.

Bomb shelters were built in many suburban gardens and wardens found themselves with another job – inspecting their safety. Some shelters were highly sophisticated, with electric light, telephone extension and running water. In other cases people dug pits, covering them with wattle poles and sandbags. When the rains came the holes filled with water. Mosquitoes bred in them, then termites damaged the wood. Wardens advised these people to stay in their homes, preferably in a passage near necessities like a toilet, light, food and, above all, telephone and radio.

One mother, living on her own with three children, decided the linen cupboard in the passage was a good safe area. She put the children in, only to find there was no more room for mum.

An enthusiastic Army sergeant major started firearms courses for civilians and gave up much of his leisure to instruct women and farming groups in the use of their own pistols, revolvers and other weapons for self-defence.

Housewives, mothers and city office workers learn to shoot in self-defence.

The Army also experimented at the range to see how best to protect the public from shattering glass. While shatterproof glass gave the best results it was expensive, so transparent tape or vinyl film was recommended and windows throughout the city were soon taped up.

Umtali was subjected to eight rocket and mortar attacks from Mozambique and from within Rhodesia. In addition three suburbs were attacked by terrorists using automatic weapons and hand grenades.

Most attacks took place at night or in the early hours of the morning, and on all occasions Civil Defence workers went into action, sometimes while the bombs were falling. The attacks varied in intensity and duration, some lasting 10 minutes, others up to two hours. In the short attacks between 20 and 30 bombs fell on the city, but in the longer ones 400 or more mortar bombs and rockets fell. Four people were killed and 10 injured.

There were many miraculous escapes, several involving Civil Defence personnel. A controller, Freda, acting as liaison officer between the General Hospital, the Civil Defence control and urban ops rooms, was at the hospital on duty during the city's heaviest attack in October 1978. Atmospheric conditions were poor and to find the best position for her low-powered transmitter she moved into the open. A number of bombs hit the hospital grounds, damaging buildings and installations and starting a fire. Freda went on working. Next morning it was found that the fire escape where she had been standing only seconds before the bombs fell had been riddled by shrapnel.

Three controllers, Mary, Leila and Helen, whose duty it was to man the radios and telephones at the Civil Defence control room in the Civic Centre as soon as an attack started, were always the first to arrive. They had to travel more than three km through much of the city to reach their post, and the routes they travelled were often subjected to direct hits from mortars and rockets, some bursting within 27 m of their vehicles. Once two mortar bombs exploded in the garden of the house immediately opposite two of the women (who were neighbours) while they were getting into their cars to go to the Control Room. Another mortar landed on the tarmac of the road they used within minutes of their passing the spot. Undeterred, they carried on with their duties.

As the Mayor said afterwards, it was the dedication and sense of civic duty of these women, none of them young, in the face of danger, that was the finest example of unselfish motivation. "Without this motivation it would be very difficult, if not impossible, for Civil Defence to continue to function with the high degree of success and efficiency which has rewarded its efforts," he added.

Umtali folk slept soundly most nights, secure in the knowledge that they were watched over both by Civil Defence and the Special Constabulary, affectionately known as the 'Wombles'.

These men, with no military commitment, who were over-age for other services, or in some way unfit for more active duties, gave their leisure time unstintingly for the peace of others. Dressed in blue overalls and hard hats and carrying batons, they patrolled the streets after dark, walking in pairs.

"We never went armed," said a long-serving member. "We were issued with baton, handcuffs and whistle and had to provide our own torches. We worked a four to five hour shift, with full weekend duties, and we rarely had any drama." For some of them it was a nightly chore, stepping out on a leisurely beat, checking homes and the comings and goings in the streets of the suburbs where they lived.

"If anything illegal was spotted, the Charge Office was told immediately. It was a great comfort to many wives and families alone while husbands were on call-up duty, as well as business and shop owners. We were on duty during the attacks and were able to help."

In 1977 there were only 60 men in the service which had been operating for many years. After an appeal by the Wombles' Chief Warden, the Umtali force was stepped up to 146, all volunteers, and some with doggy companions. They were all men who wanted 'to do their bit', and some Specials were in their late 70's.

A significant fact was the happy relationship the Special Constabulary enjoyed with the public whom they served. Be they butcher, baker or candlestick maker by day they all became guardians of the peace by night.

3 Children's war

"Their steadfastness, courage and fortitude in the face of perpetual danger from terrorist attack both within and outside Rhodesia has been magnificent and deserving of the highest admiration."

– MCM CITATION

Young people are resilient and adaptable, and these qualities certainly came to the fore in Manicaland schools during the war.

Traditionally, Rhodesian schools were based on what in 20th century Britain might be called old-fashioned standards and morals. Prayers were said at morning assembly, pupils were taught to take a pride in their uniforms, to show respect to the staff and other adults.

Staff were dedicated and enthusiastic.

In the schools, stress was laid on morals, discipline, duty, integrity, selflessness and initiative. This bias towards 'gentlemanly' behaviour and a Christian outlook on life brought out the best in pupils from one generation to another.

The basic educational principles were the same in black schools, but African customs, tradition and culture were strong.

African children were unsophisticated, the teachers dedicated and enthusiastic. European-style manners and the broad principles of Christian behaviour were being instilled. One tremendous difference however, was that the parents, largely unschooled themselves, were unable to give continuity education (including discipline) in out-of-school hours.

With very large families (it was not unusual for a black man to have two or three wives and 20 children) the number of black pupils being turned out of the primary schools was staggering. The numbers were so great that the Government and the white taxpayer could no longer cope.

Thousands of teenagers were out of school, looking for excitement, a prey to every silver-tongued rabble-rouser.

This was the background against which pupils and teachers in Manicaland had to cope with the trials of four years of 'struggle' from 1976 to 1980.

In the Tribal Trust Lands thousands of black children were deprived of any formal education. Terrorists burned down schools, killed teachers, terrorised parents and prevented children from going to school. In 'liberating the masses from the colonialist regime' the intention was to alienate the peasant people from the white Government – but it was the black children who suffered. Thousands left their desks, some voluntarily and others forcibly, and marched across the border for training as 'freedom fighters', returning to their country later as 'guerillas' or 'refugees'. Many more became 'mujibas' – the eyes and ears of the guerillas, the go-betweens from the terrorists to the tribespeople – often doing their own terrorising as well.

Christians found it particularly difficult to understand why many mission stations became havens for terrorists.

The Chikore Mission in the Chipinga district is an example. It became a terrorist training centre rather than a school. A white education official, Mr W., took over control and turned it into a Government school. He was so concerned about the African children in the area that he drove to Chikore every week for months on end, usually alone, as most often no Army escort was available.

The roads were dangerous as they were continually being mined, and he could easily have been ambushed. He told the pupils the truth as he saw it.

"You fellows," he said, "have been taken over by the terrorists and have become whores and soldiers. What future will you have? What training for a career? If you love your country and want to help it you must get educated."

Alone he had to reorganise the school, find and install teachers, act as headmaster, and arrange all the details, such as laundry and food – from his official base in Umtali.

In another area in the south-east, a black official also risked his life daily to bring education to the black children in the area. The terrorists were closing all the schools on the eastern side of the Tribal Trust Land which bordered Mozambique. The road down the middle of the area was land-mined and impassable. So Mr M. cycled down this road daily, entering the eastern side to persuade the African children and their parents to move west where they could continue their education in safety.

Some people were too afraid to follow him; some preferred to join the terrorists and to fight for the 'liberation of the people'. Others, however, were brave enough to move over into schools being built and enlarged to receive them.

Old Umtali Mission, developed on the site of the first township of Umtali, on land given to the Methodist Church by Cecil Rhodes, was the place from which the first group of students ever to leave secondary school in Rhodesia to join the 'struggle' 'disappeared' on March 22, 1975.

They were pupils of Hartzell High School. As the headmaster said at the school prize-giving, attended by Prime Minister Mugabe, in 1980: "As a staff we were dumbfounded, but the spirit that spurred those 16 boys to abandon their studies was to spread to other schools with amazing rapidity. What started as a trickle developed into a mighty flow of students crossing the border into Mozambique, which no one could stop."

Speaking after Independence, the head of St. Augustine's Mission, Penhalonga, said the first pupils from his mission crossed the border in 1975, but were sent back until Mozambique won independence the following year.

Later a total of 200 St. Augustine's students went across the border at various times. Asked how he felt about this, the head said: "The sort of people going over you could trust implicitly ... and so anything they were going for has to be a good thing."

On estates, farms and mines, many primary schools were closed as a result of intimidation and threats. "If you send your children to school – they'll be killed." Who can blame parents for keeping their children out of school under such circumstances?

In Umtali, the black schools soldiered on, gaining pupils from rural areas who came to live with relatives in the comparative safety of the town. Their education suffered little, except for the noise of rocket and mortar attacks on the city and a syllabus change that cut out history and replaced it by a subject called 'environmental studies'.

In the white schools, efforts were made to keep school activities going and open days, films, school plays, dances and debates were held as usual, except that they took place in daylight instead of at night and during the week instead of at weekends.

Many school teams from other centres refused to travel to Umtali for sporting fixtures. This brought home to local schoolchildren the fact that they were living in a dangerous area. It also brought out qualities of courage and endurance, and Umtali schoolboys and girls refused to cancel fixtures and did the travelling themselves, with parents riding 'shotgun'.

The security drills were well rehearsed. "If attacked, lie on the floor of the vehicle while we attempt to drive through. If we fail, scramble out and take cover in the ditch at the side of the road," pupils were told.

The children became hardened travellers. Often there would be late nights on Friday after school functions, a 05h30 start on Saturday, a 3½ hour bus journey to Salisbury, two hockey matches before lunch and a prompt return in order to be off the road before dusk – and still they often won. Their resilience and sheer physical and mental toughness were amazing.

At first the war had little effect on city schools. The 'sharp end' or the 'valley' were far away. Then, in 1968, came the death in action of 17-year-old Reginald Binks, brother of a Girls' High pupil, and well-known among the young people of Umtali. The next blow came in August 1974 with the death, as the result of a landmine explosion in Mozambique, of 24-year-old Hilary Forsyth, a former student of Umtali Girls' High School. She and a Salisbury friend had been making their way to the Cabora Bassa dam to collect material for a book on the Zambezi that Hilary was planning to write.

By 1976 the physical effects of the war began to be felt in Umtali – particularly in the schools with their comparatively large population of boarders. Anti-terrorist drill ('terr drill') was started, protective devices were installed, first aid lectures were given to the seniors and members of the Security Forces came to reassure the girls. Convoys were introduced and armed escorts provided to accompany boarders and teams travelling to and from Umtali.

"The war was really brought home to the public of the Eastern Districts and to Umtali Girls' High School with the news of the Chipinga landmine explosion of June 1976, in which Marianne Habing, her mother and little sister were killed, and another sister, Yvonne, and a friend, Shirley Wicksteed, were severely injured. Yvonne died a week later," said the head of the school.

Terr drill went on, with efforts being made to maintain a balance between a realisation of the seriousness of the situation and the prevention of panic. "I think the staff of the schools succeeded in this," one head said.

At the Boys' High there were class checks as a safety precaution against bombs. Bomb and mortar drills were practised. Hostels were security fenced and fitted with alarm systems for safety and tighter control was exercised over boarders' movements. A communications system was introduced to keep the hostels in contact with one another and the City's Civil Defence Aide.

Then came August 11, 1976, and the first attack on Umtali.

"Lessons learned were put into practice and all boarders moved quickly and quietly to their 'places of safety'. Morale was excellent, and when one child began to cry (a reaction which might have spread) the superintendent said very quietly, 'Shall we say the Lord's Prayer together.' Calm and confidence were restored," a head recalls.

A few days later, eight girls started on a 200 hour non-stop relay swim to raise money for the Terrorist Victims' Relief Fund (used to help both European and African victims). The weather, even during the day, was inclement, but spirits were high. Music blared, fires burned round the pool day and night, and a team of parents supplied hot meals and other necessities. Public interest and enthusiasm almost matched that of the teenagers. Umtali's generosity was overwhelming and the result was a magnificent $3 858, of which $3 555 was given to the Terrorist Victims Relief Fund and the balance to the King George VI Children's Home. This was only one of the many, but certainly the greatest, of the fund-raising efforts for the forces undertaken by Umtali's schoolgirls.

The helplessness of children aged between four and eight was the most frightening aspect of planning the security in an infant school, a head said. The theme running through all the drills and security measures was self-reliance. This had to be impressed on the children and reinforced daily. The teachers were well aware that a situation could arise where the children would have to fend for themselves.

The teachers did the best they could to train the children without causing undue alarm and despondency. Parents, too, had to be 'educated' and this was no easy matter.

There were lighter moments though. Until the younger children became familiar with wartime terminology they referred to mortar bombs as 'water bombs' and Civil Defence very soon became 'Fizzle Defence'.

"While under attack in their own homes many children gave first consideration to their animals. This sort of behaviour was common and their unselfish attitude impressed their teachers," a head said.

"The raids on Umtali barely affected the young children. Many of them slept right through. Those who experienced the noise, the dust, the vibration, the flashes, the shrapnel bursting and the cordite smell soon talked it out of their systems the next day. The teachers felt the stress far more."

While the raids on Umtali were forgotten, every eight weeks Daddy went away for six long weeks. This had a most serious and disrupting effect on the children. Fathers would miss important occasions like birthdays and Christmas as well as school sports days and other functions. When the trauma of having a father or brother wounded, maimed or killed was added, the effect on the children was far-reaching.

"With fathers on continual call-up mothers were often confronted with behavioural problems which were sometimes carried over into school," said a head.

"What was remarkable was the tremendous fund of sympathetic tact which pupils drew upon when classmates were bereaved. At one period, there were at the school five families whose fathers had been killed in active service, and a long-time member of staff was also widowed. At least five former pupils were killed in war service."

Pupils' reaction to attacks were, teachers felt, largely determined by the reaction of parents but a few highly-strung children experienced great tension and in some cases had to be moved to other centres.

At the Boys' High School academic work suffered through the call-up of staff, the school closing early, the late arrival of boys travelling in convoy, disrupted lessons through drill or minefield explosions and disturbed exam study when there were mortar attacks.

Border Hills Infant School was damaged on two occasions. The first time there was a direct hit on the African staff quarters. The men were lucky to come out alive though one gardener had to go to hospital. The next time a classroom block and office took the brunt of the attack. A large piece of shrapnel from a rocket knocked a chunk out of the office wall. Shattered glass and shrapnel were all over the place.

The headmistress and her grounds staff were up at first light (about 05h00) to inspect the damage and clear away the debris before the children arrived at school. The quantity of shrapnel picked up was unbelievable. There were even pieces scattered all over the bottom of the swimming pool. A large chunk afterwards made a useful paper weight on the head's desk. The grounds and damaged classrooms were cleared by 07h30 and the children were allowed through the gates as usual.

Children's games during this period were related to the war. Cops and robbers or cowboys and Indians were old hat. Terrs, gooks, choppers, hand grenades, mortars, AK's and FN's featured in their play situations. Even the drawings in their school books dealt with the war. The girls too, were not entirely immune. Their knowledge of certain events and the machinery of war, weapons and equipment was astounding, and all the happenings were re-enacted daily.

Boys took great delight in collecting mortar fragments and several warnings had to be given regarding the dangers of meddling with unexploded bombs and other devices.

When the shop bombings started, precautions at schools were tightened still further. Pupils were instructed to mark their cases or satchels with large white letters so that they could be identified from a distance. They were instructed to report the presence of any objects lying in the school fields and there were several false alarms when absent-minded individuals deposited their cases in odd corners before going off to play.

"... offering condolences was an agonising exercise but one was humbled by the immense courage of so many of the victims," one head recalls.

"I would often be 'phoned to pass on terrible news to pupils. Remarkable human qualities were often displayed in the face of such sad circumstances.

"Two 'phone calls, particularly, come to mind. One was from a mother, early one morning. Afraid of the damaging effects of rumour, she asked if I would let her daughter know that they had been attacked during the night. In the same tone of voice as if she were making arrangements for the weekend, she explained that her husband had lost an eye and they were waiting for the road to be cleared before rushing him to Salisbury.

"The other was from a father whose wife had been killed a few months earlier in a landmine explosion. 'Please tell Shirley', he said, 'that I was caught in an ambush this morning, but I'm fine. Just a little lead in the bum!'

"And then there was the telephone call from a member of staff asking if she might be excused from school the following day. With barely a tremor in her voice she explained that she had just heard that her son had been killed in a contact."

The Umtali Boys' High School Roll of Honour with its 38 names is indeed too long to list each name. Two other old boys who were killed, but not in active service, are included in the citations.

In 1977 it was decided to perpetuate the memory of those students or former students of Umtali Girls' High School who had lost their lives as the result of the war.

An 'Honours' board in the school Beit Hall, inscribed simply 'In Memoriam', carries seven names: 1974 Hilary Forsyth; 1976 Marianne Habing, Yvonne Habing; 1979 Susan Turner, Wendy Tulip, Rosemary Hacking (nee Gifford), Elise Liebermann (nee Vorster).

The major reaction to the war situation was one of 'no fuss adaptability'. Life had to continue and people simply got on with it.

"Perhaps this trait was exemplified best when, on the night before their first 'O' Level exams in November 1977, when there were enough worries as it was, the suburb of Fairbridge Park was attacked," a head said. "Families finally settled into bed after 01h00. The next day there were no complaints from pupils or parents in the area, no lame running to the head for excuses to be made and concessions extracted from the

Examining Board overseas. War had become a part of life and one had to live one's life in spite of it.

"The war was grim, but there were many positive side effects. Noble qualities were drawn out of people. They worked harder and did more – it was one's duty and therefore it was done – questions were not asked about where duties began and ended, as so often happens in less threatened situations."

Marymount College, founded by American Roman Catholic sisters in 1957, opened the following year with 40 Form I and II girls. The first three black pupils entered the school in 1964.

The college buildings are less than one kilometre from the international border with Mozambique.

"In 1976 the closure of the border seemed to place Umtali in a vulnerable position and many parents decided they did not want their daughters at Marymount," one of the sisters said.

The security forces had become increasingly worried about the school's vulnerability and a group of three to six men patrolled the grounds every night.

"The Army decided we must have security fencing around the dormitory sections of the building," she went on. "After a great deal of discussion and the possibility that Marymount would have to close immediately if the fencing was not installed, the Government agreed to finance an electrified fence and security lighting. The Army then set up a permanent base on the school campus to protect the girls. From the second term until Marymount closed there was a constant guard on the campus."

After the mortar attack on Umtali in August it was decided, for safety's sake, that part of the Dominican Convent would be used as a dormitory for boarders to sleep in at night and a busing system became a part of the daily routine. The girls would leave Marymount after supper at about 18h30 and return for breakfast the next morning at 07h00.

Marymount was the hardest hit school, with the war finally closing it at the end of 1976. The buildings remained empty during 1977 and 1978 with only a caretaker and skeleton staff.

In 1979 the Roman Catholic minor seminary at Melsetter moved out and the priests came to Umtali to live in the Marymount buildings.

In April 1977 St David's Girls' Secondary School (for blacks) moved for safety from Bonda (Inyanga district) into the empty Dominican Convent buildings in Umtali, and for the first time the city had a black school in a white suburb.

Towards the end of 1978 an Umtali School Action Committee was formed to look into the feasibility of forming a Community School in terms of the Education Act. This said, in part, that "Communities have the right to establish and administer educational institutions of their own choice. The right of these institutions to maintain their cultural and religious identity in accordance with the desires of the respective communities will be upheld."

At this stage blacks were already taking their places in formerly whites-only Government schools in Umtali.

The Action Committee, at a meeting on January 19, 1979, agreed to the formation of a comprehensive Community School in the city. A Board of Governors was appointed. Parents voted on the issue. The recommendation was put to the Secretary for Education who gave his approval and so the Umtali Community School was born. It opened in January 1980 with five sections catering for all ages from infants to Form VI.

In 1981 the Government rescinded this Act and the Community Schools could no longer function. Government schools are now open to all, and the former white schools have a large majority of black pupils and staff.

4 Women's work

"In addition, the work of women's voluntary organisations in providing for the welfare of the Security Forces personnel has been quite outstanding.
– MCM CITATION

Umtali women, like their sisters in other parts of the country, have always given much time and energy to helping others. They are involved in a number of voluntary organisations which raise funds for charity and assist those in need.

During the war they were busier than ever, meeting new calls, facing new challenges, always willing to do what they could to help others.

Typical was the response to the appeal for help for victims of terrorist attacks.

The Terrorist Victims' Relief Fund was a country-wide organisation with headquarters in Salisbury and funds collected in all areas. Umtali Rotary Anns also had assistance for terrorist victims as their project, and in this they were helped by the women of Umtali.

Doro took on the job of helping injured Africans brought into the Umtali hospitals (often full to overflowing during the height of the landmine activity). At first she worked entirely on her own, visiting each patient and taking extras – sugar, peanuts, jam, condensed milk, soft drinks, sweets, cigarettes, writing paper and envelopes. She would help them write their letters or write to their relatives for them. Without her, some of the victims could never have contacted their relatives to let them know what had happened.

"One man was blown up by a landmine. He lost his bank book, so I went to see the bank manager for him and eventually helped him sort out his financial problems," she said.

As the number of black victims increased, extra help became necessary. Edie, Mollie, Joan, Rhoda, Marje and Kris were among those who offered their services.

They appealed to black women to assist, but they were too afraid to do so.

Other white women joined the group and took over the weekly visits to black patients in the District Hospital at Sakubva, the city's oldest African housing estate.

Aid was available to a very great number of people, all the money being given by whites for black and white terrorist victims' relief.

"A bus hit a mine," one of the white women workers said. "Three

29

black women each lost both their legs. One was too fat ever to be able to get onto artificial limbs, but we did all we could to help her. One had a two-month-old baby. One young black girl lost both her legs too. It was a pathetic case – she was only 12. She was given some odd scraps of material to play with in hospital. She sewed these together to make a most charming patchwork skirt. We were very impressed with her talent and initiative.

"Her father came to see her. He didn't seem to worry so much about the loss of her legs as about her education. 'Please help her get educated,' he pleaded.

"So I got in touch with a mission and the Catholic Men's Association paid for her education. I managed to collect money for her other expenses as well," she said. "The girl was given artificial legs and learned to walk with them. I was thrilled with her progress each day... Later she wrote to tell me that she'd learned to walk properly."

There was a black man, John, who was travelling from Kimberley to return to his home in Malawi. He was walking through Mozambique when he was attacked by Frelimo who stole all his possessions. He managed to escape and was walking along the railway line when he came to a fence. Not realising the danger, he climbed through the fence which blocked his path. Moments later he stepped on an anti-personnel mine. Both legs and an arm were badly injured. He eventually reached the Umtali Hospital and was there for many weeks, receiving treatment. He had no money, no relatives, no friends.

"I felt so very sorry for him," his white benefactor said. "I wrote to his former employer in Kimberley and managed to get a passport for him. When he came out of hospital we found him accommodation and gave him clothing and food. When he was fit enough to travel we saw him onto the train for Kimberley. Later he wrote to me. He told me he was still crippled in both legs and one arm but that the Rotary Association in Kimberley had found him a job. He was a good Christian man."

As the war intensified the white women's group collected clothing and blankets. They kept cupboards full of these and other articles ready for any emergency. And there were plenty. A farmer would 'phone to say that his compound had been burnt down and his labourers had lost all their possessions in the fire.

"Sometimes it would be 60 black men, women and children in need, and we would send out clothing and things like saucepans and kettles for them all. Umtali's white people were very generous in the face of these emergencies," one of the group said.

"Terrorists attacked the black workers on a tea estate on one occasion.

Two men were stabbed. One died, the other was brought to hospital in Umtali. His head was grotesquely swollen. It looked terrible. He recovered eventually after many weeks in hospital.

"When he was ready to be discharged, he appealed to me. 'I don't want to go,' he cried. He was shaking all over with fear and added: 'I can't go back. They'll kill me.' I soothed him and told him he need not go back, we'd find him a job elsewhere. We found him a light job that he could cope with."

Later the work included white victims as well.

The group leader visited each victim in the Umtali Hospital twice a week. "One had to go often to see how they were getting on and make sure they were looked after when they came out," she said. "Most of the black nurses were pro 'freedom fighters'. They were very keen to nurse any terrorist who was brought into hospital but not so keen on caring for the victims of their actions."

It was inevitable that the Women's Voluntary Services, of Second World War fame in Britain, should re-appear in Rhodesia during the bush war.

"An army marches on its stomach", is the old saying, and the troopies' description of 'ratpack' fare spurred on the women to supplement it.

Security force ration packs – 'ratpacks' or 'rats', as they were finally called – were small cardboard boxes containing tinned meat, fish, fruit; packets of powdered soup, milk and potato; rice, tea and coffee, plus tubes of cheese, jam and margarine. Thousands of boxes were sent into the bush to keep the men fed during years of fighting and patrolling in remote areas in all kinds of weather.

The first canteen in Manicaland opened at Penhalonga in 1976. Rusape had its own canteen (for farmers and men in uniform) and Umtali got going later that year.

They were all impromptu, casual, workaday places, begged from owners who no longer needed the rooms and were soon filled with first-class equipment supplied by the Border Patrol Welfare Fund. Second-hand supplementary furniture came from local well-wishers.

Everyone wanted to help. From snacks, hot dogs, biscuits, apple pies and cups of tea, the service spread to curry and rice, stew and sadza (cooked maize meal prepared especially for the black troops), roast chickens and fruit cake. Extra parcels and boxes, with iced sponges, chocolate gateaux and sausage rolls were sent to the bush for good measure. The flow of food was never-ending, as were the streams of customers. For four years local women gave of their best to provide free or cheap meals to keep the security forces on the march.

"In response to an article in the local paper, a group of about 12 white women from Umtali and Penhalonga met to discuss ways of helping the Security Forces. Little did we know what a huge, but rewarding, task we were undertaking," said a regular helper.

"Our first Women's Voluntary Services troops' rest room was opened in a small building off the main street. Within two years we had moved twice to accommodate the greatly increased numbers of black, white and coloured men using our facilities. We progressed from serving tea, coffee and sandwiches to providing Christmas fare for thousands of men in the bush."

Most of the women put their personal interests to one side and the canteen became their No 1 priority. They received countless tokens of gratitude, but their greatest reward was seeing weary, grimy faces light up at the sight of a hot hamburger or a cold 'brown cow' (a soft drink mixed with ice cream).

"There was a wonderful relationship between the women and the forces of all races," said one of the helpers. "They were such courteous, well-behaved, cheerful men.

The "Ladies of Comfort" busy packing troops' goody bags.

"But I must mention another great relationship – among the women themselves. It took great dedication to the cause of helping our fighting men for 200 women of all ages to work together in such a Christian spirit. We not only got on well together, but many firm friendships resulted from working side-by-side.

"God's helping hand was very much in evidence where finances were concerned. No matter how bad our bank balance looked, when the time came to pay the bills, the money was always there. The generosity of the Manicaland people is something we shall never forget," she said.

The Women's Voluntary Services prided themselves on never refusing a troopie's request. "Providing things like a horse-box, a couple of spare pillows, two mousetraps, or lifts to other centres, was all in the day's work."

The Umtali office has a folder of thank you letters which are much appreciated. But the workers treasure the many moments of laughter, ragging and chatter, and the fellowship in the canteen even more. Certainly no one will forget the day when the notice board announced: "The ladies for next week's roster are hanging on a hook behind the kitchen door!"

Service with a smile for troopies at the WVS canteen in Umtali.

Penhalonga canteen opened with a flourish when a Lieut. Col. cut the red tape at the door of a disused shop in the village while a large crowd of helpers and well-wishers watched.

Life-size cartoons decorated the walls, and though the troopies never came in the numbers anticipated, a devoted group of canteen helpers gave excellent hot-dinner service every evening without fail to hungry Police Reservists on eight or 14-day call-ups.

To collect funds the Penhalonga 'girls' organised a sponsored walk. (These were all the rage in the district at the time.) They raised $1 000 by walking from the top of Christmas Pass to the canteen – led by the Penhalonga piper – with never a blister between them. Walkers ranged in age from six to sixty.

As a grand finale the male Police Reservists turned the canteen tables and fed the women an enormous spread!

The evenings together, when the men sat in the canteen for a while with rifles at hand and one ear listening for a sudden summons to action on radio or 'phone, will never be forgotten.

"We were a district full of people 'doing their own thing' before," said Chief Stick Leader Jimmy. "Now we're a community."

The Loyal Women's Guild in Umtali has served the community discreetly and with compassion since 1907, working for the distressed and less fortunate and preparing in advance (where possible) for any emergency.

Part of the Guild's early work was to tend the war graves in the cemetery. In 1968 they were asked to administer a fund raised in Umtali to help the family of a young local man killed while on active service.

By January 1973 the situation along the border was becoming more serious. A letter in *The Umtali Post*, asking, "Is Umtali geared for trouble?" prompted the Guild chairman to approach the District Commissioner to discover what was being done and whether a committee, formed years before, could be resuscitated.

The District Commissioner called a public meeting with the aim of forming a Civil Defence Committee to be called on in any emergency. A Guild representative was invited and on 'report back' Loyal Women's Guild members volunteered for a variety of duties. A list of names was sent to the District Commissioner by the end of March 1973.

Soon after this the Terrorist Victims' Relief Fund was started and the Guild supported it with donations. They made it their project in 1978 – with such success that Guilds throughout the country followed Umtali's lead in supporting the fund.

In June 1973 the Women's Voluntary Services organised Civil Defence duties for Umtali women and the Guild was given the care of the elderly, support for any scheme for the daily care of working mothers' children, and the distribution of blankets and clothing where necessary.

In June 1974, when the Portuguese were leaving Mozambique, a flood of refugees was expected. Guild members were organised into shifts to deal with them and to hand out clothing and blankets. But the influx did not come.

When it was suggested that the Loyal Women's Guild should pack comfort parcels for local men on call-up, a working committee of five white women was formed and the Manicaland Comforts for the Forces Association was registered with the Department of Social Welfare. The first parcels were packed in November 1973 and the scheme was magnificently supported by the white people of Manicaland for many years.

The normal work of the Guild continued, although war conditions and sanctions altered some aspects. Errant husbands found it easier to disappear without trace, either slipping out of the country or into the army. Marriages broke down due to call-ups. Fewer elderly people needed help, but families suffering at the hands of terrorists were assisted, including one from Mozambique when the husband was kidnapped.

Apart from ordinary Guild work, members helped the Red Cross, Women's Voluntary Services, Civil Defence and worked as emergency drivers or fundraisers for Tsanga Lodge (a rehabilitation centre at Inyanga for disabled members of the Security Forces).

Said a member: "It was not an exciting war for the Guild, but, geared to meet any forseeable emergency, we were absorbed into the fabric of stubborn resistance which was woven by the people as a whole. We were able to meet so many war demands by virtue of the generous response of Umtali people to every call for aid."

"The war had been going some time and lads from Manicaland were serving in all branches of the forces," said Ellie, wife of a former headmaster of Umtali Boys' High School. "Nothing was being done to make them feel that the folks at home were taking any notice of their efforts. In September 1973 the Loyal Women's Guild took up the challenge and it was agreed to provide parcels of goodies for all the Security Forces in Manicaland.

"Naturally a great deal of spadework had to be done. Suitable accommodation for storing the goodies and packing the parcels had to be found. Money had to be collected and pleas for magazines went out. The people of Umtali responded in their usual magnificent way and after registration under the Welfare Act we were able to send out our first consignment of parcels on November 21, 1973."

Like all new projects the initial problems seemed to increase. The first few parcels were packed in cardboard boxes, enabling items like biscuits and fruit cake to be included. But it was soon realised that boxes were too cumbersome and difficult to handle.

After a suggestion from the officer commanding the Drill Hall, a calico bag was used instead. The bags had to be stitched and, thanks to help from some Senior Citizens, the Comforts Fund was never short, never let down.

At the inaugural meeting in February 1974, it was decided to 'hive off' from the Guild and 'go it alone', Ellie said.

"Only twice in our six years of existence did we have to hold fund-raising efforts, and only twice a street collection."

With help from the Mayor's Christmas Cheer Fund, the Lions Club and women's organisations, the ever generous public saw that the 'boys' continued to get parcels on every call-up, even when numbers swelled. Umtali business firms gave up their annual Christmas parties to send large cash donations to the fund.

The Girl Guides helped initially with packing sweets and nuts, and at Christmas time chickens and fruit cake were sent to the men in the field. Women donned aprons, got out the precious ingredients hoarded from the last holiday 'down South' (dried fruit was on every visitor to South Africa's shopping list) and baked cakes for 'Ellie's parcels'.

"In all, 18 322 parcels were packed and sent to men in the 4th Battalion Rhodesia Regiment, Addams Barracks, the Police Reserve, Police Anti-Terrorist Unit and the hospital," Ellie said. "Judging by the letters we received our efforts were not in vain."

Letters came from remote Army bases and lonely bush camps, warming the hearts of the hard-working group, quaintly christened 'The Ladies of Comfort'.

"I wish you luck for your kindness. We also continue with our bush operations," said a black sergeant engaged in fence construction in a 'hairy area'.

"From the bottom of our blistered heels to the top of our mopani-fly covered heads, we thank you for the most welcome bags of goodies," wrote Police Reservists from Inyanga, Umtali, Melsetter, Rusape and the Vumba.

"Thank you for the parcels. I am saying, don't get tired. We are going forward with the war," wrote an African soldier.

"It is so easy to feel forgotten in the bush, not only for the chap who has no family or girl friend. All of us at times plunge into the depths and feel alone and scared. Your parcels, and the message they bring, do so much to restore our perspective and faith. Your committee is doing an excellent job in maintaining morale," said a white officer.

"Had it not been for the last consignment of chickens, we would have lost considerable weight! The orange juice, condensed milk, peanuts, mirror and face-cloth, everything, even the bag itself, was put to immediate use," wrote a Coloured troopie.

"Those presents in a cloth packet were fantastic," wrote a black PATU* man. "I hope God will keep your hearts and minds in harmony."

"I wish you the best of very lucky. Pray for us until we meet again," wrote another black soldier.

* * *

These were some of the tokens of thanks to a fund which needed $1 000 a month to keep the supplies flowing – and somehow there was never a shortage of donations.

The 'fund' would have liked the cloth bags, stitched with such loving care, to be returned. Although a few turned up many were used for carrying shaving kit, stuffing in fruit and nuts for a bush patrol, or even for cleaning boots!

After years of devoted work, Ellie received the Meritorious Conduct Medal on behalf of all her helpers.

* * *

"Twenty chickens, two kg sausages, eggs, margarine – and don't forget the flour..." All part of a shopping list. So it has continued, over the years, for members of the Memorable Order of Tin Hats' Women's Auxiliary.

"This is the way we make our money, catering for weddings, sundowners, lunches, receptions. All our hard-earned cash goes towards charities at the end of each year," said Lady Billie.

"Only very hard work many years ago by staunch members of D-Day MOTHWA realised the dream of building our Jubilee Street MOTH hall," she said.

———
*Police Anti-Terrorist Unit.

For a number of years the MOTHWA organisation had a Troops' Welfare Fund. Dotted around base camps in the bush, barrack rooms and laboratories, are numerous mementoes of the MOTHWA's hard work.

The call came early in the war from the Army for a deep freeze, urgently needed at a base camp. "The chaps could do with some cold refreshments and fresh food when they return from patrols in the bush. Could MOTHWA help?"

Certainly they could. How many would the Army like? Several freezers were bought and supplied, at various times, to different units. Sports equipment was needed to relieve boredom and exercise healthy young bodies. Here again MOTHWA stepped in and gave what was required.

Another call came for special microscopes so that men returning from the bush, after ploughing through muddy rivers and pools, could be tested for bilharzia (a debilitating water-borne disease).

MOTHWA raised the money, helped by various Shellholes in South Africa, and microscopes were obtained and handed over to the Army.

"Money's running short, girls. What can we do to fill our coffers?" asked Lady Billie.

Someone suggested a 'knit-in'. ("Ugh, how I hate knitting!")

The president of the Umtali Rotary Club, Rev. Ivan Carson, and the Mayor, Doug Reed, at a charity 'knit-in'.

But one Saturday afternoon there they were, having a marvellous time seeing who could knit the most rows in the shortest time – and soon they had raised the necessary money.

It was getting on for winter – balaclava time – so out came the knitting needles once again. Wool was bought. "Help yourselves. Take as much as you can manage." They even roped in some of the Senior Citizens at Strickland Lodge.

MOTHWA helped with the baking of Christmas cakes for Ellie's glory-bags, provided curtains for a new canteen near King George VI Barracks in Salisbury and continued catering for civilian social functions in Umtali to raise money for their many projects.

Although they dwindled in numbers they battled on, helping in every way they could 'the boys out there fighting for us'.

"Catering is hard work," said one MOTHWA. "We often have to rope in husbands, daughters and sons to give a hand. At the end of it all we seem to give our money away so easily – just a few strokes of a pen in a cheque book. But as long as we know we are helping someone, we are only too happy to carry on," said a woman who has always lived by the MOTHWA motto: "... mutual aid, true help and comradeship."

They enjoyed themselves, laughing and joking together, but they had their sad moments too.

"If ever we felt really close to the war and the conditions under which we lived, it was the day we heard of the death of an Umtali lad who had been given a few days off from his stint in the bush to get married. It had been a joyous occasion catering for him, his bride and guests, on a lovely sunny Saturday. Then, a few weeks later, he was killed, along with several others well known to us," said a MOTHWA.

Every year at the annual Remembrance Day parade at the Umtali Cenotaph, where MOTHWA laid their distinctive blue and white butterfly wreath, the list of names on the Umtali Roll of Honour grew longer.

* * *

'Operation Tea Party' was a fund-raising exercise with a difference that soon caught on in Umtali. Started by Edie, it provided funds for sporting and recreational equipment, Christmas hampers, reading matter and other comforts for black and white Internal Affairs National Servicemen and black District Assistants in sensitive areas.

The 'keeps' they manned were bleak, primitive, often mudwalled or tented posts, without even a chair to sit on. Their spells of duty were long and boring as well as uncomfortable, so the Internal Affairs Association Border Comforts Committee determined to supply a few little luxuries for their men. They also helped those who had been injured or who were in hospital for any reason.

To start the ball rolling, Edie asked 10 friends to a function at her house. Each contributed a minimum of 25 cents to the fund and enjoyed the party. Each guest then did the same, organising her own party or entertainment within the week. The scheme was popular and provided the means for sending many items into the bush to brighten life for the 'Intaff' men.

* * *

Although the Jairos Jiri Centre for black handicapped workers was founded by a well-known Bulawayo man and has its headquarters in that city, the growth of the Umtali centre, despite the war, was encouraged by Manicaland African women persevering with their skills at home under the guidance of a white woman and her committee.

From a tiny shop with one counter and an overfilled display window in a side street, the Umtali centre has grown to a superb complex of attractive shops near the city's Civic Centre.

During the war, supplies of village craftwork from the outlying areas decreased due to intimidation by Communist terrorists and the difficulty of collecting raw material in the troubled areas. But a trickle of handwork still came in and black women in Manicaland's Protected Villages continued to make beautiful baskets, table mats, sewing containers and their own traditional household equipment under very trying conditions.

Their 'rusero' baskets (for sifting grain), the 'mitani' (for straining beer and sorting grain) and 'chitundu' (for carrying plates and dishes) were not only useful in their own lives but were bought by townspeople and visitors as attractive items of 'local colour' for home use.

Sisal mats became scarce as roads and bus services became dangerous. The sisal mats from Melsetter and Chipinga were particularly popular and a source of profit to the makers.

Mr Jairos Jiri sent a band of his trained disabled workers to Umtali where special buildings, workshops and accommodation were designed and built for them at Zimunya, a black township south of Umtali. They settled happily for a while until threats by terrorists forced them to come into Umtali for protection. To continue living and working as members of a white-sponsored scheme – even though it was helping crippled blacks to earn a living and find their human dignity – was not allowed by the terrorists who promised murder and destruction if they remained in Zimunya. In Umtali, under protection, they carried on in their wheelchairs in makeshift homes. They have now returned to Zimunya.

The Jairos Jiri Centre in Umtali had a tremendous boost when election observers, foreign journalists, monitoring forces and others visited the city at election and Independence time.

"The type of work Manicaland village women produce is popular with Continental visitors, and we have had orders from Norway, the United States, Britain, as well as South Africa and other countries," said the woman in charge of the craftwork shop in Umtali.

The average monthly 'pay out' is about $1 700, but during a recent Christmas the craftwork brought in earned $2 000.

Many white women, including two former Umtali Mayoresses and the Umtali Loyal Women's Guild chairman, continued their regular work (begun many years ago) at the women's homecraft clubs in Sakubva, training African women in embroidery, crochet, knitting, weaving and other skills. By raising the standard of their work, the articles produced have also now become saleable and sought after by tourists and buyers throughout the country.

One remarkable women's club which kept going throughout the war, despite adverse conditions, was the Vumba* Homecraft Centre. Its products are also sold in the Jairos Jiri shop.

---

*The Vumba mountains are south-east of Umtali.

5 *Influx of wounded*

"Hospitals and medical services have also played an outstanding role in the treatment of the many casualties, both civilian and Security Forces, from all parts of the Eastern Districts which has been the scene of prolonged and intensive terrorist activity."

– MCM CITATION

Helicopters hovering near the Umtali General Hospital invariably meant a batch of wounded patients, sometimes for the local wards and sometimes on their way to specialist treatment in Salisbury.

The heli-pad was only a few metres from the hospital laboratory and in view of the main road.

The hospital ambulances invariably drove down to the heli-pad to wait, and when laboratory staff saw them there they knew what to expect.

Two young laboratory technologists remember a particularly serious case, of a troopie with a head wound. The laboratory had been asked to have six units of O negative blood ready for the chopper's arrival. But

Smiles all round from the gunners when they heard there would be free beer from the Red Cross for those who gave blood for the hospital blood bank.

there were only two pints available. (O negative is precious because it can be used for anyone and the Umtali laboratory only bled donors when necessary.)

"We decided to give him fresh frozen plasma to make up the fluid and take him out of shock," one of the young women said. "We had about 10 minutes to thaw the frozen plasma before the chopper arrived. They were going to pick up the blood in Umtali and take the wounded man by fixed wing to Salisbury."

The technologists – one tall and the other quite short – put the frozen plasma in a bowl of very hot water and ran down to the heli-pad. The grass was very long and the tall one had to tell her companion when to jump over hidden obstacles. Onlookers were amazed to see a metal bowl bobbing up and down in the grass – but their efforts paid off. The man lived.

On another occasion a Police Reservist was wounded. He was 'case-vaced'* to hospital but the laboratory was particularly short of blood of his group. Within half an hour of his arrival the news had spread round the Police Camp and 50 policemen arrived at the laboratory to donate blood.

"They were most indignant when we turned them down because their blood groups were not the same," the technologist said.

The laboratory girls got to know some of the chopper pilots who sometimes ran through the long grass to the laboratory for a cup of coffee and a chat. One pilot was a former laboratory technologist.

The Umtali General Hospital, on a large, open site on Churchill Road, with a pleasant view, was opened in 1932. Originally the kitchen was equipped with a wood stove and there was a hand-operated lift. The stove was modernised, but the lift remained for many years.

Life was quiet in those days when the only patients were simple accident cases and the usual disease and illness of a small town popu-lated mainly with retired residents, civil servants and schoolchildren.

The Matron, since retired, saw the building of new wings and depart-ments over the years and it was she who agitated for the heli-pad so that Air Force choppers, bringing in casualties from the bush, could land as close to the wards as possible. At night she was always first to arrive on the scene to organise car headlights to illuminate the pad, until proper lighting was fitted.

The first casualties to be landed there were five injured men, one of

---

*Casualty evacuated – normally by air.

them a personal friend of Matron's and a builder of the chopper landing area.

Many times when casualties were brought in the staff knew nothing of 'the scene', only that there were wounded bodies to attend to. Occasionally the dead men on the stretchers were well known, underlining the tragedy and futility of the war.

"We dreaded the sound of the ambulance or choppers arriving," said the staff.

Trained nurses living in Umtali who had married or were in other jobs soon volunteered for duty.

After refresher courses, a useful band was on constant standby. They never failed to report when needed. During an attack on Umtali a sister telephoned: "I'll be right along as soon as I can, but there's a THING hanging on the tree outside."

It was a rocket, dangling from a branch.

They worked all hours to cope with the influx of wounded bodies from contacts, ambushes, incidents involving solitary motorists on the road or attacks on the province's convoys.

"They are all humans, suffering," said the Medical Superintendent. "Whether terrorists or ours, it's my job to patch them up."

The hospital quickly adapted to functioning as a front-line receiving centre for the border area under Dr Bill. In one year alone in the African theatre he and Mr George and their teams did 3 500 operations. There were another 1 500 in the European theatre – a grim total for a doctor who once removed nine limbs from wounded passengers – victims of a blown-up bus which hit a 'tin can'* in a Tribal Trust Land.

Army casualties were brought in with their 'medics't in attendance. The wounded men had been given first aid, had drips set up, had been given morphine and antibiotics and generally arrived 'in good shape – and alive'. But on occasion doctors and staff were saddened to see friends brought in too late to be helped.

When the hospital was hit in October 1978 there were no injuries. "God's hand was over us all that night," said the Matron.

Shrapnel smashed through the physiotherapy department and other buildings were damaged. About nine or ten mortar bombs landed in the grounds. Patients struggled under their beds to escape flying glass. One man cheerfully remembered to drag his (forbidden) bottle of whisky with him.

---

*'tin can' – landmine. The planting of landmines was one of the main activities of the Communist terrorists.
†Medical orderlies.

44

When mission hospitals in the province were forced, through terrorist activity, to close, black nursing and medical trainees from Regina Coeli, Bonda and Mt Selinda were taken in at Umtali halfway through their courses and 'finished off', so that they could take their Medical Council exams and qualify.

In 1968 the Sakubva African township hospital was equipped and opened. During all the stress and strain the hospital authorities had nothing but praise for the local public.

The library and broadcasting room, the TV room, the blood bank, the ice-making machine, the air-conditioning, the film projector, were all among the items provided by the public. If a service club discovered that the hospital was short of something they generally did their best to make sure the hospital got it, by public fund raising, invariably involving entertainment and fun for others.

Most Umtali residents knew the hospital well, either as patients or visitors. It was a relief when the authorities decided that cash was at last available to fence and screen the buildings. Previously the hospital had been completely open, day and night, without guard, relying on the trust and co-operation of a public which appreciated the quality and mercy of its work. But to the city it seemed too vulnerable in times of violence.

One ward was set aside for young men recovering from war wounds. They sat in the sun, with plastered limbs, unfailingly cheerful despite the pain. Originally black and white patients were in separate wards, but eventually they were put side by side and cared for by black and white alike.

The criticism levelled at Rhodesia by foreign Pressmen and others was often completely unjustified. Cecil Rhodes advocated a multi-racial society from the start, but the Pioneers found the blacks so primitive. They had their own 'ngangas' (witch doctors) and medicines and were fearful and suspicious of white 'muti' (medicine). They looked on hospitals as places where people died. It had taken years of work to educate them in the use of modern drugs and medical facilities.

An important adjunct of the Umtali Hospital is the Public Health Laboratory in the hospital grounds, which serves the whole of Manicaland.

'Big Jim', the Chief Technologist, saw a continuing increase of work throughout the war years. The laboratory trained nursing staff in simple routine analyses (which could be done without complicated equipment) for outlying African clinics, from Chipinga to Inyanga.

The Umtali laboratory also did routine bacteriological examinations of water supplies throughout the province and kept a close watch on the supply and demand for fresh blood, both for emergencies and normal operations.

In 1976 they noticed an increased reluctance by blacks to give blood, which was needed by all. Many said they did not want their blood to go to 'the soldiers', while others had different reasons. But there was still a panel of white blood donors who were always willing to give, on receipt of a call, for a black or white-skinned person. One 84-year-old white Umtali resident freely gave blood regularly, taking pride in his contribution to a country he loved.

Once 10 'casevacs' were brought into the hospital and the demand for blood for transfusion was high. Twenty Umtali people responded to the call immediately.

Normally hospitals were given short notice of the arrival of emergency patients, but the laboratory did not on this occasion know the type of casualty or blood groups needed.

On average 4 000 pints of blood were used in local hospitals each year during the war, from 1975 onwards.

Did they ever run out of blood? Occasionally, but supplies quickly came from Salisbury. During the war it was noticeable that families were very 'blood-conscious'. If someone was in hospital needing treatment, the whole family rallied round to offer blood without being asked.

Blood bank collection was in the care of Joyce who, with her Red Cross van, regularly visited commercial firms to bleed the donors and to encourage volunteers from the African townships.

"We collected a large number of pints of blood, in spite of the fact that it was very difficult to go into certain areas," said the Assistant Commandant, Alice.

Staff from the Public Health laboratory visited camps in the Umtali area to bleed donors. A young woman technologist vividly remembers one such visit to the Artillery.

"For some reason the powers-that-be decided the best place to bleed them was in the pub," she said. "We lined up all the guys and started to bleed them after giving strict instructions that if anyone felt 'funny' he was to tell us. Every donor was given a free beer from the Red Cross, and the guys sat around sipping their beers and ragging their mates – consequently several passed out.

"I was bleeding one when he turned green and collapsed in my arms – much to the amusement of all the onlookers. All these contributions of blood were much appreciated," she said.

46

"Because of the costs involved in collecting blood it could never be 'free' from the Central Blood Bank," Jim added. "The blood itself is free but there is a charge for testing."

Every specimen that came into the Umtali laboratory had a human context for Jim and his staff – each belonged to someone's mother, father, brother, sister or child. When there were deaths the lab workers would rather not have heard about them, but the increase in their work at the height of the war was a chance to get on with the skills they were qualified to contribute.

"I'll always remember the time two of us were in the Red Cross ambulance taking two unconscious soldiers to Salisbury," said one of the city's hardworking Red Cross women.

"We were given a medic to go with us. He had been up all night and was very tired. Not far out of Umtali he wanted to be sick. One of the injured was on a lung suction machine and we had to stop every half hour to attend to him. So we decided to leave the medic at Rusape and pick him up on the way back.

"An Army chap told us to call at Jock's place, but on the return journey neither of us knew who Jock was so we called at the Police station for more information. There were laughs all round when they told us it was JOC – Joint Operations Command!"

The Red Cross women took many serious cases to the capital: patients with landmine injuries, bomb blast or gunshot wounds, or amputations. The courage shown was amazing and yet, with the worst cases, some were nightmare journeys, never knowing whether the patients would live until they got to Salisbury.

The women knew that the terrorists had no qualms about attacking a Red Cross ambulance, yet they always travelled unarmed.

It was rewarding to get a note from the Andrew Fleming Hospital in Salisbury saying, "Well done, Umtali Red Cross. You did a magnificent job."

Umtali Red Cross had been very active with full-time hospital work during the 1939–45 war, but afterwards there were very few members.

In 1956 the movement was revived by the Manicaland Provincial Medical Officer of Health. The Red Cross Headquarters was eventually built in Kingsley Fairbridge Street in 1963. In 1960 members became involved in refugee work, helping people fleeing from the Congo. Six years later they got their first ambulance-cum-all-purpose vehicle.

Industrial firms asked the Red Cross to run first aid courses for employees, and in the 1970's hundreds of Civil Defence members were trained by the Red Cross. There were courses at various centres in the city as well as in the surrounding districts – the Vumba, Odzi, Inyazura, Burma Valley, Sheba, Stapleford and Odzani.

Red Cross started first aid posts throughout Umtali and districts, teaching schoolchildren as well as adult volunteers. Members were always on call to go anywhere at a moment's notice. They attended sports functions, collected waste paper and ran a lending cupboard for crutches, wheelchairs and other medical items.

A number of instructors did wonderful work, including one of the black instructors, headmaster of a school in the Nyamaropa area of Inyanga, who was abducted by terrorists. He managed to escape and immediately returned to his work.

Red Cross Headquarters, which is equipped as an auxiliary hospital, was badly shaken but not damaged during the rocket and mortar attacks on the city.

Members took part in many Civil Defence exercises as well as giving aid during 'the real thing'. Red Cross members were fortunately on hand when Umtali's three shop bombings took place, so casualties received prompt treatment.

Umtali Red Cross acquired its Peugeot ambulance in 1975. During the closing stages of the war the ambulance made frequent (sometimes three times a week) trips to Salisbury, taking terrorist victims and injured servicemen there for treatment.

6 *Shoppers' nightmare*

"The business and industrial sections of Umtali are also to be commended for the exemplary manner in which they have sustained the economic life of the city in the face of exceptional difficulties."

– MCM CITATION

She rushed into the office, white-faced and trembling. "It's Tip Top," she said. "I've just seen the shop blown up!"

The speaker was a middle-aged secretary not given to histrionics and the rest of the staff listened in shocked silence.

"I was driving past the store when I saw a bright orange flash. There was an enormous bang and bits of the roof flew across the road."

It was 15h30 on Monday, October 15, 1979, and Umtali's first shop bomb had just exploded, ushering in a grim new phase of the war.

The blast blew the corrugated iron roof of the outfitter's shop in several directions – across the road, on top of an adjoining double-storeyed building and into a nearby tree. The shop front was destroyed and debris was strewn over the floor. Glass windows in two adjacent shops were also shattered.

A black shop assistant was hit in the thigh by shrapnel, but there were no other injuries. Another assistant, standing near a window, had a narrow escape. "I just closed my eyes and blocked my ears," she said. "Glass rained all over me. I felt heat and heard the bang."

Shop staff told of seeing a suspicious-looking package in the store arcade. It was a square box with a metal rod protruding from the top, wrapped with transparent tape and rubber bands. Shoppers and staff had been cleared from the area and there was no one close by when the package exploded.

Many city people heard the bang but thought it was part of an Army artillery and mortar exercise in progress at the time.

Following the bombing, the Umtali Chamber of Commerce launched a 'Beat the Bomber' campaign and stressed the importance of security. People were warned not to let messengers and hawkers wander in and out of buildings. Any one of them could be carrying a bomb, it was pointed out.

Yet many businesses seemed unconcerned about the danger. A survey of several Main Street premises, including big departmental stores, by a newspaper reporter showed that security assistants were not checking parcels thoroughly. Items placed at 'left luggage' counters while owners shopped, were not being examined.

This indifference brought sharp reaction from the security forces, especially the police, who said it would take blood to wake people up to the danger they faced.

That blood was not long in coming. Just 18 days later, on November 2, another bomb exploded at Bhadella's Wool Shop further down Main Street. Fifteen people were injured, and were treated by first aid teams from South Ward, who were first on the scene.

A neighbouring shopkeeper said, "I heard this loud explosion and rushed out to see bodies lying in the street and glass strewn all over the place."

The blast blew out all the store's windows and gouged a hole 20 cm wide in the concrete floor. Scraps of wool were plastered on the ceiling and walls. The bomb had apparently been concealed in a parcel. The shop had a security guard but he was not at the door when the bomb went off.

Commenting, a Police spokesman said: "We were distressed by this. It revealed our inadequacy and the threat posed." But it also produced reaction. Within 45 minutes after the incident the managers of 26 businesses had signed up security guards.

It was their job to be vigilant, to prevent unauthorised people entering buildings and to search all those coming inside.

But this did not stop the bombers. On Thursday, November 8 at 09h40, a bomb exploded in Meikles, a big department store in Main Street. Two young black women, 'mujibas'*, one of whom had been carrying the bomb strapped to her leg for planting as soon as possible, died as a result of the explosion they had caused. The blast, in the men's department, shattered most of the glass frontage, blowing display goods onto the pavement. The noise was heard throughout the city.

This incident had such a profound effect on everyone that by lunch-time security guards and staff members had been posted at the entrances to most city stores. *The Umtali Post* produced a single page 'Special' with pictures of the damaged shop – and a warning.

"This morning's bombing was the worst yet. It is only through God's grace that there were not more people killed or seriously injured. What is worrying the public is the fact that this particular store had security guards checking shoppers for many months. Still someone got in ...

---

*Youths living in tribal areas trained by Communist terrorists to act as look-outs, go-betweens and messengers. Usually males, but females were also used in latter times.

"Business houses, traders and the public must take this matter far more seriously ... thorough searches of people as well as bags and parcels must be carried out."

Engineers inspect the site where Umtali's third shop bomb exploded, in a big department store in Main Street. Two women, who carried the bomb inside, died.

Hotels and stores put up cubicles where body searches were made on everyone coming in. Women had to open their handbags for inspection and black mothers removed the babies they carried tied to their backs. Men were searched in separate compartments. Where an arcade contained a number of shops, managers clubbed together to meet the expense of security checks carried out at both entry and exit points.

Many shoppers objected to the searches but it was for their own good. Explosives sufficient to wreck and kill could be contained in an ordinary cigarette packet. People were warned against 'browsing' in shops. "Know what you want, go straight in and buy, then go home," they were told. Mothers were advised to leave children with friends when they went shopping and also not to buy where there were no security guards.

Owners were told to stay close to shopping bags and watch them constantly. It was all too easy to slip a device into an unattended basket, hoping it would be carried inside.

'Beat the Bomber' talks, films and demonstrations educated the public. The bombers' target was people and the devices could be of any size. The idea behind urban bombing was to lower morale and convince people it was not worth living in Umtali, the Police said.

'Cordon-and-search' exercises became routine practice. Certain areas were sealed off by armed police and troops. Passers-by were checked to find out who they were and what they were carrying.

"We are looking for suspicious persons, not only bombs," said the city's Police chief, who slammed both the commercial men who complained of losing business as a result of the increased safety measures, and shoppers who grumbled about the inconvenience.

By December Umtali was accustomed to bomb drill. 'Bomb-breaks' became part of the working day, with staff being cleared from premises when suspect devices were reported.

A portable radio, a parcel of old papers, a bundle of firewood in a tree, a package of old clothes, a tin trunk of books, a cardboard box – all were suspect.

There were bouquets for those who reported objects, but brickbats for those who refused to move away from the area fast enough. Some walked backwards to see what went on when their curiosity got the better of them.

Despite official fears that Christmas shopping might be a 'bomber's paradise' there were no more incidents. With the ceasefire at the end of 1979, people gradually relaxed. Cordon-and-searches ceased, body searches stopped and even the security guards disappeared from shop doorways.

Looking back on those evil days, a president of the Umtali Chamber of Commerce, whose grandfather came to the country in 1893, commented: "Umtali reached its lowest ebb when bombs started appearing in shops, six months before the end of the war. It was the Chamber of Commerce which initiated the anti-bombing campaign in the city and the authorities made it so difficult for the saboteurs to leave their nasty little parcels that this particular aspect of the war faded away."

He paid tribute to the spirit of the people of Umtali during those difficult years. "In spite of the attacks on the city the people proved most resilient and refused to capitulate. Businesses continued, though trade was poor and many companies battled to keep going."

The closing of the Mozambique border in March 1976 had a detrimental effect on Umtali's tourism and trade, and the hotel industry, in particular, suffered very badly, with some hotels being maintained on a caretaker basis only.

He pointed out that Umtali's economy has always been closely linked to the prosperity of the farming community, especially the large timber industry, and that of coffee, tea, cotton, wheat, cattle and tobacco. In the last two years of the war Umtali's economy was adversely affected by the hammering the farmers took. The timber industry, especially, suffered many setbacks and sawmilling came to a virtual standstill when mills on the estates were burnt down.

Although Rhodesians were fighting for their very existence as well as battling against sanctions in the '70s, they never went hungry. Shops in the main centres could always supply the necessities of life and sometimes a few luxuries as well.

By contrast, two years after the war's end, there were shortages of bread, cheese, meat, butter and other locally-made consumer items, as well as petrol. Traders complain about the long delays in delivering the goods they have ordered, while shoppers complain about the ever-rising cost of the things they buy. With spiralling inflation, traders also find that their import allocations (imports are strictly controlled) produce fewer and fewer goods, so that the lifting of sanctions has had no marked effect upon commerce.

Hopes held out at Independence for a rapid increase of trade and tourism with Mozambique have not materialised. The barriers and fences are down at Forbes Border Post and the route to Beira is open again, but there is very little movement across the border. The sea, the sand and the prawns, which were the magnet for thousands of holidaymakers in the 'colonial era', may still be there, but few are going to Beira to find out. The security situation has put them off. Similarly, there has been no rush of Mozambican shoppers to Umtali to bring a minor trade boom similar to that experienced at Kariba and the Victoria Falls with shoppers from Zambia. Too much of Umtali's cross-border trade has been illegal with people selling smuggled goods like prawns, cases of sardines and herrings (gifts to Mozambique from countries in Europe), ivory and other items.

When the war ended, 1 000 000 people – refugees, fighters, children and students – came into the country, all with money to spend. In addition, more black Zimbabweans had highly-paid jobs. The result was that business boomed, but there was a terrible shortage of goods, and the rate of inflation ran very high. The road ahead, as the commerce president saw it, was for the country to become more efficient and self-sufficient.

Manicaland's principal industry, forestry, lost more men and had more damage done to than any other. Thousands of hectares of trees were destroyed by terrorists' deliberate fires in one year alone. Property and buildings were burnt, vehicles and equipment blown up or stolen and destroyed, men were killed and skilled labour chased away. All this has cost millions, with Anglo American companies and the Government Forestry Commission being the chief losers.

It was only in October 1978 that the Timber Growers' Association in Umtali started to keep official records of war damage. Statistics soon revealed an alarming situation. Fifteen different estates sent in returns and, before hostilities ceased, many had suffered more than a dozen incidents involving sudden death and destruction of men and property, all in little over a year.

The monthly returns, with details of incidents and losses, terse and to the point, came in regularly. The first was from Gwendingwe, a Melsetter concern, which was repeatedly hit. In September 1978, incidents were minor. Terrorists entered the compound, cut the security fence, robbed the beer hall, attempted to abduct the local ranger and then fired anti-tank rifle grenades at the Police Landrover.

The following month there were no incidents at all, a unique report for that year. But for two years the valiant young estate manager and his staff were continually hammered. Men were wounded, labourers chased off, vehicles attacked, money and equipment stolen, cattle rustled, the clinic looted, a foreman murdered, houses fired on with rockets and mortars, and trees burnt in a tale of constant destruction. Still the estate continued, with indomitable perseverance, their only minor triumph and consolation being when two terrorists blew themselves up while setting landmines in the area in March 1979 – rough justice perhaps, but a minor source of satisfaction to the residents in the district.

The Melsetter forest estates were particularly hard hit by terrorism, with 14 incidents being reported from Charter Forest Estate. In 1978 eight forest employees died in action, defending their right to continue living and working in the area. In 1979 there were 98 terror incidents in forests along the border.

Couples returning home from shopping trips to Umtali were ambushed by terrorists, wounded and killed. Tractor drivers moving about their daily work were threatened, injured and shot. A white forester from Melsetter was abducted and taken to Mozambique for several months. Another was killed at Sheba in the Penhalonga district. Forest rangers were held up and robbed of labourers' pay. Clinics were looted and fuel pumps blown up. Houses and cars were burnt and forest vehicles stolen.

At one forest estate there was a public decapitation of a black man and his wife by terrorists – because they had a daughter married to a policeman. In another area a forest ranger was shot dead and his labourers threatened.

Sawmills turning out the much-needed timber for development were reduced to ashes. Buses serving forest estates were ambushed and workshops were attacked. Bars and kiosks nearby were ransacked and labourers kidnapped. Quarters were damaged and fittings smashed or stolen. Oxen disappeared and fences were cut. Intimidation was rampant.

Vehicles were riddled with bullets and a tipper truck worth $15 000 was burnt out. Vehicles and equipment were in a sorry state and there was neither money nor opportunity to replace them. The attacks on heavy lorries and trailers loaded with sawn timber on the road between Melsetter and Umtali became so serious that special convoys had to be run to protect the timber supply, so vital to industry.

Murder, abduction, attack, theft and destruction – Rhodesian foresters and their men resisted all this for more than three years, trying to keep forests growing and their timber output flowing.

When the Timber Growers' Association sent out its circular asking for returns so that all members could assess the true situation, they certainly got the facts. One ironic note on a return, in the 'Reaction of Security Forces' column, was – 'NIL – Frustrated by Lancaster House Agreement'.

Attacks continued after the cease-fire in January 1980 with vehicles hi-jacked and grenades thrown on the Melsetter Road. The destructive habits of the troublemakers took time to die out and the foresters' frustration at seeing years of endeavour destroyed, continued.

The courage of these men, black and white, their wives and families, was incredible. The lonely roads and thickly-covered forest slopes held possible danger at every bend, yet very few left their posts.

When Manicaland's forest community met at funerals, as they so often did, their hearts went out to the bereaved, particularly in Melsetter, the tiny village overlooking the Chimanimani Mountains, which lost so many forest and farming people.

Umtali industries dependent on timber as their main raw material were greatly hampered in obtaining supplies from the 'hot areas'. To bring in the wood, convoys had to be used, slowing up deliveries and resulting in the uneconomic use of transport.

"We also had difficulties getting our finished products to the main centres of Salisbury and Bulawayo," said one industrialist. "Later transport ran in daylight only."

A 'blessing' was that the imported raw materials for Umtali's industry came through from South Africa with very little delay, unlike the present situation when consignments sent via Maputo in Mozambique often take more than two months to arrive from the port.

"Very few of our factories actually closed down for lack of raw materials throughout the war years," the industrialist said. "Now the war is over more than one plant has run out of materials and has had to close until such time as the goods arrive."

Industries dependent on power brought to Manicaland from Kariba were seldom cut off. Although the supply lines were extremely vulnerable they were subjected to ineffective terrorist attacks. The people living in Melsetter, Cashel and Chipinga had not been so fortunate, with electricity supplies frequently interrupted when pylons were blown up. "We were all very appreciative of the magnificent job done by the local Electricity Supply Commission staff who were frequently sent into extremely dangerous areas to repair the damage done to the transmission lines," he added.

Miraculously too, the city's water supply was virtually untouched, although in many places the pipeline was an easy target.

"Despite years of sanctions which preceded the war and the fact that much of the plant used by Umtali's major industries was far from new, we managed to keep the wheels of industry turning with the help of local engineering firms," said a former president of the Manicaland

Chamber of Industry. The engineering firms adapted to the situation and produced spare parts – some needed urgently – while the bigger firms in Salisbury and Bulawayo undertook the fabrication of plants which, until then, was quite new to them.

"It is interesting to note that an Umtali engineering firm started making spares for a local industry and this led to exports to South Africa," he said.

On the human side, industrialists found themselves faced with ever-increasing numbers of their employees doing regular call-ups.

"Those under 30 only worked for you for about half the year," said a managing director. "Somehow you managed to keep your plant running, with those who were not on call-up putting in vast amounts of overtime.

"Another factor that had to be considered was that when these men came back from an arduous call-up it took them two to three weeks to reorientate themselves – and then it was almost time to go off again!"

Call-ups also disrupted the men's family life and this encouraged 'quite a few' to leave the country.

The mortar attacks on Umtali and the African townships seldom affected the turn-out for work the next morning, he said. "In fact, it was interesting to hear the staff, both black and white, boasting about their near misses."

Local omnibus companies suffered heavy losses of vehicles and income during those troubled years. One Umtali company, which has been operating in the area for 20 years, lost four buses. Several of their staff were threatened, wounded or killed. Once a bus had to be left in the bush for six weeks until it was safe for a breakdown vehicle to move in and recover it. On two occasions drivers and conductors were forced out of their vehicles and made to walk long distances through the bush.

In March 1980 terrorists stopped a bus and forced the driver to take his vehicle into the bush. Ordering out the driver, conductor and passengers, they killed the conductor and wounded the driver, who was left to die. He dragged himself to the main road to get help but died from his wounds later.

Although they went in fear of their lives, knowing they were a prime target, the bus men carried on with their jobs as best they could. However, services to dangerous areas like Melsetter and Inyanga had to be suspended, while on other country routes the buses only went halfway to their normal destination. Rural folk were left without transport, while the bus companies lost at least half their revenue.

7 The brown jobs

"Because of the continuous threat to the city, those residents with a security force commitment have been called upon to undertake duties in excess of the normal commitment imposed on other Rhodesians and they have responded wholeheartedly to this call in defence of their city."

–MCM CITATION

The backbone of Manicaland's defence in the tough years was the Territorial Force – all those civilians who disappeared regularly from normal work. Summoned to the war by official notices, the territorials swopped safari suits for 'camo kit',* packs and rifles, and were whisked off into the bush. What did the military think of these part-time soldiers of 4 RR? (The 4th [Manicaland] Battalion of The Rhodesia Regiment).

"We could not have wished for more co-operative troops," said the top man in the Thrasher operational area, i.e. Manicaland. A former commander of 3 Brigade (who had to tell Umtali to 'hold tight' and live each day as it came when Mugabe won the election in February 1980), praised the part-time soldiers.

"They were dedicated men, fighting in defence of their own country. They were the backbone of our forces. They were sent to far corners of the province, knowing their wives and families had been left at home in vulnerable positions and they worried about them. It was that type of warfare. But army-wise the territorials contributed well. Our entire team-work depended upon them."

Of the years leading to the end of the bush war, he said: "We all have unhappy memories, but there are some splendid ones too. I find it tremendous how people, particularly farmers, could tolerate the dangers they faced, the isolation, the damage to their homes, equipment and labour, as well as the loss of loved ones. The bravery of the ordinary people of Umtali and Manicaland will always impress me."

Back at the office: "It's not *that* time already!" was the plaintive cry when the small brown envelopes arrived with call-up commands. At homes, lounge floors were covered with kit which was hastily sorted, buttons sewn on, seams repaired, as wives resigned themselves to yet another enforced separation.

Early apprehension soon faded however, and by the second day of call-up Manicaland's manhood was in uniform and ready for anything.

---

*Camouflage uniform.

Although there was some fear (and the record showed good reason for it), the spirit engendered among troops, black and white, was such that a strong and motivated force was established.

The humour was always there. Any situation could provide the seeds of a practical joke or a good laugh. Sometimes roles were reversed and civilian executives became mere troopies, saluting officers who might be their own junior members of staff.

The National Servicemen were posted to all branches of the security forces. Some were posted to the Rhodesian Light Infantry's 'fire-force' after a strenuous 4½ months' training and families followed their trails with interest. Mount Darwin (with more pubs per hectare than any-where else), Inyanga, Chipinga, Vila Salazar (where men spent more time underground, mole-like, than above) Mphoengs (near the Botswana border for those who have never been), Panda-ma-Tenga, Kazungula, Victoria Falls, Binga, Mukumbura and Kanyemba – the names conjured up exotic, far-off places. For school-leavers it was a case of seeing the country at the Government's expense.

The National Servicemen felt they had a tough time with a total of 18 months' service. Later, as territorials, they spent six weeks 'in' and 12 weeks 'out', "depending on how often an election was necessary", said one troopie who found that a 12 week call-up was nothing unusual. It kept him out of mischief, he said.

To some fell the job of catering. Always complaining – in spite of gift freezers, fresh meat and other supplies – cooks became the heart and soul of a company and loved their work. Where else could they test their experimental gastronomical delights on a willing, eager and hungry clientele?

Potential Jody Schecters and Mario Andrettis found themselves as drivers, speeding through the bush or along tarred roads, in Tribal Trust Land or city streets, in an assortment of vehicles – 2.5, 4.5, RL, MAP, Hippo, Puma, Crocodile or common Landrovers. They at least offered a change from the clapped out old Morris back home.

Everyone complained about the weather on call-ups, with good reason. In winter the days were invariably too hot to carry huge packs through the bush, filled with jerseys, blankets, extra socks and kit to keep one warm during the freezing nights. And was it the Army or the Police Reserve which first discovered the warmth of the 'old girl's' panti-hose? In summer it rained and rained – even during the drought years.

Remember ratpacks? No one liked bully beef. Everyone hated braised

59

steak in sauce, and few asked for second helpings of frankfurters. What the men preferred was tinned fish and inevitable 'doggo's'.

The local troopie was a good improviser and soon discovered that dog biscuits soaked overnight and fried next morning made delicious pancakes. Imagine sitting in the bush on a lonely kopje, hundreds of kilometres from anywhere, relishing a fabulous meal of rice pudding, cooked with dried milk powder and flavoured with jam from the ever present ratpack tubes?

With pride and satisfaction the soldiers enjoyed rivalry. Pubs from Rusape to Chipinga had their share of representatives from the RLI, RAR, SAS, RR,* Selous Scouts and Grey's Scouts, as well as the RDR (Rhodesia Defence Regiments), all telling the tale and claiming the best regiment was theirs.

Language became unique to a unit. RLI troopies lived in a world of their own and few outsiders could understand their conversation. Even lesser known was that of the RDR which consisted mainly of Coloured and Asian men.

A dog to an RDR soldier was a 'tick taxi' while a crocodile was a 'mobile handbag' or a 'flat dog' to the RLI. 'Rotary chariot' was the name for a helicopter, while RDR vehicles were 'goffel chariots'. White people were 'honkies', Coloureds were 'goffels' and Indians 'bhais'.

Inevitably there were many narrow escapes from death, a 4 RR private recalled. In pouring rain he was one of a group of 12 on reconnaissance, creeping through the undergrowth with blackened faces, laden with kit. It was dusk and they were on a long walk to check on enemy base camps. Muted curses were frequently heard as the men slithered and bumped down a pig trail with their weapons and kit. Although they were following a map, they were unaware that a narrow river had become a raging torrent. Suddenly two of the group were washed downstream. Struggling waist-high in water, the lads saved their fellows, and pushed on to sleep in a mealie patch as unobtrusively as possible till first light.

Did these youngsters, many straight from school, or their elders in 4th Battalion Rhodesia Regiment enjoy their call-ups? Today, with the war over, many still recall the old times and declare: "We would gladly do it all again if we had to."

The 4th Battalion was formed in 1959, mainly from farmers, with annual training camps at Inkomo, outside Salisbury. In January 1964 it was moved to the Drill Hall in Umtali, absorbing B Company 1 RR who

*Rhodesian Light Infantry, Rhodesian African Rifles, Special Air Services, Rhodesia Regiment.

occupied the building. On April 30 that year the Battalion was granted the Freedom of Umtali. The Mayor handed the Scroll of Honour to the commanding officer, Lieut. Col. W. W. S. Smart, himself a former Mayor, at a parade at the Civic Centre. The Scroll and Colours were then paraded through the streets of Umtali.

Attached to the Honour was the privilege for the Battalion to add 'Manicaland' to its name and the right for members to wear a blue and white hackle.

B Company 4 RR was the first territorial company in 2 Brigade committed to action on what was then border control in the north-east. It was later regrouped under 3 Brigade, and when Operation Thrasher began in February 1976, 4 RR was deployed to the Eastern Districts, serving first in Inyanga, then Umtali and Chipinga. In December 1977 it was moved again, to Grand Reef, and finally back to Chipinga where it assisted in two general elections – those that brought Bishop Muzorewa's UANC to power in 1979 and Robert Mugabe and ZANU (PF) to power in 1980. The Battalion stood down that year and its Colours and Roll of Honour were laid up in St John's Cathedral, Umtali, on October 23, 1980.

(There are 185 names on the Manicaland Roll of Honour – 73 Army, 57 BSA Police, 51 Internal Affairs and four Air Force.)

When they were not on call-up, Umtali's territorials were still protecting the community. After the city had been attacked it was decided to organise suburban area commands as a retaliation and protection force in the event of terrorist infiltration of the city under mortar attack. It was realised that such an attack on a suburb would have a disastrous effect on morale, so 4th Battalion men were asked to stand by at home for this eventuality.

4 RR consisted of men from all walks of life. They were proud of their regiment and of their colours. They wore their dark green berets with the blue and white hackles with pride, whether they were marching in an Aloe Week procession or as bearers at a funeral.

As the Army Chaplain said at the service for the laying-up of the Battalion Colours: "The 4th (Manicaland) Battalion, Rhodesia Regiment, has served its country, its province, its city with great credit and distinction. Our Colours and Roll of Honour are laid up to rest with all rightful dignity, respect and esteem that befits the good name of the Battalion.

"Many things may be removed from us in the ever-changing scenes and orders of life. But one thing that is difficult to remove is the memory of the past. Every member of 4 RR, past and present, can be justly proud in remembering the achievements of this Battalion. These we must not only remember now but also in the future.

"We meet here today to salute for the last time the 4th (Manicaland) Battalion, Rhodesia Regiment, and to remember with solemn pride, honour and gratitude those members who paid the supreme sacrifice. May God bless us all."

Army 'girls' riding on a Ferret scout car, show the flag for the Army in Umtali's annual Aloe Week procession, while helicopters fly overhead.

3 Brigade moved to Umtali in January 1976; first to the overcrowded Addams Barracks (formerly a Catholic boys' school, Carmel College), then into the Cecil Hotel at the corner of Victory Avenue and Main Street, shortly before it was due for demolition.

This familiar city landmark had been empty since the opening of the new Manica Hotel next door. The Army quickly commandeered 'The Cecil' to make it shipshape for Brigade Head Quarters.

Ed, the Quartermaster, well remembers the scene. With no electricity in the building their first task was a complete re-wiring job. The old hotel echoed to the noise of hammering as walls were knocked down, partitions banged up and a honeycomb of offices and hide-outs built for the necessary departments in what were formerly corridors, hotel suites, public rooms and bedrooms. Gone were the faded basketwork chairs and nodding verandah palms which had decorated Umtali's most popular social focal point for years. Up went wire and 'Keep Out' notices as the 'brown jobs' moved in.

In March of that year 3 Brigade set up house as JOC Thrasher*, in the heart of the city. Military vehicles roared to and fro or monopolised parking bays in the area, while Umtali shoppers became accustomed to seeing the Army's khaki singlets hanging on the balconies to dry.

Brigadier Derry MacIntyre was the first commander of 3 Brigade. A dynamic crowner of queens and princesses at Umtali social functions, he endeared himself to Territorial Force wives and mothers by holding endless meetings with them and listening to their complaints.

That year there was a near miss on Headquarters when a Russian rocket landed a block away. It missed the top brass by a few dozen metres, and the casing was propped up in the Quartermaster's office as a relic of a short, sharp attack on the city at 17h22 on November 3.

Just before Christmas, the locals, and the country, were saddened by the tragic death of four top security force men in a helicopter crash at Cashel while on their way to visit troops in the field.

Ed, the Quartermaster, scrutinised the daily sitreps† to familiarise himself with troop movements and then worked flat out to supply the outgoing men with all their needs, from telescopes to transport. The situation changed daily, frequently overnight, and it was his job to know who was going where and who was coming, although not necessarily the reason why.

Visitors were numerous and varied. They ranged from a high-ranking German observer, Prince von Habsburg, and a previous NATO commander to the 'hoi polloi' of the world's Press. Prime Minister Ian Smith came regularly and once held an urgent Cabinet meeting in the dining-room when an RF Congress coincided with a national emergency.

At the daily JOC meetings (they seemed endless when someone in

---

*Joint Operations Command.
†Situation reports.

town was urgently required to attend to normal business) the commanders of the Army, local BSAP, Air Force, Special Branch and Internal Affairs met to read reports of the previous day's incidents and to plan a major design for future operations.

They all had snippets of information to contribute, so the picture was consolidated and the facts presented for review and action by all concerned.

"Whether or not there was too much censorship of war news, as the public claimed, was a matter of opinion," said one JOC chairman. "If a group of terrorists had moved into an area and we knew about it, then we moved troops there also. It was hardly wise to tell the world we'd done so, although we always notified farmers in the area whenever possible, so that they could take the necessary precautions. A frequent complaint from farmers after incidents was that there had been nobody to react immediately. But we had 565 km of Mozambique border to guard. We had to deploy men at a moment's notice from Cashel to Enkeldoorn if necessary, with minimal strength."

In 1976 the Army girls first put in an appearance and their swinging figures in camouflage trousers and battledress shirts were seen popping in and out of 3 Brigade Headquarters. Many were attracted by the glamour of the uniform (the beige and bottle green of Rhodesia's Women's Army was very smart), and the excitement of being on an all-male scene. Others decided that to do the donkeywork at the nerve centre of war was the best way of serving their country.

The Army apparently fought against having women in uniform for years because of 'administrative hassles'. Pressure of events eventually made it essential for them to recruit women, whites only in the early days, to use their talents in administrative duties in a non-combatant sphere.

"The Army girls' contribution proved extremely useful. Although they did not join in great numbers, there were enough of them to relieve men to go to the frontline," said the brigadiers.

Army wives played an important part in the war effort. Their support and understanding was absolutely essential. This was true of both regulars' and territorials' wives. They all bore a tremendous burden, and the Army acknowledged this.

One of Ed's tasks was to keep a close eye on the daily menus, particularly when conferences were being held and visitors needed feeding. He had one lucky find when 40 demijohns of Portuguese vino were discovered while he was turning out a storeroom to make an armoury.

He faithfully returned the bottles to the new hotel next door, but was given one in exchange.

"On the whole we never ran short of supplies, except whisky," said Ed, who saw the former hotel house four bars – the officers' mess, the sergeants' mess, the corporals' club and the other ranks' canteen.

Wartime difficulties included keeping a strict eye on expenditure, especially on fuel. Rhodesia was fighting an economic war as well as a military one. At the peak of activity 500 vehicles were maintained for use throughout the area and 'write off' figures were naturally high.

Ed's favourite duties were trips to the men in the field by 'chopper' or protected vehicle. He had his fair share of close shaves, jolting landmine explosions and being shot at, but returned with a better idea of what was needed in the bush, be it volleyballs or medical supplies.

When it was decided to establish the brigade as a permanent feature of Manicaland, the rear and main Headquarters were fused into one. Units belonging to the Brigade operated in the area, including Midlands 10th Battalion, The Rhodesia Regiment, which served first in the Chipinga area. When the war spread they moved back under command of Headquarters Midlands District.

The Brigade's other two territorial battalions, 8 and 4 RR, served in Manicaland with 3, 5 and 6 (Independent) Companies, Rhodesian Afri-

Grey's Scouts ride through Umtali early one morning before being deployed to Chipinga.

can Rifles. Other non-infantry units included 3 (Brigade) Signal Squadron, 3 Engineer Squadron, 3 Maintenance Company, 3 Medical Company and, as important as the rest, 3 Provost Platoon (Military Police) and 3 Pay Company.

From time to time non-brigade units, the Selous Scouts, SAS and Grey's Scouts, were brought into the area to carry out operations.

Once the artillery unit based on the south side of Umtali agitated for a ranging programme to prove the fall of shot. The Brigadier reluctantly gave his approval because of the difficulties of adequately warning sufficient people beforehand about the 'bangs', and the fact that many might not receive the message. Confusion could result.

The artillery boys let go with their fire almost simultaneously with the bomb explosion which wrecked Tip Top in Main Street. The Army was blamed in many quarters for poor aim with their big guns!

"No ways could we even laugh it off," said the Brigadier.

As chairman of the Landmine Warfare Committee in Salisbury, Brigadier Peter saw the development of all the curiously-shaped protected vehicles seen around the province. The experts built experimental models and then blew them up to study the most economic form of safe transport. A wide variety of Hyenas, Porcupines, Leopards and other 'animals' resulted.

One of the most successful was a modification of the 2.5, and these vehicles definitely saved lives. Originally the Army and civilians suffered at least one death, frequently more, for every landmine on the roads. Later in the war it was surprising if any deaths at all occurred as a result of explosions under the specially reinforced transport vehicles.

Eighty per cent of the Rhodesian army were black soldiers, and blacks and whites fought together on the same side, learning far more about each other than at any other time in history. "This made for a valuable interchange of friendship and appreciation of each other's qualities, courage and character," said the Brigadier.

When the Mugabe Government ordered the integration of all the forces to form one Zimbabwean Army, all the different parties were fighting each other as well as the Government. Now they were being ordered to work together and such a situation was incomprehensible to some. There was conflict in their minds as to what constituted a desirable future for the new Zimbabwe they had inherited.

Sadly, many blacks of the former Rhodesian Army still live in fear of retaliation and dare not wear their bravery medals.

What sort of conduct merited a medal during those difficult years?

Hundreds were awarded throughout the country, some, unfortunately, posthumously. Buried in the files, gathering dust, is this typical citation for a local man who was awarded one of the highest decorations, the Bronze Cross of Rhodesia. It was given to him for 'continuous bravery'.

"Sergeant T has been continuously deployed on operations since 1969 and during this period has been personally responsible for the elimination of many terrorists. He has been involved in numerous contacts, during which he has shown a high degree of leadership and aggression. In November 1976, while deployed in Operation Thrasher area, Sergeant T successfully ambushed several terrorists in a post Fire Force contact and killed them all. In a separate engagement in 1977 in the Hurricane area, Sergeant T was a group commander in a Fire Force operation. On being deployed he immediately came under fire and by careful deployment of his men managed to kill two of the terrorists and capture another.

"Sergeant T had repeatedly carried out reconnaissance patrols on enemy camps, many of which have been successful in pinpointing targets for the Fire Force. Sergeant T has displayed great initiative and courage on operations and has shown himself to be an outstanding soldier."

* * *

The Umtali minefield, along the border with Mozambique, was the 'hairiest' in the country because of the terrain (the very steep gradients), the type of vegetation and the weather, said the man who probably knew more about it than anyone else.

He was Major Vic, a second generation Rhodesian, who joined the regular Army in 1972 after spending years in the Territorial Force. An electrician by trade, he decided to join the Engineers, and in 1973, with two others, laid the first personnel mine in the Mukumbura minefield in the north-east.

"We realised then that a minefield was a very necessary barrier, although mines are only a deterrent, not a permanent barrier, unless covered by fire," he said just before leaving Zimbabwe with his wife and baby daughter to settle in South Africa.

In 1975 Umtali's need of such a barrier suddenly became obvious and attention was switched to the eastern border.

The first job was to construct the security road from the top of Cecil Kop to the Braintree ridge in the Lower Vumba. The road – a magnificent scenic drive more or less following the international boundary – cost $1 000 000.

Once the road had been completed the Engineers started work on the minefield. It consisted of three lines of ploughshare and other types of mine combined, and stretched eventually from Stapleford to Burma Valley.

"The three main dangers facing the Engineers, which didn't exist in other minefields, were the low cloud or mist, the wet vegetation in the tropical rain forest and the thick humus. Put together they made for a very slippery, treacherous situation," the major said.

The minefield was completed in 1976 before the first attack on Umtali.

The war took a grim toll of the Engineers. They lost 67 men, killed in action and in minefield construction, and more than 90 limbs in the minefields.

"We had a man walking down the minefield doing maintenance when suddenly a snake appeared in front of him. There is only one route in a minefield, the centre line, but frightened, he ran into the field and was injured by a ploughshare.

"Another Engineer was seriously injured when a bushbuck triggered a trip wire and the man received four pellets, one in his forehead, one in his chest, one in his lungs and another just above the knee."

The major said that animals and minefields didn't go together and the Engineers had been totally opposed to the Cecil Kop Game Park, and particularly the suggestion to use the minefield security fence as part of the game park fence.

Once the minefield was in position, life, for Umtali people, was punctuated with bangs at all hours of the day and night.

Most of them, according to the major, were caused by animals, rodents or birds – such as a dove flying into a trip wire. Even vegetation, like a branch or a strip of bark from a gum tree, can set off a mine.

He knew of five people, three of them white, who had been killed in the Umtali-Burma Valley minefield, although he was sure there were more. They had all been working on minefield maintenance.

"A lot of our injuries were sustained as a result of terrorist incursions," he said. "Once the enemy had been injured in the minefield it was the Engineers' job to breach it and remove the body or injured person and then replace the used mines, no easy task with the vegetation and the weather.

"On maintenance days there was no problem. If it was raining we wouldn't go into the minefield, but if there was an injured person lying there screaming we had no option but to go."

Over the years 'the other side' assessed the Engineers' equipment and method of operation in the minefield and ' to their cost' breached it and made routes in and out. The Engineers were hard pressed to maintain the 700 km of minefield in the country. Even keeping the Stapleford to Burma Valley section in order was a mammoth task.

Then, when the war ended, the Engineers were tasked with the unpleasant job of removing all the minefields they had laid. It had to be done using specially protected heavy earthmoving machines.

"If you remember that people are still picking up mines from World War II, the chance of all those in Zimbabwe being cleared in six to 12 years is pretty remote," he said.

The Engineers' other roles were mine warfare on roads, the booby trapping of stores and abandoned farmhouses and EOD (explosive ordinance disposal).

"Thrasher was second in order of landmine intensity. The highest figure of mines per month was in the JOC Repulse* area. At the peak of the war we had between 20 and 40 mines a month which had to be lifted by the Engineers. Those that had been detonated by vehicles were investigated for booby traps and also for intelligence purposes. The last job we had was the collection and destruction of the bombs fired by our own people during the war and also arms caches left behind by the terrorists."

The Engineers had no bomb disposal injuries. There was one serious injury from lifting landmines and booby traps 'by kind courtesy of Lord Soames'. He wished the railway cleared in January 1980. "As he was the Governor we were given a direct order to clear the line. A former Umtali banker lost a leg at the thigh in this operation," the major said.

After the war ended the Engineers suffered some minor injuries. One man lost an eye clearing booby traps on a farm in Chipinga.

The major's final words were of praise for the people of Umtali. "They were fantastic to all the Engineers," he said. "For the first two years we were based in Salisbury and we came to Umtali as strangers. But people opened their hearts and invited us into their homes. The feeling towards us was quite unbelievable. I have been to all the towns in the country but there's none like Umtali."

---

*Joint Operations Committee for Victoria Province.

8 The Mushroom Club

"Us ouens* in the bluest only get kept in the dark, eh?"
"Ja, and fed on bull . . ."
"Ja, well, have another beer and join the Mushroom Club. Cheers!"

This snippet of alcoholic conversation was typical of many heard at Grand Reef in the early days, according to Flight Lieutenant John, who spent much time there.

In the beginning the Rhodesian Air Force included regular members, National Servicemen undergoing training and a convivial band of volunteer reservists, enthusiasts with previous Air Force service in other Commonwealth forces. John was one of these, serving as a camp commandant and wearing a half-wing, indicating that he had served in another war as an air-gunner.

Before the Rhodesian bush war started, a Joint Operations Command system had been evolved, dividing the country into five areas where JOC's could be set up if necessary. Each JOC area was to be served by one or more forward airfields. There was a permanent forward airfield at Wankie, designated FAF 1, and a semi-permanent one at Kariba, FAF 2.

"When terrorist activities began, itinerant FAF's were established where necessary. As soon as an incursion was of any importance, an FAF 3 was established and remained in operation until that little scene had been sorted out," John said. "However, this happy state of affairs ended after Christmas 1972 when widespread attacks on homesteads began in the Centenary area. FAF 3 dug itself in at the Centenary airstrip and the area was designated Operation Hurricane, with the JOC at Bindura." Later FAF 4 was opened at Mount Darwin and FAF 5 at Mtoko.

A forward airfield consisted of an Air Force presence with a few helicopters and an antiquated fixed wing aircraft known as a Trojan. Antiquated it may have been, but the Trog packed a tremendous punch. Stationed with the Air Force was a commando of the Rhodesian Light Infantry. This combined force (which became known as the Fire Force) was ready to go into action whenever terrorist groups showed themselves.

---

*Slang for 'we people' or 'us chaps'.
†Air Force Personnel (Blue jobs).

If heavier fire power was needed Hunters and Canberras were called in and directed to the target by the Trojan. Occasionally the FAF had the services of an old Provost pistol-engined trainer. With its twin Brownings and other 'funnies' this was an extremely potent air weapon.

An FAF consisted of a group of tents for the men and the normal domestic and administrative requirements. The early FAF's were merely strongly-defended encampments situated beside landing strips. They were usually kilometres from a dependable water supply, so the water bowser was a vital item of equipment.

Ablutions were basic. Latrines were found by the smell of chloride of lime and the buzzing of blue-bottles.

An important duty of a camp commandant, with his storeman ('equipper' in Air Force parlance) was to maintain adequate stocks of fuel. The drums usually came from base in Road Motor Service lorries, but sometimes 'funnies' on the road would stop them getting through. Then the Air Force had to bring in the supplies themselves.

"It is difficult to imagine what possessed us in those early days, lining up this precious fuel with parade-ground precision in neat, military rows alongside the aircraft," John said. "The aircraft too, were dressed by the right like guardsmen on review."

As the months went by the FAF's took on more permanent duties. The terrorists had infiltrated into the tribal communities. The war had obviously come to stay.

Tents gave way to prefabricated wooden buildings with all modern conveniences. Defensive earthworks were constructed round all the accommodation areas. Aircraft were hidden away each evening in permanent well-defended parking bays. Tarmac runways were quickly constructed.

"The old FAF's became permanent bases, complete with bars and swimming pools," said John.

Camp commandants soon found themselves in offices equipped with safes (instead of keeping the field imprest in back trouser pockets), and filing cabinets to house the unending missives received from Headquarters.

Additional personnel started arriving in the form of A and B reservists who were called up for six weeks every two months. These men proved useful in spite of the strong 'old soldier' and 'barrack-room lawyer' element in their midst. The spirit in which they tackled anything they felt worthwhile was admirable. They contributed commonsense and a spirit of seriousness to the job, and the war could not have been conducted efficiently without them.

Round about 1975 when it became obvious that the Portuguese in Mozambique were losing interest and that Frelimo were more or less having things their own way outside the military cantonments, the daily sitreps and the radio made it plain that the communists were about to take over the metropolitan government in Portugal with the tacit agreement of the forces in Mozambique.

"I was called up for two days to survey Grand Reef aerodrome for the possible establishment of an FAF there," John said.

"After submitting a report I got a verbal, paternal pat on the head. Mozambique collapsed and our eastern border was left wide open to the enemy. In February 1976, while on call-up at Mount Darwin, I was told to supply personnel to open up another FAF at Chipinga – FAF 6. At this time the war was rapidly losing momentum in Mount Darwin and Mtoko was becoming more active."

Then, Salisbury people saw a sleek little aircraft, with twin tail booms, streaking across the sky. Older folk swore it was a 'Lightning'. The Lynx had arrived, and Umtali was to see a lot of it in months to come. Apart from its future worthwhile contribution to the war, it became a wonderful morale booster to the Air Force.

"We had watched with concern our overworked Trojans of No 4 Squadron," (Umtali's own, since the city had formally adopted No 4 some time before) John said. "The blues said of it, 'The old Trog has 12 cylinders, 11 of them clapping, and one turning the prop'."

With the opening of FAF 6 at Chipinga, a new operational area, JOC Thrasher, with headquarters in the old Cecil Hotel in Umtali, came into being. JOC Repulse was soon to follow in the Lowveld, with FAF 7 at Buffalo Range.

"I'd been back from call-up a week when I had a 'phone call at work asking what I had done with my survey of Grand Reef," he said. "It appeared it had been mislaid at Air Force Headquarters."

Next day he reported to the military at Addams Barracks where he was told he was on call-up again with immediate effect. He was handed a signal telling him to establish FAF 8 at Grand Reef immediately. It was to be in operation when the first aircraft arrived at 08h00 the following morning! The ground personnel, with the camp equipment, would follow sometime in the afternoon.

"It seemed an impossible task," John said. "I arranged for the call-up of a small group of volunteer reservists, instructing them to grab a blanket, raid their homes for food and proceed to Grand Reef under their own steam. In retrospect, the response and enthusiasm is hard to describe."

At Grand Reef they found the grass shoulder-high. Then the heavens opened and it poured with rain (63 mm) while they unpacked. The first items to be off-loaded from a lorry and hurriedly packed at New Sarum air base, were 10 rather useless grass-fire beaters!

However, the RLI commando arrived that night and the aircraft was on schedule next morning. The combined air and ground forces were in action within a couple of hours.

To budget for any FAF, a camp commandant required a field imprest in the region of $500. The airfield had been opened on a Friday and Air Headquarters did not work on Saturdays, John recalled. It was thought that money would be available by Wednesday, but imagine trying to organise food, transport and other items without ready cash. "I just had to arrange an overdraft with my bank manager to tide things over.

"I was destined to serve the remainder of my call-up at Grand Reef till I developed an odd mixture of affection and downright loathing for the place," he said.

As soon as possible after the end of that memorable stint he went to Chipinga to compare FAF 6 with the newly-opened Grand Reef. In spite of all the problems FAF 8's opening was 'cushy'. Chipinga was not the ideal site for a Forward Air Field. It would have been better at Nyanyadzi – a view shared by others.

"But Chipinga's civilian population had been so hard-pressed that any attempt to move the airbase to Nyanyadzi (in the drier, flatter lowveld) would have had a disastrous effect on the morale of that courageous community," John said. FAF 6 eventually degenerated into a token forward airfield, a subsidiary of Grand Reef.

Meanwhile Grand Reef looked different at each call-up period. TV sets, cinemas and a pool all appeared as a result of the efforts of the people of Umtali and Odzi and the 'fantastic support' of the Border Patrol Welfare Fund.

The tempo never slackened at FAF 8. Few days passed without a 'wing ding'. Reports were constantly coming in from Observation Posts, established on prominent high features, of enemy movement in the area. The terrorism mounted daily. Almost nightly, aircraft answered distress calls from farms under attack. They flew numerous errands of mercy carrying injured blacks to hospital and safety. "The main sufferers in the war here were the black people themselves," the Flight-Lieutenant commented.

One call-up is particularly remembered. He had a feeling 'things would happen', especially when a doctor at Grand Reef had difficulty getting permission to return to his Bulawayo practice.

The weekend had passed normally. Then, suddenly, all but one air-craft took off with crews and their personal equipment. Another caterer turned up with extra kitchen staff and the camp commandant was advised to prepare for an influx of men. Within the hour, security was tightened to the extent that no personal mail left camp and there was a complete clampdown on all unofficial communication with the world outside.

"I was no wiser than anyone else about what was happening," he said.

Supplies began arriving and volunteers readily unloaded them. Large marquees and camp-beds were an indication of the numbers to be catered for. The challenge was accepted with delight.

"I had an excellent 'SWO man' (for some mysterious reason NCO's were known as SWO's) and a first-class crowd of mature A and B reservists. As a team we felt capable of anything. The two caterers were experts and calmly accepted the prospect of an influx. Catering was a security risk as we normally bought from regular local tradespeople. Any sudden demands would need explaining and rumours would circulate, so our orders to regular suppliers were kept to normal and we augmented them by ordering from all over Umtali. These supplies were collected by airmen wearing borrowed Army clothing."

It was obvious they were to play nursemaid to a large cross-border 'punch up'.

The doctor's delayed departure became significant. They had to pro-vide a casualty clearing station, complete with operating theatre. They had no medical equipment in the stores. With the doctor's advice, direction and energetic scrounging, a presentable emergency hospital was ready in a couple of hours. Among the makeshift equipment was an instrument steriliser in the shape of the camp's new frying pan, placed ready for use on a gas-ring.

The operation was a big one.

"We received only three casualties from the battle. One, unfortu-nately, was a lad whose body was brought back. Two others had leg and foot injuries which were not serious enough to prevent them finding their way to the Mushroom Club – the camp pub.

"The doc's most serious case that night was unconnected with the raid. A village tinker from a nearby Tribal Trust Land had tried to open a Communist-made phosphorous grenade to see how it worked. It was a horrible sight."

In World War II John had been involved in many air raids and allied landings but he could not recall any more impressive sight than the

74

Rhodesian choppers returning to Grand Reef at dusk in perfect formation with their navigation lights blinking against a darkening sky.

On landing the crews were tired and hungry. Two aircraft contained 'loot' – a dilapidated bicycle and a couple of balding chickens in the traditional coop.

The memory of that night's meal will remain for years. Caterers and staff had excelled themselves. The dedicated staff had little sleep that night, but turned out a most appetizing breakfast next morning.

The excitement continued for a day and a half, the administration ticking like a well-oiled machine. Even the ablutions and latrines were maintained in perfect hygienic order by a corporal who, in civilian life, is a prominent and successful Chipinga coffee farmer.

"As quickly as the exercise was thrown on to us, it disappeared. We became once again a forward airfield, devoid of planes and with nothing to do but clear up the mess, like the 'morning after' a very hectic party."

Possibly as a result of this raid they received intelligence reports that Grand Reef was to be attacked. Each evening at dusk the tension mounted, but the expected raid did not take place till after John had handed over the command to his successor. He later heard the attack clearly from the comfort of his own bed 14 km away.

Normally the camp commandant and his airmen were not in the limelight and so they were able to observe the personal side of those involved. The reaction of the crews and troops they took into the front line, and the tension of waiting around for take-off, were the same as he remembered from his youth. There were those who indulged in noisy, transparent bravado, probably scared at what might happen, but who quickly responded to their excellent training and latent courage, once the 'whatnot hit the fan'. The professional soldier-types, with their ability to contemplate the forthcoming action, waited with almost detached scientific expectation.

The airmen still remember the bunch of millet hanging over the bar counter with the label 'So and So's Combined Harvester'. The millet had been removed from the engine intake of an aircraft. The pilot had been so intent on going after a group of terrorists working their way through a millet field that he 'reaped' some of the crop in the process. It was said that he returned to base 'rather white around the gills'.

Although there were periods of intense activity, for the most part time hung heavily. When the airmen were not sleeping, arguing, indulging in horseplay or reading, they would play endless games of cards. In the cool of the late afternoon some would jog or play volley-ball. Kite-flying became a fad but was not encouraged because of all the overhead wires.

No reminiscences of the FAF's in Hurricane* and Thrasher would be complete without mention of Flight Sergeant Benji. He adopted the Air Force as a long-haired pup of ungainly appearance in the early days at Centenary.

Air crews at Grand Reef, waiting for something to happen.

He was every airman's dog. At no time would he have anything to do with Army or Police. When not curled up on the camp commandant's bed, Benji was invariably with the lads. At night he would sleep in any of the gun pits where his alertness to any audible movement was appreciated. Benji, presumably, could bark but his warning to human mates in the pits was always a quiet growl.

While at Mount Darwin Benji's leg was broken when a vehicle backed over him while he was asleep under it. He was casevaced to Salisbury for treatment – the first pup to be transferred by helicopter. He had a complete lack of interest in the charms of the local doggy dollies and was probably just a confirmed bachelor.

---

*North-east Machonaland.

76

The Rhodesian bush war has now become history. All that remains of the FAF's are the runways, deserted buildings and empty aircraft bays. The FAF's served their purpose and they are clearly remembered by all who knew them.

9 *Pro rege, pro lege*

"The law of the wise is a fountain of life, to depart from the snares of death."
Proverbs 13:14

The siren blared above the Charge Office *agric-alert* board. A woman's voice screamed in sudden alarm.

"I'm under attack! I'm under attack! Control! Quickly! They're shooting! My mother's been injured. My Bright Light's* been knocked over. Oh my God! I can't find him – we're under attack!"

The voice rose higher. Panic was gripping the caller. Shots and bangs could be heard faintly in the background. More voices came through from other sets while the lone woman sobbed. "My gun's jammed. I can't fire back. They're still shooting. Oh God, there's blood – my mother! Can't you come and help us? Send someone quickly!"

The frantic call echoed through the little Penhalonga Police Station as uniformed figures rushed to hear more clearly and pinpoint the call-sign on the map.

A grey-uniformed Woman Field Reservist (Police Woman Auxiliary) at her radio sets alerted the off-duty section officer, she alerted 'Sunray'† (out at a meeting), she called the reserve‡ stick§ (on their way to a canteen supper), she alerted the Women's Voluntary Service to say 'no need for supper at present'; next the Army, "We have an emergency," and she still had time to call back to the attacked homestead: "Hold on. We can hear you. Help is coming."

It was the Woman Field Reservist's last few minutes of duty after a busy six-hour shift. Her 'relief' walked in – a married couple, bringing their supper for the all-night stint. They had not heard the first frantic cries but immediately grasped the situation. They took over, calmly soothing the young woman at the farm and setting the rescue teams in motion.

Russian rockets, mortars, hand-grenades, heavy and smallarms fire were all being poured into the lonely farmhouse at two defenceless white women who had just returned from work in Umtali.

Agric-alert – portable radio telephone linking isolated homes (and vehicles) with police stations with their names, numbers and map references for homesteads and heli-pads.
*Police Reservist unfit for active duty (often a city dweller) used to guard homesteads.
†The member-in-charge of a police station or security force detachment.
‡Police Reserve (Auxiliaries).
§A small group of men under a leader.

'Scenes' like these became all too familiar to those who wore the grey princess-style button-through uniforms of the British South Africa Police Woman's Field Reserve. They were rarely seen in public. They were the backroom girls; the 'lowest form of life' at the police stations, who had to cope with such incidents as calmly as they did with the foibles of their superiors.

Communications, channels, codes, shackles, reports, locs, contacts, sitreps, call signs and casevacs all became part of their daily jargon, while briefs and de-briefs were not the pink and lacy sort. Hundreds of local women wore those grey uniforms for years, and were proud to do so.

At Grand Reef, a few kilometres from Odzi, a war nerve centre, Woman Field Reservist duties were an amalgam of radio-operating, message-carrying, tea-making and catering. "The emphasis was on whatever was most important at the time," said Gina.

"Our hours of duty changed frequently," she said. "We began by being 'on' from 08h00 to 16h00 only. Next we went from 16h00 to midnight as well, sleeping at Grand Reef and leaving at some unearthly hour the next morning. Then the powers-that-be decided we should also do midnight to 08h00.

A year after the WFR started at Grand Reef there were fears that the camp would be attacked. 'What to do' placards were put up at strategic places.

"The radio must be protected, never mind oneself," Gina said. "That chattering, squawking box is more important."

At the height of summer at 02h00, Gina had the radio control room windows wide open and the blackouts drawn against the heat. She was reading, yawning and smoking, when she heard a noise outside. She had her pistol in her hand when the curtain parted and a face peered in.

The black man, seeing the pistol in her hand, quickly stammered, "Don't shoot! I'm only the camp guard!"

At Grand Reef, if an ambush, attack, landmine incident or terrorist sighting was reported, the message had to be passed to JOC control room and that was the last the WFR heard of it. The Odzi police station was far more interesting. Here, not only did the WFR know the area they were watching and listening over, but all the people involved as well. Field Reserve sticks were ambushed and the WFR on duty in the control room would know all the members personally. As likely as not one would be her own husband.

Elsewhere, women on duty in control rooms throughout the province would listen with sinking hearts whenever they heard the name of a casualty coming over the air. Even if it was not known to them, as wives, mothers, grandmothers, they knew the mental anguish that the message would bring to someone else in an hour or two. Gone were the days when, as recruits, they would giggle over 'Roger' and 'Jock' believing them to be unseen pin-up boys.

In the smaller stations the WFR, with *agric-alert* boards, SSB*, VHF† and Army radios to answer, as well as the phone and Internal Affairs radio, sent up many a silent prayer that they would not all call her simultaneously. It was frustrating to hear the station call sign repeated over and over again, while she was busy sorting out problems on the other means.

Some had been Woman Field Reservists for years. Others were newcomers keen to do their bit when the war intensified. Several had preliminary training in map-reading, coding and radio procedure as well as weapon-handling. Others were thrown in at the deep end and told to get on with it. They learnt fast, spurred on by the roars of the Member-in-Charge.

"Finger-trouble again? Hold the button DOWN when you're speaking! Don't gabble, they can't hear you. They're calling you! Answer them!"

But though they may not have admitted it, most of the rural policemen, hard-pressed to find enough people for all the work, were grateful for the help given by the women in grey. They were invaluable for catering work at the 'Queen Mary', the large mobile canteen used at training camps and for producing early breakfasts for personnel arriving. One WFR (since killed by terrorists) particularly remembered spending all day in the Queen Mary trying to unfreeze two large buckets full of Bolognaise Sauce to serve with spaghetti to 100 hungry men and women that night. "It was the only time the Police have had frozen meat lollies," she joked afterwards.

Another recalls the day she was on duty at the station from midday till six, in a blinding thunderstorm. With the hiss and crackle of the radios indoors, loud noise was pretty constant. Over the VHF came the cool voice of a schoolboy living on the border. Thinking she had not heard the start of some practice exercise, she dutifully took note of most of what she could hear him saying. He was obviously swotting up his radio procedure with map references and coding, she decided. But halfway through he became rather confused. "I'll report the rest in clear.

---

* Type of radio transmitter and receiver used by police.
†Very High Frequency.

80

It won't matter now," he said. Rockets were landing regularly a kilometre from the Police Station, according to him, and they were being
launched from across the Mozambique border at the back of his house.

It was not until the weary WFR went home to supper that she heard
the attack had been for real. It's easy to keep one's cool if one is
rendered slightly deaf by atmospherics on the radios!

Many of the WFR who spent years rising (or going to bed) around
05h00, remember the friendliness of their neighbourhood.

"It was fun to wake the neighbours on the *agric-alert* and, if we knew
the date, to wish them a happy birthday," said one. "The morning roll
call became a sociable routine and we all felt very much a part of the
local scene."

There were agonising moments too, when the person being called
failed to answer.

Under almost any circumstances the WFR somehow 'made it' to fulfil
their roster duty. Sometimes they had to await permission to travel
their normal route after a running battle in the area. Farmers' wives
would switch to back roads to leave their farms in the grey dawn,
hoping to avoid landmines and possible ambushes on their way to the
station.

Many of them were not only running homes with little domestic help,
but also farms and businesses in their menfolks' absence on call-up.
Often they returned from duty to cook meals for their 'Bright Lights'
(city men who took turns in guarding lonely farmhouses on the border).
The girls in grey were never without a weapon, carrying it in the car, in
the house and in the garden. They knew how to defend themselves and
their families in case of attack. Even so, there were cases where the
sheer numbers of an attacking gang overpowered them.

Weekend training camps under canvas, Sundays spent learning how
to operate different firearms or to throw hand grenades, hours of radio
work and, inevitably, years of lost beauty sleep, all added up to a
wonderful comradeship and community feeling in the district, commented Joan, a section leader of the Penhalonga girls in grey.

Many married couples served in the Police Reserve. This cut normal
social life and weekend entertaining to the minimum.

"I used to leave a note and some sandwiches in the refrigerator for my
husband when I rushed home from the office before reporting for
duty," one woman said. "Before he went out in uniform himself he'd
generally pour a drink to welcome me when I returned. Once he came
home at 06h00, after an all night stint at the station. He was white and
drawn. 'I'm pouring you a stiff brandy,' he said.

"'Before breakfast?' I asked. Then he made me sit down to hear the grim news that two more friends in the area had been murdered. He had the painful duty of identifying them. Getting into uniform and going on duty was the only way to fight off the acute sorrow of those tragic days."

"If you can't make sandwiches, don't join the WFR," was the unwritten law at Inyanga. When the dwindling number was reinforced by the addition of a woman pilot (who really knew her radio drill) the Member-in-Charge commented, "Be blowed to the flying. Can she make sambos*?"

Apart from their police work, Inyanga 'Woofers' formed a recipe club, a garden exchange and a message depot, while some provided feminine caring behind the scenes. "They knew your blood group, your next of kin, whether you kept your *agric-alert* battery terminals clean – and your size in boots! And all this information was sifted by women who looked like undisguised prison warders, prompting a local man to exclaim, when he saw an Inyanga WFR in Salisbury, 'You look quite different with clothes on!'" reported an Inyanga church magazine.

One Manicaland family album contains this terse reminder, scribbled by a Police Reservist husband for his WFR wife, telling her what to do if she was alone at home in an emergency:

1. Put off all lights in your area
2. Go to passage and switch on all security lights
3. (a) If fire occurs, use extinguisher as necessary
   (b) If no fire, dial 99, call Sunray and report
   (c) Call up on other means if 'phone out, and continue with 4, if possible
4. All firearms and ammo from gun room to passage
5. Reload all mags and attack when possible
6. FIGHT UNTIL DEAD

There are countless families all over the province who thank God they never had to reach that last point.

The Police Reserve, though not intended to play a combatant role, was, all the same, an important arm of the security forces in the terrorist war. They found themselves given many and varied duties, facing danger frequently. A number were killed while on duty. They escorted

---

*Snacks.

The Police Reserve was an important arm of the Security Forces.

convoys, rode shotgun for officials visiting rural areas, cleared farm roads of landmines, manned roadblocks and went on patrols.

Even when off-duty, most reservists were glad of their issue FN.* They never knew when they were going to need it.

---

*Belgian-made 7,62 calibre automatic rifle used by Rhodesian forces.

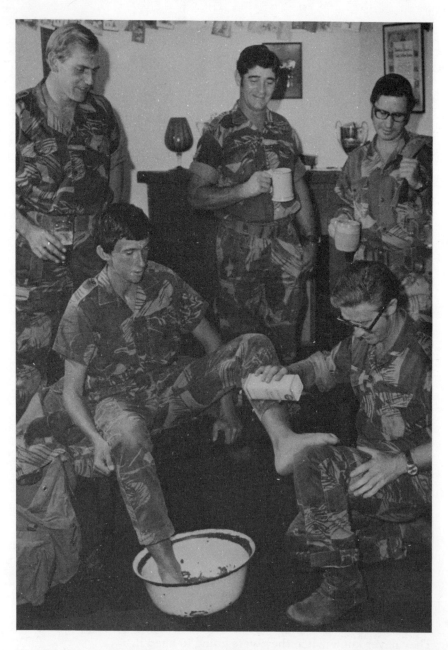

It's a long, long walk there and back. Here a BSAP Reservist receives attention from a friend, while other members of the stick look on, amused at the preparations.

84

One night, for example, there was a loud banging on the door of a Reservist's home. A visitor from Britain, unaware of the seriousness of such an act, went to open it. Suddenly the householder (her son) appeared behind her, stark naked, but carrying his FN. He was ready for all, or most, emergencies!

The caller was the householder's cook who had climbed the security fence (he was a very large man too) to report that an African woman had been stealing. He wanted the Police Reservist to go out and catch her!

On another occasion a stick of fairly elderly volunteers, mostly in their 50's, were on foot patrol on a new road, suspected of being used by terrorists. They were in single file and very much on the alert.

The cheerful, rotund, but very switched-on stick leader saw a small object, looking like a black draught, lying in the road. As men do, he lifted his foot to casually kick it out of the way. Luckily, he stopped in mid-stride. The harmless-looking 'toy' was inspected and the Engineers called. It proved to be a boosted British landmine with only three kg pressure.

That stick of five men are eternally grateful to their quick-thinking leader. Another second, and they could all have been blown 'off the board' for ever.

When it was possible to find humour in a situation the Police Reserve did so. One crowd had trouble with their toilet.

"The sagging seat of the long drop is in imminent danger of converting the convenience into a short drop," they reported. "Until the arrival of a replacement, we are being held in suspense."

"You are now going to be called 'Mini PATU'," the O.C. Urban Police told a group of Police Reservists, average age about 45, back in 1973. "You will operate in a less active capacity than the younger PATU sections, doing much the same duties, such as 'showing the flag', border foot patrols, ambushes, road blocks and manning radio relay stations," he added. They would also have their normal town duties of township patrolling, anti-riot work and building searches.

Asked what they did in the Police Reserve these men stressed the PATU* in their title, whispering the 'mini' part! But age caught them out and it was found that the older groups could not cope. So they were renamed BUGS – back-up groups.

And the BUGS operated for nearly seven years, doing most of the police duties in town and country to relieve the regulars for other work.

---

*Police Anti Terrorist Unit.

"We had some excellent regular Police Reserve officers who had seen action and knew how to treat and train older men, many old enough to be their fathers," said one BUG member. "After a few years we trained ourselves and were able to take over almost any duty without having a regular policeman in charge of the group. This, I think, was unique in the country and it came about mainly because Police Reserve had been operating for more than 25 years, and responsibility was given to the reservists, many of them ex-Servicemen with campaign medals of earlier wars."

When BUGS started there was no equipment for them. Eventually their 303 rifles and Greener shotguns were replaced with FN's, but, other than sets of camouflage uniforms, they equipped themselves. The reservists bought their own first aid boxes, cooking and camping equipment and even their webbing. In some cases groups supplied their own transport and radios.

"We were very keen in those days, sometimes far more determined than some regulars in the Police and Army," the BUG member said. "We really thought we were doing the right thing – eliminating terrorism. Little did we know that we were fighting a lost cause and that we had the West as well as the East against us. But for 15 years we halted the spread of terror to the south, and we may have taught them there how to deal with terrorism. The lesson we learnt was not to think the average terrorist was a primitive, untrained man. They were dedicated fighters in the main and had plenty of reinforcements."

Describing a typical BUG group, he said BUGS 9 consisted of a section leader (a Government agricultural officer), an accountant, a bottle store owner, a quarryman and a forestry manager. The reserves included a railway machine shop foreman and a storeman. The average age of this group, when formed, was 53.

In the early days there were no specially designed vehicles for landmines or ambushes. Five-tonners or heavies were used – with the driver's side protected and seat belts provided – with everyone sitting on sandbags at the back along with the luggage. When such a vehicle hit a landmine the men were thrown out with items like gas cylinders landing on top of them.

"The training was to always land on your feet and be ready to rush towards likely ambush positions with guns spouting. Those who had relaxed and rested their guns on the truck sides found themselves concussed or without their weapon after the blast. And the armourer was not pleased at having to straighten out bent gun barrels," the BUGS member said. "Once at a relay station we heard our relief stick had been blown up by a landmine. We were anxious about them and wondered how they had fared. They relieved us on time, limping and bruised, after being X-rayed and checked by the medics."

There were usually two radio men and four or five guards on a relay radio station. Cooking, fetching water (if available) and short patrols were done turn and turn about. Most reservists soon learned to cook and concocted some tasty dishes from ratpacks. Cool bags supplied fresh meat for the first few days, but from then on tinned stews were the main meals.

Two of the relay stations were inaccessible to vehicles and the men were taken there by helicopter thus limiting their creature comforts. Sometimes the pilots were very strict about luggage and the reservists foxed them by taking along extra 'red cross boxes' or false radio boxes. While a certain amount of hand luggage was allowed, with the helicopters having no doors, all hands were needed to hold in cans of water, camp stretchers and the reservists' FN rifles.

Bad weather, especially mist, prevented the helicopters from operating and one stick had to spend more than two weeks on the station before they could be relieved. Fortunately fresh water was nearby. Most relays only had water in cans and little was available for washing. How they longed for a bath and to sleep between clean sheets!

Towards the end of the war more permanent accommodation was built and small deep freezers and gas cookers were provided. Some relays remained 'hairy'. They were dangerously accessible and were often attacked by mortars. Many reservists qualified for membership of a local club by being blown up three times.

Relay stations were vital to the war and kept the ground units – both police and army – in contact. They often helped by notifying one stick of another's movements when they were out of radio contact. On several occasions a relay radio man averted a clash between two police or army groups. A contact, particularly one visible from the mountain relay, was particularly interesting, with great puffs of dust marking the helicopter landing points.

Many BUGS sticks split up as time went by, due to age and work commitments. Because they could not be away from their jobs for weeks at a time they went onto convoy duty as only mornings were involved and they could sleep at home.

By then a few had been trained as first aid medics and machine gunners, as well as being 'gunship'* drivers and able to use a radio.

---

*A protected vehicle armed with machine guns and rockets.

Each convoy section of three 'gunships' had a mechanic in the last vehicle to repair lame ducks or ambush casualties. During the 2½ years of the Umtali-Birchenough Bridge run, the Police Reserve never lost a life, but there were a few injuries from ambushes. This good record, they are sure, was due to the intensive training, strict convoy speeds and vehicle spacing, and the high standard of alertness insisted upon. All guns were tested before the convoy assembled and cleaned before they were handed over to the next stick, even if they had not been fired.

The daily convoys (Sundays were included) collected at the Police Camp at 06h00, loaded up and tested radios, and were ready to leave at 07h00 from the assembly point. Vehicle drivers were briefed on convoy rules and spare wheels were checked. Any doubtful car or truck was rejected so as not to hold up the convoy.

When the convoy reached Birchenough Bridge out came the sandwiches, while the bridge guard made tea. Three convoys met at Birchenough Bridge and there was always news of narrow escapes and contacts. Many friendships were made here. The Fort Victoria convoy had a rough time, sometimes being ambushed several times a day, and often arriving with flat tyres.

When the Umtali convoy returned, hot pies and coffee were provided at the Police Camp canteen at 10h30 if there had been a trouble-free run. The men then changed and spent the rest of the day at their normal work. They were paid $1,30 a duty, while unemployed Police Reservists were given $5.

In the last three years of war, 357 regular policemen were killed in Rhodesia, a number of them in Manicaland. Others were severely wounded. In those tough days many deeds of gallantry were noted in BSA Police records "... conduct above the normal call of duty..." and hardly the type of work young men had expected when they attested into the force.

For example, a young black constable was on patrol with his white Patrol Officer when their vehicle was ambushed on three sides. The Landrover was extensively damaged by smallarms fire and the constable wounded five times – in both thighs, a leg, wrist and neck. The Patrol Officer suffered serious bullet wounds to his face, shoulder and back.

Despite his own injuries the constable returned fire until his own weapon jammed. He then took over the PO's rifle and continued firing to silence the terrorists. The PO was so badly wounded that he was in no condition to assist, but the constable helped him to a nearby village where aid was refused.

Determined to get medical help for the PO, the constable (himself seriously wounded) walked several kilometres to a school where he collapsed and was revived by teachers. He had walked through an area known to contain terrorists, including those who laid the ambush. The attention of a pilot flying over the area was attracted and medical help obtained for the constable, who told his rescuers where he had left his wounded comrade.

His actions not only saved his own life but that of the PO, and showed tremendous strength, determination and courage. The constable was awarded the Police Cross for Conspicuous Gallantry.

In another incident a PO was the leader of a PATU team which came under terrorist fire. One member was seriously wounded and unable to move. In spite of accurate enemy machinegun fire, the PO crawled across open ground in full view of the enemy to drag his wounded friend to cover. He again crawled out for the radio set and, though twice shot and in great pain, called for assistance, later refusing treatment for himself and insisting that the available morphine go to his wounded man.

The Manicaland Police province, with its long border with Mozambique, had a particularly heavy police commitment during the war, said the Officer Commanding.

The former British South Africa Police force has a proud record in the province and all branches were kept fully active during the political upheavals of the 1960's and the rise in terrorism and lawlessness that followed.

With Special Branch, Signals, Police Reserve, 'A' Reserve, CID, Traffic Section, Specials ('The Wombles'), Support Unit, the all-important Dog Sections and, in increasing numbers, women in most branches, as well as district work, Headquarters and the local 'cop-shops' were kept busy 24 hours a day.

"Our work altered in character as members had to move in more dangerous situations and were forced to arm themselves to protect both the public and themselves," said the Officer Commanding. "The Police became a para-military force and were of tremendous value to the Army in a peace-keeping role."

Over the years many Africans were promoted. People saw black police officers in positions of responsibility, with the first black Member-in-Charge appointed to Sakubva (Umtali) in 1979.

Recruiting and training programmes went ahead constantly in spite of an overload of work. Commenting, the Officer Commanding said: "There was some decrease in petty crime during the war, due to increased vigilance by security guards and greater awareness by the public. But the usual cases of rape, arson and murder among blacks continued all the time."

Stock theft rose rapidly and there were large numbers of court cases throughout the province, even after the introduction of the mandatory nine-year sentence for those convicted. Some success was achieved by the formation of special anti-stocktheft teams to contain the problem. (One year nearly 5 000 people were arrested for stock theft throughout the country but only 16 per cent of the stolen cattle were recovered.)

There was a sharp rise in the number of Maintenance of Law and Order cases, with the accent on young lawbreakers caught crossing the border for terrorist training and older men recruiting and transporting them.

Other Law and Order cases included 'harbouring and aiding terrorists', and committing acts of terrorism.

Squatters posed a permanent problem. As for illegal lodgers in black townships, the courts had to turn a blind eye to this for some time, because of the increasing terror situation in many village areas where murder and torture was on the increase.

To the Manyikas, the recent phase of fighting will be known as 'Chimurenga Two', the first chimurenga (or war) being the Mashona Rebellion in 1896.

"Psuedo-terrorists appeared, with many intruders pretending to be politically motivated men working for 'the cause'. In reality they were common criminals carrying 'guns' of wood, steel, bent wire, plastic or any material likely to look convincing when seen after dark. Umtali Central Police Station had one room with all walls covered by these ingenious devices. Most of the offenders were arrested and appeared in court, some admitting to as many as 30 incidents.

Petrol stations became particularly attractive to these 'armed' youths as well as to robbers with real guns, so pumps were closed during the night throughout the country.

Meanwhile housebreaking, robbery, armed attacks, murder and witchcraft cases were all on the increase.

Prisons were soon full of a variety of offenders. Under the Independence amnesty granted by Lord Soames many were released, but within a week or two numbers of habitual criminals were 'back inside' again for continuing in crime during their short spell of freedom.

Many tribespeople took advantage of curtailed routine police patrols and investigations to rob vacant homesteads. Groups of 'mujibas' emerged among teenagers with the sole purpose of assisting terrorists and hindering security forces.

Illicit transactions in gold and precious stones rose dramatically, with increasing numbers of people trying to take their assets out of the country. The details of these plots read like James Bond thrillers.

Extra duties for the police were the organisation of convoys throughout the province when roadside ambushes of passing motorists, buses and lorries became too common for comfort. Roadblocks were constantly being set up to check cars for illegal arms and explosives.

The issue of vehicles, weapons and ammunition to districts and reservists was stepped up, while the extra uniforms needed for hundreds of men and women and the preparation of reservists' pay sheets meant never-ending paper work.

Counter-insurgency training (or COIN courses), were added to the normal police training. PATU teams for younger reservists and 'Bright Light' schemes for older men were also started.

In 1977 the country suffered 106 police deaths. In 1978 there were 102 while in 1979 150 members from all branches and races lost their lives in the service of their country.

On a more cheerful note, the well-known BSA Police Bands continued to play for dances, parades and special functions.

Staff arrived at the Magistrates' Court one morning to find it had been the target of a rocket and mortar attack the previous night. In spite of all the broken windows, more dust covering the legal volumes than usual, and the chipped walls, business continued.

In 1972 Umtali had four magistrates, a provincial magistrate and three others. Their area covered Chipinga, Cashel, Melsetter, Nyanyadzi (where occasional courts were held weekly or fortnightly), Penhalonga, Odzi, Inyanga and when required, Inyazura and Rusape.

Regional Courts visited Umtali once a month to deal with more serious cases such as rape, attempted murder and culpable homicide. The High Court (for which the main court room at Umtali was originally built) did not sit at Umtali at all during the war years. However, from about 1976, special courts, appointed under the Emergency Powers Act, sat when required in Umtali, Rusape and Inyanga, to deal with Law and Order cases in which the death penalty might be appropriate.

When Robert Mugabe came to power in 1980, ZANU (PF) committees mushroomed in numerous places and in many respects tried to take the law into their own hands, taking over the duties of police, investigating complaints, making arrests and imposing punishments.

Several cases came before the Umtali magistrates, the most serious being a series of 'arrests' in Chipinga of people said to have given information to Security Forces. Such action, if true, would have been covered by the amnesty. Those 'arrested' were beaten and tortured (burning plastic was allowed to drip onto their legs and arms), and they were moved from Chipinga to Umtali and Salisbury.

'Offenders' were sent to a farm at Arcturus where they were detained and forced to work. The men convicted of these offences were later released under another amnesty.

What was the mentality behind the actions of all these former offenders? What did they hope to achieve by breaking the law, and what have been the results since the new Government took over? The role of many earlier convicts changed with Mugabe's victory, so that they became the 'heroes' rather than the criminals, in their own locality. Many of them may have genuinely felt that they were working towards a new order, but others were the usual idle, layabout youths, looking for excitement, easily led, drawn to crime, uncaring about the morality of their deeds.

The argument put up by these political committees was that they were 'assisting the police' but it was obvious that because ZANU (PF) was in power, they wanted to run things their own way. If they got into trouble they would merely say they had been 'instructed from Salisbury'.

10 *Wind of change*

There is an appointed time for everything. And there is a time for every event under heaven.

ECCLESIASTES 3:1

In 1962, three years before UDI, which was the catalyst that set a terrorist war flaring up in Rhodesia, the Native Affairs Department had become the Ministry of Internal Affairs. Although certain functions were changed, its principal responsibilities remained. It was the arm of Government which dealt with the people, especially the less-sophisticated African people whose needs and problems were human rather than technical. People who had to be persuaded that technical progress was beneficial and why such things as irrigation schemes, schools, clinics, cattle dipping, fertilisers and hundreds of other 'civilised innovations', taken for granted by the Whites, were not only desirable but necessary.

At first the Africans had been antagonistic to Western civilisation and culture and refused education and schools for their children. It was for this reason that Tribal Trust Lands had been set aside in the early years (1923) – areas where the African people could preserve their old way of life and culture, living in mud huts with thatched roofs, worshipping their ancestral spirits, free from the pressures of civilisation. One of the Native Commissioner's duties was to protect these people from exploitation, to help them preserve their customs and, at the same time, introduce them to Western modes of education, health, hygiene and agriculture.

Because the Ministry was so 'people orientated' it had to embrace a wide spectrum of simple technology, since the African people were not able to separate their needs and problems to fit the technical departments of Government. They came to the one person they knew and could trust, the one person who understood them and could speak their language – the Native Commissioner, renamed the District Commissioner (D.C.).

To enable the District Commissioner to carry out his tasks, he had both administrative and technical staff to assist him – District Officers (D.O.'s) qualified in law, administration, African customs and languages; Administrative Cadets, accountants and revenue clerks, typists, agricultural officers and various technical and field staff (Primary Development Officers, Field Assistants – officials who would carry out a

93

variety of tasks from control of dipping services, road construction, management of irrigation schemes to co-operatives and many others). Even with the changes, the Ministry of Internal Affairs remained, to a certain extent, paternalistic – largely because of the unsophisticated nature of the people it had to administer. African nationalists were still able to accuse it of being a Government within a Government and so justify their later accusations of colonialist oppression.

Because of the high qualifications, ability and integrity demanded of District Commissioners and their administrative staff, not many black Rhodesians had yet advanced to senior positions. More and more, however, were receiving appointments in the more junior grades of the Ministry – as well as in the technical field.

One of the original appointments in the old administration, performing a vital function both then and later in the Internal Affairs Department, was the uniformed black Native Department Messenger – later called a District Assistant (D.A.). He acted as the link between the Administration and the people. He was the 'eyes and ears' of the District Commissioner. He was the trusted envoy between this official and the tribal leaders. His appointment was usually sanctioned by the latter and he was required to know the district intimately – geographically as well as its people and leaders. Constantly on patrol, he would bring back news from the District and deliver messages to the tribal leaders from the D.C.

The tribal leaders – traditional Chiefs, Headmen and Village (Kraal) Heads – were also an essential and vital part of the District Administration. The custodians of tribal law and custom, they bore heavy responsibilities over the land and its use, and the settling of tribal and customary disputes. They received ex-officio appointments on local government bodies and, in general, represented their people to Government.

Two great inter-related problems began to exert impossible pressures on the Administration in the late 50's and early 60's. Firstly, the tremendous increase in population brought about by the improved health services provided. There was, however, no real compensatory increase in productivity or in earning ability as the African absorbed Western culture and technology at a very slow pace. Secondly, the emergence of a younger generation of Africans growing increasingly dissatisfied with their traditional leadership. These youngsters were growing up in ignorance as to why their forefathers had refused White education and of the reason for the seeming lack of prospects for their future. These two acute and growing problems were placed squarely in the District Commissioners' laps.

The first problem was basically a technical one. The land had to be protected from incorrect usage. The wasteful system of shifting cultivation had to be replaced with more modern methods. Crop rotations, cash crop farming and new methods for subsistence farmers had to be introduced. This meant that the previous communal ownership of land had to give way to a more individual ownership with regulations governing possession, dispossession, inheritance, purchase and sale. This involved a major change in the attitude of the people to land, of the previously loose control exercised by tribal leaders over the land and, in fact – with the new concept of the right to purchase or sell introduced – a change in relationship between the people and their traditional leaders. Not only was it a tremendous technical problem, but an even more complex human one. There was no alternative but to give responsibility for introducing these now essential changes to the District Commissioners and their staffs. The legislation under which the changes were implemented was called the African Land Husbandry Act – hailed around the world as one of the most progressive soil conservation measures ever introduced. Even the United Nations, through its agency, the F.A.O., praised its objectives.

Not so, however, the rabid nationalists who saw a heaven-sent opportunity to stir up opposition and disaffection towards the new legislation. Although every effort was made to introduce the new law with compassion and understanding, its provisions were somewhat revolutionary and inevitably some degree of disruption in normal activities occurred. In order to fit in with the new planning and the new system, some movement of habitation or change to different land, water points or grazing area became necessary. To those who were obliged to move or change, it was not a particularly popular measure but, with careful handling, problems were overcome. The African nationalist politician, however, used any disaffection towards the Land Husbandry Act to stir up suspicion and opposition to it – thereby gaining a starting point in support of his political views. It is so easy to create suspicion in the minds of unsophisticated tribesmen who are naturally conservative and opposed to change, so it is little wonder that opposition to the new Land Act grew – and although two-thirds of the Tribal Trust Lands were successfully covered – the black politicians managed to prevent the planned completion. This gave them a start in their campaign to work up opposition to, and suspicion of, other Government policies.

Education became another fertile field for condemning the Government. Faced with an avalanche of demands for more and better facilities it was only able to progress at a pace consistent with the development of the economy.

The younger blacks – many becoming de-tribalised and thereby less affected by the bonds of family or tribal discipline – became increasingly outspoken. Having come into closer contact with white civilisation and its way of life – through education, employment and travel – they saw the great disparity in the quality of life between blacks and whites. Encouraged by hostile elements, including overseas liberals and 'do-gooders', they were quick to apportion blame for this on 'naked racialism'.

Certainly glaring inequalities did exist, not only in the standard of education but in the opportunities offered in later life. White governments of the past were, perhaps, slow in preparing for change, but they were used to dealing with the traditional leaders who were very conservative and with the older tribesmen who had opposed many changes, including white formal-type education. White administrators and Government officials had not seen the need to impose change on the African people. Many white politicians and others felt that change should come in an evolutionary manner, with the desire for it coming from the Africans themselves, and not through imposition.

The rights and wrongs of the matter and all the arguments for or against the policies adopted are now more of academic and historical interest. Sweeping political changes were introduced by Government in 1961 to meet the nationalist politicians' complaints – to give blacks a substantial voice in Parliament immediately and to give them the opportunity, by constitutional means, of gaining a majority voice in Government within a reasonable period of time. (Some say it would have taken 15 years – i.e. 1976 – for the 'A' voters' roll to have contained a majority of blacks and thus the opportunity of electing a black Government). The nationalist politician and the young black activist had, however, become impatient, distrustful and ambitious. As we now know, they were aided and abetted by people outside Rhodesia's borders – strongly supported by a Communist campaign to overthrow White or responsible non-racial government in Rhodesia – and they now demanded immediate and total political power through 'one man one vote'.

They formed political parties and indulged in campaigns of intimidation and violence to wrest leadership from the Chiefs,and Headmen. They used every grievance of the people to discredit the whites and white Government – and especially the District Commissioners and their staff. They used every instance of discrimination and inequality to stir hatred of the whites and gain support for their cause. The application of the Land Husbandry Act was used by them as an example of discriminatory and imposed legislation and by clever manipulation of petty complaints or grievances, it became 'racial oppression of the worst kind'. These activists also fanned the flames of dissatisfaction over inequalities and discrimination in the urban areas.

Internal Affairs problems increased and became more complex as the political situation changed and the security position worsened. When Community Development, a policy encouraging the people to solve their own problems with their own resources and leadership (setting their own priorities) was introduced and began to be accepted, black nationalist politicians and Communist activists saw the danger to their movements and leadership and began a campaign of intimidation and thuggery. Anyone found co-operating with the Government or its agencies became a target, the thugs and intimidators doing their work with as little danger to themselves as possible.

Many of them were detained. Others fled the country. Others again were organised outside by overseas Communist parties – especially in Russia and China. Subversion and violence increased. One reaction produced another and the violence flared into organised terrorism. 'Freedom fighters' were trained overseas and returned with sophisticated weapons supplied by these countries.

In Manicaland, many of the TTL's* border on Mozambique. The international boundary divided some tribal areas in two. In the Melsetter district, for example, Chief Ndima's people owed allegiance to Chief Mafuse, who, with all their tribal spirits, was in Mozambique.

When Mozambique became independent in 1975 there were mass migrations over the border. Thousands were attracted by 'Freedom' which, to them, meant liberty to live in the old free and easy style, unharried by Government officials talking about the conservation of natural resources; it meant liberty to cultivate in streambeds, to plant lands without contour ridges and to forget about dipping cattle. Whole kraals emptied overnight.

Hundreds of schoolchildren disappeared too. ZANLA had recruited many youngsters who went voluntarily to become 'freedom fighters'. Some were lured by promises of free education and training. Others were abducted. (The Minister of Education and Culture, Mr Dzingai Mutumbuka, said, in 1980: "In Mozambique we had 30 000 kids who

---

*Tribal Trust Lands.

ran away from home and schools to join the struggle, but they were too young. In 1978 we had 25 000 schoolchildren and 700 teachers. In September that year help began to come. Stuff was sent to us by air from the Lutheran World Federation in Tanzania.")

The heartbreak of African parents who had their children forcibly taken from them will never be known. Many white women working with black Homecraft Clubs noticed the change in their members. Mothers became thin and ill with heartache, not knowing where their children had been taken.

One white woman saw a group of these small black Rhodesians at an airport outside the country. They were being forced to board an aeroplane, wetting themselves, shivering, crying with fear. She was so upset that she went to the airport authorities, but was told to mind her own business.

Some parents crossed the border into Mozambique in a vain search for their children. Others crossed to escape from the troubles they heard were coming.

The black District Assistants, as Government employees, now became prime targets for the terrorists. They were abducted, attacked while on patrol and in their own homes, dragged from buses, ambushed, tortured and murdered. But these men, in their khaki uniforms with red flashes, showed enduring courage and devotion to duty.

During 1975 and 1976 great numbers of terrorists infiltrated the Tribal Trust Lands. Internal Affairs base camps were attacked and had to be closed. Another point of contact, control and communication with the tribespeople disappeared.

The chiefs, as traditional leaders, could no longer travel in safety to the District Commissioner to discuss local problems and seek help and advice. As leaders in the old system, they were targets for the new 'liberators'. Several chiefs moved to the comparative safety of Umtali and were no longer any help to district administration.

Meanwhile the undermining of Government authority in the Tribal Trust Lands continued. On February 12, 1976, an unarmed BSAP sergeant and two constables were murdered at the Pungwe hotel in the Honde Valley, Mutasa district. This was not an isolated incident and more reports of murders and attacks on unarmed police, district assistants, dip attendants, Conex officials and other Government personnel poured in.

The terrorists entered a kraal behind a store in the Makoni district in December 1976. Forcing the owner and his wife into their house at gunpoint, they locked them in. Then, shouting to the couple to listen

98

and watch through the window, they brutally murdered their two daughters, aged 19 and 23, and their eighteen-year-old son.

In October 1977 a well-known and popular herbalist in the same district was locked in his hut with all his medicines. An unknown number of terrorists set fire to the hut, burning the man alive.

These were merely two of hundreds of similar incidents of murder, rape, torture and mutilation, through which the tribespeople were terrorised.

The 'boys from the bush' built up safe places for themselves in the TTL's where the locals were intimidated into co-operation with the terrorists and from which they expanded their activities, all aimed at breaking down Government authority and control. They stopped the dipping of cattle. In February 1977, in the Melsetter district, nine dip tanks were damaged, burned or destroyed in a week. In several other districts, intimidation stopped all dipping.

Schoolchildren were threatened with dire consequences if they continued to attend school. Teachers were threatened or murdered and parents intimidated. TTL schools closed, as did clinics and hospitals, when nurses and orderlies were terrorised.

Rural stores shut too. This was not surprising as they were prime targets for terrorists, who would hold up or murder the storekeepers, take all the goods they wanted, burn the buildings and depart. Any customers in the way were shot, or forced to act as bearers to carry the loot.

Government employees were warned to stay away from work and villagers were recruited 'to help the cause', some willingly, some too afraid to refuse. This gave birth to a new breed of young man, the 'mujiba'. On December 18, 1976, an Internal Affairs camp under construction in the Makoni district was extensively damaged by four or five 'mujibas'. They also destroyed a tractor in the presence of 40 or 50 villagers and told government employees to leave.

Another violent product was the 'pseudo-terrorist', the thug who stole weapons or made fakes and staged armed attacks and robberies for personal gain and power. The common criminal also took advantage of the situation to steal and loot in freedom. It was all the same to the local population. Attacked or robbed, who would question whether the assailant was a bone-fide freedom fighter?

Deprived of schools, stores and clinics, tribespeople found travelling to town for supplies or medical attention very dangerous. Buses were attacked or blown up. Private vehicles were ambushed. Landmines were laid and dirt roads were most vulnerable. It was easy to dig a hole and plant a mine, covering it well, even making a tyre-tread mark over the top to make it impossible to see where the deadly explosive was hidden. Even tarred roads were not safe. Holes were cut and tar replaced to make the mine invisible.

Manicaland had a heavy toll of vehicles blown up, drivers and passengers killed and wounded. In December 1976 six blacks died and five were wounded when 15 terrorists attacked a bus in the Rusape area. Later a beer-tanker was hi-jacked and the driver killed on the spot. The vehicle was found days later, burnt out, many kilometres away at Mayo. Similar incidents in all the TTL's soon led to the end of most services.

Railway lines were sabotaged and road and rail bridges blown up. Trains were de-railed, telephone and power lines cut.

With their daily lives completely disorganised, and their hearts full of fear, the tribespeople could no longer trust their District Commissioner to help them, and his staff was unable to maintain control, owing to lack of manpower, weapons, vehicles and communications.

The District Commissioner of Melsetter said: "Virtually the last effective administration carried out was the re-registration exercise in late 1975, early 1976. This had just been completed before the position became too difficult. From then effective patrolling of the TTL's by us virtually ceased, due entirely to the lack of suitable vehicles, weaponry and communications, and the small District Assistant strength left.

"By the end of 1978 the position had arisen where the terrorist forces were in virtual control of all the TTL's, and this department was unable to perform any administrative work or even visit most of the area."

Travelling in unprotected vehicles was highly dangerous and suitable transport was not available for some years, due to sanctions. It was this that led to the death and injury of many 'Intaff' men.

Mr J. E. Hudson-Beck, the Melsetter District Officer, was killed in August 1976 when he hit a landmine while going out to the TTL's. The son of a well-known previous Secretary for Native Affairs, he was young, eager and devoted to his work. There was no one to replace him.

11 *Quo vadis?*

I'm a long way from home in the war zone,
The sky is almost light,
I wonder what the day will bring –
Oh God, why must men fight?

GEOFF HILL

The parts played by young white men during the war were many and varied. A heavy responsibility lay on those National Service cadets* or vedettes,† serving short-term call-ups at Internal Affairs bases in the Tribal Trust Lands.

"People thought this was nothing in comparison with service in the Army," said one young Internal Affairs man from Salisbury. "The troopie was glorified by the public but, in fact, we had quite as tough a time and our job was much more interesting."

He was a 'townie' from the capital where he had been born and educated.

"What a shock I had when I was sent out into the bush! I felt I was the first human to have walked through some of the untouched, untamed areas of the country where there was nothing but trees, buck, birds, duck on the pans, hippo in the rivers, elephant, hyena and jackal."

Brian, like many others, was sent first to Chikurubi Training Centre for three months where he attended lectures on African customs and was taught basic weaponry.

"Our role was described as 'semi-combatant'. Suddenly we were deployed to our stations and faced with an entirely new way of life and environment. I went to Chipinga in March 1976 to a District Commissioner's rest camp and sub-office in the bush. I had met my DC and my orders were: 'Administer the people. Get out and meet them. Go into the kraals.' How very different from normal days when young cadets had to go through much training and selection to ensure that they were capable of dealing with the tribespeople and difficult situations.

"Soon I found myself, at 20, being looked upon by groups of Africans as a father advisor, and most of them were at least twice my age. I was called upon to sort out marriage tangles, attend tribal courts, help deliver a baby in the bush, take sick people several kilometres to the

---

*New recruit for permanent staff.
†National service recruits.

nearest clinic, explain what malaria and bilharzia were and try to educate the people into taking prophylactic pills and boiling their drinking water.

"The rains that season were heavy. Two of us were on patrol in the Chisumbanje area in a Leopard (protected vehicle) when it stuck in the gluey, black, basalt mud. All our digging and shoving were of no avail. The mud kept collecting under the wheels. On the second day we radioed the District Commissioner in Chipinga for help.

"'Push', he replied, and that was all the help we got. We eventually found a tractor on the Tilcor* estate, which was sent to drag us out. We soon learnt to drive through mud without getting stuck.

"That year the Sabi River nearly burst its banks and the Chisumbanje sub-office was surrounded until it became an island. We were cut off for three days with the threat of the rest camp being flooded out.

"One day I was driving along an irrigation canal when a flock of wild duck flew in front of the Land Rover. A District Assistant (D.A.) sitting beside me was knocked unconscious by a bird. 'My D.A. has been knocked unconscious by a flying duck'! I radioed to the District Commissioner.

"'What the ... are you talking about?' he demanded, thinking I was swearing at him in some new lingo."

Eric, who was stationed with Brian at Chisumbanje, was also unused to bush-life. They had a Rhodesian boiler † to heat bath-water. The wood was damp and the fire so poor that the water was tepid. Eric decided to remedy matters and poured a can of petrol into the fire beneath the drum. The blast badly burnt his legs.

He also collected snakes and kept them in the mess. The D.C. did not care for snakes, especially when two escaped on his inspection tour. He returned to base rather hastily.

Eric was alone once when the camp was attacked by terrorists, but all the rockets passed overhead and he was uninjured. He was also the first to hit a landmine and again escaped injury.

"It was lonely in the bush," commented Brian, "and generally there were only two of us on patrol, never knowing how many terrorists we might meet.

"We had to learn to handle District Assistants without previous experience of disciplining a group of men. We also had to establish

---

*Tribal Trust Land Development Corporation.
†Method of heating water in a large drum over a wood fire.

102

good relations with the people and tried to learn and remember African customs.

"As the war increased and more terrorist incidents occurred, the D.A.'s in camp became nervous and panicked easily. Even a hippo rumbling along the fence would start the D.A.'s firing and it was my job to calm them down."

Once they started firing at a mysterious object between two protected villages. Guard Force men in both Protected Villages (P.V.'s) retaliated. That 'private war' wasted 2 000 bullets before Brian could settle the matter.

The black villagers were persuaded to go into the Protected Villages for their own protection and the Internal Affairs cadets, who had a real affection for 'their people', felt the villagers did not understand the danger or motivation of the terrorists. The villagers, "like meat being fought over by two dogs", were bewildered, suffering from their own ignorance and fear, said Brian.

One character whom the cadets met, was known as 'Beautiful Body'. He was employed to erect fences round the Protected Villages. He had long, blonde hair and came from overseas. He had a mass of deodorants, after-shave lotions, hair brilliantines and other preparations.

"He'll soon learn," chuckled 'Intaff' staff on his arrival. Soap and strange smells not only invited mopani flies, but terrorists as well. 'Beautiful Body' soon adapted.

After being wounded in an ambush, Brian spent a long time in hospital before being sent on a month's holiday by the Terrorist Victim's Relief Fund. He worked in the Chipinga office before being sent to Chibuwe in 1978. By then he was accustomed to his job and found it easier to cope with his men as well as the new National Servicemen coming in.

Terrorist incidents became a part of daily life. African stores were broken into, and they had to be investigated. Pseudo-terrorists arrived on the scene, robbing, assaulting and generally causing trouble. They had to be arrested.

"There were some horrible incidents too," recalled Brian. "I had to help an African husband collect the bits and pieces remaining of his wife. She had been having an affair with a Guard Force man in a Protected Village. The terrorists heard of it and called her a 'sell-out'. They tied a grenade to her back and roped her to a fence. She was blown to pieces. Every bone in her body was scattered about.

"Then there was the time when a Special Branch Land Rover with 15 Africans in the back hit a landmine with its rear wheel. Eight were killed. I'll never forget the woman who'd been pregnant. Her stomach was blown open and the baby was found up a tree."

Due to shortage of staff the D.C.'s were overworked, short of time and unable to carry out the administration of their districts as they would have wished. They strove to find solutions to the problems in the TTL's. They turned the small camps and bases into 'Beau Geste' type forts which were constantly attacked at night with British, Russian, Chinese or German mortars and rockets. Despite their totally inadequate defensive weapons – due to the fact that Rhodesia was under economic sanctions – casualties were surprisingly low.

The forts helped police and Security Forces to establish a presence in the TTL's, but the areas are so extensive that this made little difference. When the Security Forces established themselves, terrorists moved to other areas, returning when the Security Forces had left.

Another young cadet, Ewan, was sent to Mutsago in December 1976. Mutsago was a discarded Army base consisting of only a couple of bunkers. "One of these," Ewan said, "was about two metres deep. One of the vedettes and I slept in it. I had my bed up against one side. It had been raining one night and I felt the call of nature and climbed out. When I returned, my bed had disappeared under a fall of soil and rock. One wall of the bunker had collapsed.

"I had two vedettes," Ewan continued, "and 15 to 20 D.A.'s. On January 15, 1977, the base was attacked and I woke up with the first bang. I had an Italian vedette at the time who was supposed to press the alarm on the *agric alert*. When I went outside to let off a couple of magazines I didn't see him, but as I was changing the magazine again I heard streams of Italian coming out from under the dining-room table in the house behind me. 'Madre mia!' Forgetting the *agric alert* for the moment, I ran over to the D.A.'s barracks to see if they were all right and was met by a ghostly apparition: The D.A. who had been on guard had rushed to the bunker and had run into a pile of cement on the way."

Ewan lived through many incidents, contacts and landmine explosions and, at the end of January 1977, was sent to Chitakatira base. This was in a Tribal Trust Land near a European farming area. "I got to know the Burma Valley farmers fairly well," he said, "and promised them that I would react and go to their assistance if they had any trouble.

"One evening there was a loud explosion from a Roads Department camp up the road. My District Commissioner, who was spending the night, was seen streaking out of the toilet, pulling up his shorts. We decided to react and I jumped into my Leopard (protected vehicle) and took off. Then I slowed down to allow the D.C.'s vehicle and another to catch up and was immediately ambushed by terrorists. One of the Burma Valley farmers came to my aid in his aircraft, dropping a home-made bomb to frighten off my attackers. The Roads Department camp – graders, tipper trucks and fuel storage – was completely destroyed. The aircraft then radioed to me that there was a vehicle coming up the road. Thinking it might be terrorists, we laid an ambush – only to find it was two Burma Valley farmers coming to our aid!

"One afternoon the Roads Department tipper trucks carrying gravel were attacked. Hearing the firing I reacted with my District Assistants and landed in a fairly heavy contact with terrorists. After four or five minutes I saw one of my D.A.'s running down the hill towards us whereupon there was a burst of fire and he fell. We had trouble getting to him as there was a terrorist with an SKS rifle taking potshots at us every time we tried to get to him. We managed to reach him, but as we were getting him out to the vehicle we came under 60 mm mortar fire. Fortunately a couple of minutes later a Lynx support aircraft from Grand Reef arrived and the contact ended."

Ewan went farming in 1978 but "I came back to Internal Affairs as I was worried about my black District Assistants who had been very faithful. I picked up where I had left off at the Intaff bases," he said.

The District Commissioner, Mutassa district, trained uniformed District Security Assistants (D.S.A.'s) for all Manicaland. They were a great help, assisting the District Assistants and making up strength on the various stations. Forced into a military role due to a shortage of Army personnel, they carried out aggressive patrols, showing great bravery and devotion to duty.

Umtali's attacks were publicised, but less well known were the attacks on the smaller centres. The Inyazura petrol station was blasted in June 1976. At Vengere African beerhall in Rusape, 11 armed men held up the occupants, stole $348 from their pockets and took the watches from their wrists as well as all the beer, brandy, cigarettes and sweets available. They then tried to abduct two uniformed African policemen. This was in July 1977. There were other similar events when only blacks were the target.

The establishment of Protected Villages was the biggest project undertaken by Internal Affairs to protect the villagers from intimidation and murder. The exercise entailed moving whole kraals of tribespeople into a fenced and protected area.

The P.V. project was unpopular. People disliked moving away from home and had complaints about their comfort, but the scheme disrupted the activities of the terrorists, who had been fed and cared for very often in the kraals by willing or intimidated villagers. P.V.'s were costly, so few were constructed in the country as a whole. The Honde Valley was the main access route for terrorists, so a special effort was made here and 16 P.V.'s were established and administered.

In the Umtali district an attempt was made to establish Community Villages (C.V.'s) where people could live together for protection. They were fenced but unguarded, not as successful as Protected Villages, but better than nothing. In Melsetter district only one Community Village was set up, at Chikukwa.

The District Commissioners' problems were not only in the bush. They had headaches in connection with white towns and villages as well as black urban townships in their areas. The terrorists cut lines of communication and tried to make the main roads between towns impassable.

It fell to the District Commissioner to instigate and attend Civil Defence meetings to plan safety precautions, supply security fencing and settle labour problems, as well as cope with difficulties in commerce and industry, municipalities and schools. In Umtali the District Commissioner and Provincial Commissioner were overloaded with meetings, including the daily JOC sessions.

The District Commissioners were also involved in all the white farmers' problems when homestead attacks, abducted labour, stock theft, crop destruction, burnt buildings and ransacked stores became their lot. Advice on claims for compensation was constantly required.

At one time the Security Forces in the rural areas were reacting to more than three incidents a day, apart from the regular sweeps of roads, contacts, follow-ups, lifting of landmines, repairing of sabotage damage, manning of roadblocks and other endless tasks. As a member of JOC the long-suffering D.C. knew of all incidents and worked constantly to alleviate distress, while still keeping his normal work running smoothly.

The Army tended to come and go from a district, and from all reports little military success appears to have been achieved either in Manicaland's white farming areas or the Tribal Trust Lands. The young troopie was a wonderful fellow, eager, courageous and dedicated, as was the black soldier and policeman. Why the lack of success? Many gave their opinion that the senior officers in the towns were fighting an eight to four war. Was the war being fought with 'kid gloves' due to policymakers in Salisbury, or a feeling of compassion of white for black? Or did they feel they were being accused by the Western world? Whatever the reason an appallingly high percentage of Manicaland's small white

106

population was killed – apart from the very large number of innocent black civilians.

Among the dozens of tragic happenings in the province, one of the worst was the massacre of 27 black employees of Aberfoyle Tea Estates in the Honde Valley at the end of 1976. They were presumably murdered because they worked for a white-managed company.

Community development and local government training was badly affected by the war. Training courses were held but attendance dropped significantly owing to intimidation, the dangers of travel and the fear of being seen associating with Government officers. Improved living programmes in the Protected Villages also suffered from lack of support.

Three times terrorists visited Rowa Community Development training centre to steal vehicles and bedding, threatening the staff and damaging the buildings. Rowa was closed and taken over by the Army as a temporary base for No 3 Engineer Squadron. The training branch moved to Eickhoff House, a boarding hostel at Umtali Girls' High School, and then to the former Border Hills Infant School before returning to Rowa in 1980.

What of the wives and families of Intaff? Their men were so overburdened with work and worry that they had little time for family life. Wives bore the responsibility of rearing the children, often living in remote stations and overcoming their fear of loneliness, travelling in convoy on dangerous roads and concern for their husband's safety. When their men returned the danger increased, yet many showed great courage and loyalty.

One black official said in 1981: "The terrorists are still after me." For two years he was unable to go home to his wife and children.

"My wife had to provide the terrorists with food and blankets. She sent secret messages to me warning me not to come home or I would be killed. Those men continually asked the local people if they did not feel the Internal Affairs officials were a nuisance and a trouble to them. They were trying to incite the people of my home area against all Government officers.

"Then one day 40 to 50 terrorists came to my wife and told her they had heard I was coming home. They ordered her to move out because they intended burning down our home. They sent her with a woman escort to bring a letter to me. This warned me to leave my job with Internal Affairs and called me 'Smith's dog'. I handed the letter to the Special Branch. My whole home was burnt down and we saved only two blankets, two pillows and two dogs.

"Several headmen were abducted not far from my home. They were handcuffed, dragged off and killed. We thought the chief had disappeared but some youngsters heard what happened and told us about it later. The terrorists had merely said, 'You're old' – and shot him.

"There are so many terrible incidents that I remember," he continued sadly.

"A retired sergeant of District Assistants was running a store. He came to see the District Commissioner about a problem. Later, Security Forces killed three terrorists in a contact and the rumour started that this ex-sergeant had reported their whereabouts. So they came and shot him.

"They left him lying on the verandah of his store with orders that nobody should touch him. They often did this. 'You must pay money to us first', they said. They made their money that way, but the main reason was to frighten the people into obedience." It had the maximum terrorising effect.

"There was another contact in which some terrorists were killed. This time a Dip Supervisor was suspected of having reported them. He was just getting off a bus when someone cried, 'There he is'! Terrorists grabbed him and questioned him in front of the passengers. In spite of his protests of innocence, he was killed. Perhaps the person who pointed him out bore him a grudge, but the fact that he was killed in front of them all taught the locals not to get on the wrong side of the terrorists.

"Headmen were afraid to collect their salaries from the Internal Affairs offices. One came to fetch his pay packet and he was accused of reporting a terrorist presence to the District Commissioner, so he was abducted. The terrorists rounded up the people for questioning. 'Yes! He's a sell-out!' yelled the crowd. Although aware of his innocence, they were too afraid to do anything else. The terrorists beat and tortured the headman until he died in front of the people. He was then put in a shallow grave.

"In May 1976 two D.A.'s were patrolling in plain clothes and went to see a sick Kraal Head. A man who had a grudge against them reported their presence to the local terrorists, who followed, shot and killed the two. Yet another pair of D.A.'s were tied back to back, shot and pushed down an antbear hole."

The black Intaff man continued with his gruesome tale.

"In 1977 the terrorists were at a kraal and learned that a certain witchdoctor was unpopular. He had two children. They shot him and then the children so that his spirit would not transfer to them. Next door was a witchdoctor from Malawi, also unpopular. He was also

108

killed, for in this way the terrorists tried to gain popularity with the people.

"We were often attacked in our base camps and sub-offices with rockets and mortars. It was difficult to carry out our administrative work. We had to fortify our camps and go on armed patrols."

One of the first white women to join Internal Affairs as a cadet, and later a District Officer, served with distinction and later married into the Department as well. She and her husband were stationed at one of the most remote and dangerous offices in the province, occasionally cut off completely without communications from the outside world. The only way to get in and out was by air, and the station did not possess a plane.

Landmines had been placed on most of the surrounding roads and this meant the end of all bus services. 'Phone lines were cut in September 1978 and she was pregnant.

What did it feel like to be the only white woman for kilometres around, carrying a baby, acting as a District Officer and running a home – with the constant possibility of terrorist attack and no means of communication?

This young couple and the other 'Intaff' members at Buhera did not just keep the station going. They recruited and trained 50 District Security Assistants (D.S.A.'s) to escort administrative patrols. When S.F.A.'s* were trained in July 1979, black plotholders at Buhera Irrigation Scheme started to return. In July a special Buhera Fire Force of D.A.'s and D.S.A.'s was formed.

Asked why the terrorists destroyed local council buildings, schools and dip tanks, a former council secretary at Buhera said: "The councils were identified with the District Commissioner and not the people. Because he was the president and had advisory functions this was felt to be domination. Later, the chief of the area would take over and nominate some of the committee. This was felt to be taking power away from the people."

School and diptank fees were collected by the council, so the trouble-makers destroyed them. In Buhera there were 300 African teachers and 16 black dip attendants, six council offices and 450 officials, but the nationalists still felt that the D.C. 'dominated'. During the war no taxes were collected because of landmines, ambushes and intimidation, so the councils collapsed.

---

*Security Force Auxiliaries.

With their intimate contact with the people and their problems, Intaff had to help stage the first and second one man, one vote political elections – one in 1979 and the other in 1980. In the Makoni district 100 terrorists put up ZANLA posters during the 1980 election campaign and threatened death to anyone pulling them down. They also told the locals that the war would go on if they were not elected.

But the end of fighting did not mean the end of slaughter.

In February 1980 the murder of four black women in the Rusape area and the ambush of a bus carrying a black wedding party from Umtali to Salisbury (with 15 killed and 22 injured) showed that the art of terror and killing was far too habitual to be abandoned.

Was it possible to hold 'free and fair' elections in this atmosphere of fear in the Tribal Trust Lands? Nobody asked the D.C.'s. Nobody sought their advice. They were required to assist the politicians to organise an election, to assist Monitors and Observers from other lands, reporters from all over the world, polling officials and the public – but nobody asked the 'mothers and fathers' of the districts, who had loved and served and tried to protect the people of the T.T.L.'s for a century whether the elections could be or were fair and free.

D.C.'s were taboo, dubbed imperialists, colonialists, paternalists, and the T.T.L.'s were handed over to the politicians – and the terrorists. Quo vadis? Only the future holds the answer.

12 *Serving the nation*

Whether doing, suffering or forbearing,
We may do miracles by persevering.

ROBERT BURNS

The Electricity Supply Commission

"The light's gone out!" Hearts pounded when the electricity failed after dark during the war. Instant blackness could mean an attack was imminent, and while families crept around hunting for candles and matches and keeping their weapons close, the power failure meant yet another call-out for Manicaland's Electricity Supply Commission technicians.

"ESC," said one wag, "is short for Essential Come Now!"

Without vital power, homesteads became more isolated and vulnerable. Farms were without water and equipment, and essential concerns were deprived of the means to continue production. Whole communities were without light and the comfort of cooking and other facilities.

The first indication of a power failure would be an urgent telephone call to the 24-hour ESC service. "I'm without electricity," someone would say. Another call summoned the standby electrician, all too often from his bed or the family dinner table. The trouble might be a local line down, a sub-station (transformer) gone, or more serious trouble at one of the three main control centres.

On their way to repair a damaged transmission line, this ESC crew was blown up by a landmine. The brand new vehicle was wrecked but the men escaped.

Yet the repair squad went, fully aware that the troublemakers, having done their bit, might well be lying in wait for them too.

Thanks to the enthusiasm of the saboteurs who were determined to disrupt the entire supply and distribution of electricity in Manicaland by blowing up transmission towers, ESC tower gangs in Umtali constantly improved their skill in erecting towers. They cut the time taken to erect a 132 kv tower from 14 hours at the beginning of the war, to a mere three towards the end.

The job meant nightmare journeys over landmined roads, through ambushes, past scenes of previous contacts, in hostile country and rough terrain in all kinds of weather. The saboteurs' favourite trick was to strap explosives to the legs of towers and blast the metal structures to a crumpled mass. It was a constant task to maintain the 500 towers between Umtali and Middle Sabi, as well as the 180 between Umtali and Rusape, said Terry, the District Manager.

One particular tower was blown up (or down) three times. But if power was out to a district at midnight, then supplies were generally 'ticking over' again by midday, even if it meant installing a new tower. The ESC boys prided themselves on their ability to replace towers quickly, and Umtali iron merchants once worked all weekend to help out in an emergency.

Another trick was for the opposition to unbolt sections of towers, burn down wooden transmission poles, or saw them off at ground level. In November 1978, they did their utmost to put the Dorowa phosphate mine out of action. They struck repeatedly at Melsetter and there was no doubt that this valiant little village bore the brunt of the war, say ESC staff.

All that remains of a transformer, costing thousands of dollars, that was blown up by terrorists.

Millions of dollars of damage was done in Manicaland – a disruptive and costly exercise to a country battling to defend itself. But 50 whites and 250 blacks kept the electricity flowing in the face of danger and death, despite tremendous setbacks.

"Their incredible devotion to duty was quite unparalleled," said the Umtali ESC head.

Men were wounded, vehicles were stolen, landmines exploded beneath drivers rushing teams to repair jobs. A meter-reader in his vehicle was abducted in a Tribal Trust Land and badly beaten up, technicians were threatened and shot at, but still they carried on.

"We were extremely unlucky to lose one man, Lazarus Sabvute, as a result of a landmine explosion. But our chaps were working in pairs in 'hot' areas where the Army would not move unless they had at least 12 men," he said.

Besides a stolen Land Rover the ESC lost five out of their 80 vehicles through enemy action. One lucky (?) technician, called out to the Vumba, found two landmines in the road ahead. He jubilantly claimed the $500 bounty offered at the time. The next time he was out he was blown up in a landmine blast which smashed the front of his brand new vehicle. He escaped unhurt.

Abusive leaflets were frequently found on nearby trees after installations had been cut, but "we just tore them up and pressed on".

The ESC had immense help from Umtali Police Reserve Air Wing, whose pilots flew teams over danger areas to pinpoint damage and report back.

The men maintained their spirits with typical cheer, singing defiantly and triumphantly their debonair song "We are the power boys!" with all its nonsensical rhymes.

"In spite of continuous danger their defence mechanism worked well," said their manager.

The administration staff invariably moved in the front line alongside their technicians, helping to maintain morale by showing their support and appreciation in difficult times.

"Overseas visitors just could not understand how we got our men into the field under these circumstances, but it was simple. The whole idea of our work ethic in Rhodesia, our determination to get the job done and never question our role, was foreign to people unfamiliar with Rhodesian guts and tenacity. For instance, when the Vumba substation was blown, the area was without power temporarily, but only while we used all our ingenuity to tie in power from other sources."

Each depot at Inyanga, Rusape, Chipinga, Middle Sabi and Umtali was responsible for maintaining its own distribution system and all were equally hard hit. The white technicians particularly had rigorous call-up duties in various security forces, in addition, but this gave them a closer insight into the overall problems of the province. This led to better co-operation with the Army.

The ESC training scheme for Africans went ahead throughout the war with a new impetus. The variety of the emergency work demanded of them and the frequency of call-outs only increased their speed and efficiency, and competitions were run to test the men's abilities.

It was a great satisfaction to them to know that they had been able to change 12 000 glass insulators on the power lines back to the original porcelain type, because the glass had proved unsuitable for the climate. This was a big job for the ESC but the work was completed.

Many times the Army had to be called in to clear the landmines planted round the damaged posts. Occasionally teams would be working for more than an hour before the mines were found and there were many 'narrow squeaks', said the ESC head.

Asked if any serious shortage of equipment affected their work, the District Manager grinned. "We thought we might run out of steel, but never did. We only ran out of sleep!"

It was sheer doggedness that kept these indomitable men going in spite of countless hours of duty, sleepless nights, hazardous journeys at all hours in all weather and finally, an overwhelming exhaustion.

"Normally we have a tremendous Christmas party and the chaps enjoy it. In 1979 we were too exhausted to bother."

The strain was echoed in family circles where wives and mothers waited and worried. They dreaded the sound of the telephone ringing after hours, the telltale dip of the lights at night that meant another tower had been blown, and the inevitable call-out that followed. They worried when they saw the tension lines on their men's faces, and bodies drooping from weariness. Worst of all were the long waits for their return after a call-out.

Six families have left the local ESC 'family', to the regret of all. Couples with young children saw no happy future ahead. It was more their lack of confidence in the future which persuaded them to look elsewhere, rather than the memory of hardships endured.

When medals were handed out for bravery and perseverance, six Electricity Supply Commission men, in the hardest hit of all provinces, Manicaland, were decorated. Men who had worked at Inyanga, Rusape, Umtali, Chipinga and Middle Sabi received the Meritorious Service Medal.

And what about the consumers? They frequently wrote letters of tribute thanking the ESC men in the field for getting the lights back on again – and risking their lives to do so.

Zimbabwe's Electricity Supply Commission was a public utility and non-profit-making organisation with more than 42 000 consumers. It employed a staff of nearly 3 000, including casual labourers. In the eastern area it sold over 240 000 000 kWh of power during the year, to mining, industrial, municipal and farming concerns, as well as domestic users. Its main source of power was from the Central African Power Corporation's hydro-electric station at Kariba.

The Commission's training schemes in 1981 included 13 undergraduates reading for bachelor degrees in mechanical and electrical engineering at universities in Zimbabwe and elsewhere. The apprenticeship scheme continued satisfactorily and 89 'appies' of all races were undergoing comprehensive training in electrical, mechanical and motor mechanic trades.

Posts and Telecommunications Corporation

How often did the 'phone ring, perhaps in the middle of the night or in the early hours, throughout Rhodesia, for anxious families to ask each other, "Are you all right?" and hear the comforting reassurances, "All well here. Keep *your* head down!" Whether they were minor domestic morale-boosters after attacks, or important affairs of state under discussion, people could always keep in touch promptly, thanks to the Posts and Telecommunications Corporation (PTC).

Efficient telephone communications were vital to the developing country and especially in wartime. With their hundreds of installations throughout the province and countless kilometres of wire connecting the people, Manicaland's Posts and Telecommunications Corporation was on the alert constantly, repairing extra disruptions to the service from May 1976 until the end of January 1980.

Their battle to maintain lines started slowly enough in Juliasdale, but spread to other areas. That year more than 40 faults due to 'enemy action' were reported, and repair teams rushed to the scenes to restore services. By August and September they were travelling more than twice a week to sabotaged lines, but it was not until 1978 that the communications 'war' really began.

There seemed no lengths to which the terrorists would not go to disrupt the system. They removed handsets, booby-trapped or cut down transmission poles, cut wires and cords, laid mines for repair vehicles, ambushed repair teams, beat up and abducted drivers.

Whenever a store, clinic, hospital, farm, homestead or hotel was attacked, the phone lines were either destroyed beforehand or burnt out in the fray. Trunk routes were cut in several places on many occasions by bullets during ambushes. Whenever damage was inflicted by terrorists they warned the local tribespeople that their premises would be burnt down if they dared to ask for service to be restored.

Repair crews were threatened, attacked and similarly warned. One team was held up by armed men and robbed of their watches and salaries. Their Land Rover was captured and driven off but later recovered, burnt-out.

On another occasion some two and a half kilometres of main line was completely destroyed and a large team was sent to repair the damage immediately. During the night, as they rested at a police camp, they were attacked with mortars, rockets and machine-guns. Two PTC men were killed instantly and 15 others were injured, some seriously. They were evacuated by the Air Force at midnight from a remote airfield which first had to be secured by the remaining PTC men and the police. The line repairs were completed the following day – a wonderful example of team-work.

Three men installing a link in a remote area were ambushed by a hail of rockets and the fuel can in their vehicle caught fire. But the men were unhurt, and continued to install their link.

Any logbook of the Corporation could well have read, "Farm attacked, 'phone cut, PTC work party to area with escort. First light attendance required." This happened so often in our border province.

Invariably telephones were replaced and lines repaired the same day, by gangs in their hard hats and bright orange overalls.

Employees remember the time a PTC vehicle was stolen and the driver abducted. The truck was used by the terrorists to rob a bus. Later a PTC team working on a line was mortared by the armed men. The mortars fell short and the gang reacted well and continued their repair. The next day there was an ominous road block and message: "That was only a warning. Next time we fire it will be full attack."

Occasionally the teams in the vehicles had such sudden frights that a little panic spread. One labourer was seen clinging to a driver 'like a teddy bear' when the bullets flew, while another lay flat like a ghecko* on the floor of the cab! But in spite of the horrors of landmines, AK† fire,

---

*Type of lizard found on walls and rocks.
†Avomat Kalashnikov 47 rifle used by the terrorists who were armed by Communist countries.

vicious threats and bloodthirsty warnings, the dedicated technicians carried on regardless.

Whenever villages or outlying centres were under fire the telephone operators on switchboard duty remained calm and handled the situations well.

"The PTC men also did their call-ups with the Security Forces and when they were back at work were still in the thick of it," said one official.

"It made real men of them. We are very proud of what they did. Their wives too, had a great deal to bear and we admire their courage." Not only were the technicians involved but the clerical and stores staff assisted as escorts during those difficult years.

Although many were based in Umtali, the Corporation had black and white staff in outlying areas – Cashel, Penhalonga, Melsetter, Mayo, Wedza, Headlands, Inyazura, Odzi, Macheke, Watsomba, Dangamvura, Birchenough Bridge – wherever there was a large enough community with telephonic equipment to defend, there was a PTC man and his fellows to assist.

November and December 1978 were particularly heavy months with ambushes, sabotaged lines, poles sawn down, from Fern Valley in the Umtali suburbs to Headlands, Cashel, Macheke and Mayo – a far flung area. Frequently the repair men found main roads blocked, fires burning, or army activity following reports of murdered Europeans en route.

Throughout the several rocket and mortar attacks on Umtali, PTC staff were on the alert immediately, and out to inspect damage as soon as the 'all clear' was signalled by Civil Defence.

Much damage was done nearby but the Telephone Exchange had no direct hit in spite of 180 bombs landing in the October 1978 attacks. Exchange operators always remained at their posts while the bombs fell and some rushed on duty during the firing so that thousands could dial and say, "Hullo Mum! You all right?" or, "Hold tight. We're on our way."

Roads, Water Development, Health and Conservation

Roads, water development, health and conservation were all services that managed to carry on somehow, with depleted staffs, in the face of extreme danger.

Although all were essential services officials were still called up for duty with the security forces and remaining staff battled on as best they could.

Roads, as a vital communications link, were a prime target for the terrorists. Bridges were blown up, trenches dug across main roads during the night and maintenance units attacked in an effort to cut off the rural areas. The ministry lost men to terrorist bullets and bombs; valuable plants, machinery and vehicles were destroyed but still the routes were kept open. On occasion traffic was delayed while roadmen found a way round a damaged bridge, but it was never halted. Low-level bridges, abandoned when main roads were realigned and new, high level bridges built over the rivers, were hastily brought back into use and given new approaches with tarred surfaces to reduce the risk of landmines. In places where there were no low-level bridges, causeways were built which would take heavy traffic even when the rivers were high.

Construction work was mainly on security roads – improving the access to farming and mining centres to make travel quicker and there-fore safer for the people living there. Guards accompanied the construc-tion units. While men and machines worked on the roads, armed men, mostly from the Rhodesia Defence Regiment (made up of Coloured and Indian soldiers) watched over them.

Everyone who sat behind the wheel of a vehicle anywhere in Manica-land during the war is grateful to the Ministry of Roads men. They did a wonderful job.

* * *

Water development too, carried on, but they worked out of the public eye and want to keep it that way. "We'd rather forget it all," said a senior official when asked about his ministry's war experiences.

* * *

Public health nurses, black and white, continued their duties in the face of extreme danger. Progress was limited by the security situation in many remote areas, but in spite of all the dangers and difficulties, progress was made towards increasing health facilities for black Rhode-sians in rural areas.

There were 65 clinics for Africans in Manicaland at the beginning of the war, and 111 at the close, despite many being damaged or de-stroyed. An illuminating fact in the face of present day assertions by the members of the new Zimbabwe Government that the rural areas were neglected by the 'colonial oppressors'.

Medically speaking, it was easier to treat people when they were living close together in Protected Villages. Preventive health measures and the administration of drugs was much simpler.

Cholera was contained whenever it appeared; there were no widespread epidemics; 90 000 rural people were immunised against measles which can be a killer in Zimbabwe; and thousands of huts were sprayed to kill mosquitoes and prevent malaria.

All the usual infectious diseases that spread in crowded conditions were dealt with as they cropped up. As is usual in war, tuberculosis and venerial disease increased.

"Water supplies kept going wrong and we only had five clapped-out old vehicles which were mine-protected but not proof against attack," said one official.

Buses stopped running in many Tribal Trust Lands as a result of terrorist landmines and armed attacks. This meant that people were unable to get to the clinics for treatment. "Every day was an emergency to us and our village staff and health workers had the wounded to cope with as well.

"We carried on with our supplementary feeding schemes and Well-baby clinics wherever we could. Seven of our staff were lost. They just went missing and no one knew what became of them. Clinics were robbed and burnt down by terrorists, but we went on building more. Twelve clinics were built in Protected Villages near to schools and these have become the centre of growth points in the province," a health official said.

Council clinics were destroyed, yet within 12 months these had all been rebuilt and 16 were in operation, with the help of the Manicaland Provincial Authority.

The Ministry had a constant battle against bilharzia. "Our teams would protect African school water supplies, treat the children after classes and get them free of the disease, only to have them reinfected at home."

Many provincial health workers had narrow squeaks and escapes from death. They slept in vehicles in isolated bush villages "where we could have been murdered and no one the wiser", yet they stuck to their jobs. As a result of their dedication public health throughout the province never collapsed.

One day a black community health sister was on a routine visit to a clinic in the Sabi Valley. Suddenly an Army lorry in the road ahead of her vehicle exploded. It had hit a landmine.

"There were about 15 soldiers who just fell out of that truck in all directions and many were unconscious in the ditch," she said.

"I jumped out of the car and went from one to the other giving first aid, using their guns as splints to bind the broken limbs. After treating them for shock and spending half an hour in the mud, sliding about in that ditch in my white uniform, we had to move on. The comrades might come and then we would be in even worse danger."

She called herself a jack of all trades. London-trained, she spent most of her time in the bush after returning to her own country, driving her own vehicle, with public health nurses for company.

"We gave advice, inspected maternity cases, took supplies to temporary clinics and acted as a mobile clinic when necessary," she said. "We worked with the sick and the well from the Honde Valley to Chipinga and further, often having hair-raising experiences."

Throughout the war she had to leave her small son and a mother at home. They worried endlessly that she might be killed. Before the second election she was nearly shot accidentally by the Guard Force at a Protected Village, but wherever she went she was respected for her work.

For this sister and other health workers the crying need in the rural areas is education to put across the message of good health. "We can do very well on our own African diet if we educate our mothers to grow vegetables and prepare food properly," she said. "Whoever heard of coke and bread or tea and bananas being essential? It is better to concentrate on clean water and fresh sadza mixed with nuts and home-grown vegetables for the children."

Kwashiorkor – a civilised disease due to malnutrition caused by people's desire for more sophisticated foods – resulted from ignorance rather than war, she said. Its cause was wrong feeding.

Family planning in Manicaland made strides during the war with the staff continuing their work in the field despite many difficulties.

Then came peace, a new government and Independence. Soon after, the Family Planning Association's good work ceased abruptly as the Zimbabwe Government stepped in and took it over.

In 1973, family planning acceptors in the province numbered 450 a month. In 1980 there were 3 000.

"My staff were responsible for 75% of the family planning in Manicaland," said the former Family Planning Association director. "The one major change in our approach has been to convert the field force of educators into combined motivators and distributors."

Their clinic services changed very little. The Association's earliest unit was a mobile clinic service operating from Umtali into surrounding farming areas and Tribal Trust Lands. The second mobile unit, working from Macheke, was destroyed by a landmine in 1978. Sister Elizabeth Mauku was killed with her driver, Rudorwashe Kunyadza.

In 1974, with help from the Rural Council, a mobile unit was introduced at Chipinga. It also incorporated a Well-baby service.

"In Africa, an identifiable free-standing family planning service is vital. It serves both a motivational and a practical purpose. Evidence now available from international authorities is quite clear that failure to slow population growth in Africa is largely attributable to offering family planning merely as part of the health service. It receives no priority and conveys no urgency," said the Family Planning Association director.

This country, he claimed, had pioneered for Africa the use of lay distributors for the community-based contraceptive distribution. "We are five years in advance of other countries with our lay distributors and 'doorstep delivery'," he said.

"If we worked office hours what would happen on the Honde Valley tea estates? Women are out from dawn to dusk when they are plucking tea, so the time for our work is in the evenings and weekends."

Similarly a woman with many obligations in the traditional land units was not likely to be enthusiastic about a plea to travel to a clinic some distance away at which she might, or might not, find contraceptive stocks or adequate motivated staff to attend to her, particularly early on when her motivation was not very high.

In 1980 the Family Planning Association had 39 educator/distributors in Manicaland – in the Honde Valley, Melsetter, Sabi Valley, Maranke, Mutasa, Penhalonga, Grand Reef and elsewhere.

In spite of the energetic drive to combat the problems of over-population, it had to be remembered that family planning was against African tradition, the director said. Before the white man arrived, parents lost so many children through illness, malnutrition and snake-bite that they felt they had to produce a great many in the hope that three or four would survive. Children were useful too for herding cattle and helping with home chores, while daughters brought in 'lobola'*.

Sons were the recipients of their father's spirit after his death, therefore a man must have a male child or he would not live evermore. These old beliefs remained.

---

*Bride price paid by prospective bridegroom to bride's father.

"Only when the mass of the African population realise they cannot advance economically and attain high standards of living in a Western context, will they appreciate the point of having smaller families," said a former Senator in the Muzorewa Government.

African families want the best of both worlds – many children and free health and educational facilities for them all. Even in the 1980's many African men still have many wives and scores of children and expect the State to care for them all.

* * *

Conservation

Before Frelimo took over power in Mozambique the Eastern Group of Intensive Conservation Areas had experienced few problems with regard to security. However, from the beginning of 1976, the picture changed rapidly with all areas experiencing a deteriorating security situation as will be illustrated in later chapters.

In spite of difficulties and danger, Government Conservation and Extension Department officials continued their work in European farming areas. But in the Tribal Trust Lands, where the terrorists were intimidating the people, swearing to kill them if they had anything to do with Government services, Conex men could no longer advise African farmers on soil fertility, dam building, suitable crops, marketing and other vital aspects of agriculture.

13 *Angels of death*

Shall any gazer see with mortal eyes,
Or any searcher know by mortal mind?
Veil after veil will lift – but there must be
Veil upon veil behind.

EDWIN ARNOLD

'In this sign conquer', the motto of the Corps of Chaplains, appears on its badge, a white Maltese Cross, with a blue rondel and gold quatrefoil in its centre, all encircled with a wreath, half of laurel and half of oak leaves.

The symbolism goes back hundreds of years – the Maltese Cross to the Crusades, the motto to Emperor Constantine and the wreaths to the days when victorious soldiers were crowned with laurel and leaders with oak leaves – but the Corps is very modern.

To some, the idea of ministers in uniform is anathema. There should be no link between guns and the Gospel, they say. Sometimes the chaplains themselves were asked for their Scriptural authority for being involved in the armed forces, for ministers with the word of God putting on a uniform and identifying themselves with the security forces.

"If any Christian has doubts about his call or responsibility in the armed forces he should go back and see what Scripture has to say," said an Army chaplain. "In scripture we find a soldier's calling and work is often referred to."

How does the chaplain see his calling? An Umtali chaplain tells how he became involved:

"When I arrived in Umtali I was in secular work and eligible for call-up. In July 1975 I went to serve with A Company, 4 RR in the north-east operational area. On the third night there, I was involved in a landmine blast but, praise the Lord, was unscathed. During my six weeks in the bush I was able to take services every Sunday morning. They were quite informal and it was amazing how many fellows came along."

His stint served as a good foundation for his future work, because on Chaplain's visits to the bush later he always met one or two men who knew him from call-up days. At the end of that year he was transferred to the Chaplain's Corps as a chaplain's assistant and continued visiting the bush, though no longer as an infantryman.

It was during one of these visits, in 1978, when returning to Umtali after a week in one area, that he was ambushed.

"We left the base camp at 05h00 and had not travelled far when I instinctively felt the need to grip my rifle," he said. "As we entered a river bed and went across a bridge there was a tremendous explosion and I thought we had hit a landmine. A rocket had been fired at us, had gone overhead and hit a tree nearby. I was back to back with a big fellow and he sheltered me, getting rocket shrapnel in his head and shoulder.

"Then they opened up in the ambush and bullets were whizzing everywhere. One thing I learnt in that experience is that it happens so very quickly, 10 to 15 seconds, that's all. You often hear fellows saying, 'Well, there'd be time to give the last prayer.' There's very little time for that.

"In the firing I saw how the Lord controls every movement we make. We had come through the ambush and had to return fire. I had to bend over to unbuckle my belt (we were strapped in for landmines on the road) and as I moved forward to do so was hit in the side, five centimetres below my heart. It was a flesh wound, the bullet going in and out again.

"I didn't realise at the time that I had been hit. An African soldier was hit in the neck and the same man who had been hit by the rocket shrapnel was wounded again, this time in his shoulder and leg. The terrorists had fired at the driver – obviously if you get the driver you get the vehicle – but miraculously the bullets passed both sides of the windscreen. One hit the radiator so the water ran out.

"We couldn't travel more than 2 km up the road before we stopped. I realised then how God had answered our prayer." (The driver and the chaplain's assistant, both members of the same church, had spent time in prayer together the previous evening.)

"When we stopped I realised I had been hit. I spent the night in the Umtali Hospital after the wound had been cleaned and stitched up."

These experiences gave him a good foundation for his future work among the troops. "I sincerely believe the Lord enabled me to experience them so I could be of assistance, to comfort and help others who had to go through similar ordeals," he said.

When he visited injured troops in hospital the chaplain said he could almost see the question 'What do you know about it?' written on their faces. The Lord had enabled him to go through similar experiences and he was able to help them in their need.

In 1978 he was commissioned into the Chaplains' Corps as a captain, serving as 4 RR chaplain and being involved in 3 Brigade. He had to show an interest in the Army's work and see that the chaplains were available to help with all problems, including mundane matters like sorting out school fees for a soldier's daughter and other welfare cases.

One of the tragedies was the marital problems caused by the war. He believed that this scar would never be removed.

"In the call-up system it meant that for six weeks at a time the wife had to assume a role often unfamiliar to her, taking on the responsibility of the home and making decisions. She had to do many things the husband would have done had he been there. This was a strain on the home relationship. It was a graceful wife who could step down when her husband returned, allowing him to resume his responsibilities, knowing full well that in a month or two he would be gone again, out in the bush on a further call-up.

"Often this didn't work. I once had a husband weeping because he came home and said he just felt 'like a spare part'. The wife refused to give up responsibility. She had got into the run of things and knew he was going away again in a few weeks.

"It was a strain on the children who didn't know their fathers well with so much coming and going. There were serious problems with the call-up system, yet there was no other way. The Army was basically a civilian army and men still had to work in commerce, industry and agriculture."

Many wives were unfaithful while their husbands were in the bush. Husbands were unfaithful too. Army commanders were very conscious of the fact that if a soldier suspected his wife of unfaithfulness then he was not a good soldier. Many times the chaplain was called in to sort out marital problems. There were many divorces as a result of the war. There were personal problems too – a soldier had time to think in the bush and one of the chaplain's basic jobs was simply to be available.

As far as the Rhodesian Army was concerned a chaplain's work was mainly welfare, 'noticas'*, and hospital visiting, not spiritual work. This was just incidental as far as the Army heirarchy was concerned.

Chaplains seldom called church parades. It would not have been wise to do so because the men would have come under duress, and there could have been resistance. But a lot was done on a personal level, being seen, mixing with the men, making yourself known, earning the right to be heard.

"It was surprising how many men would come, mainly at night, to

---

*Notification of a casualty.

the mess 'do', when there was a chance to relax. Men would come on their own to speak about the things that really matter," he said.

His one disappointment was that sometimes even Christians did not stand up for Christ as they should have done. "Many times I was surprised at these people, sometimes even church leaders, who, once they were in uniform, started swearing and drinking with the 'boys'.

"I tried to challenge them to realise it was their responsibility to the Lord to stand up for Him under these circumstances. They said it was 'lack of fellowship'. I tried to show them that their fellowship was in their home. When they came into the bush it was a mission field right at their doorstep where they had the opportunity to witness and show what the Christian life is all about."

Sometimes he found two to four Christians in a base camp and fellowship, prayer and Bible reading was held to encourage them.

"I remember when I went with another minister to Foxtrot Company on continuous service. We spent four days with them. I didn't feel I had achieved much, yet there was one young man I had spoken to who kept coming across to chat. Ten days later I heard he had been killed in an attack on that base camp in which five were killed, four in the attack and one on the follow-up.* Peace flooded my soul. I knew then that that young man was with the Lord. He was the one I was obviously meant to speak to. I realised then that it was worth going, even if only for the spiritual enrichment of one person."

Notification of casualties was the hardest part of the chaplain's work.

"With most jobs, the more you do it the easier it becomes, but telling next of kin that son, husband or brother has been injured or killed in action is just the reverse," he said.

"Death notifications were the worst. There was no set way. I just had to go along praying for God to give me the right words to say. I couldn't prepare anything, every circumstance was so different, and the news was met in so many different ways.

"The hardest part was to knock on the door and tell someone they had lost a loved one – to bring the blunt news. It was no good beating about the bush, no use wasting time – you had to come to the point, come to it quickly and do it compassionately.

"I was grateful that the Army used chaplains for this work. The Police sent the duty officer and one can imagine how he must have felt. The chaplain had the training and the call.

---

*Pursuit of those responsible for an attack.

"There were a couple of instances I remember well – one was particularly tragic. The parents had been expecting their soldier son home (he had written to say he was coming on R and R*). But he was killed in action and I had to tell them. They heard the Land Rover coming up the drive and the mother went to the back of the house. I came in the front, met her husband and told him their son had been killed. The mother came into the lounge, expecting to see her son, and was greeted with the news of his death.

"Another chap had completed his stint and finished with the Army. He then volunteered, after being stood down, to do another exercise, unknown to his parents. He was killed on this operation and I had great difficulty in trying to convince the parents that it was their son. The mother kept saying: 'He's not in the Army, he's been stood down. He's going to university. Are you sure it's not a mistake?'"

The Umtali chaplain said he became known as the Angel of Death and he had to be careful when visiting.

"I remember going on an ordinary pastoral call. The lady nearly had a heart attack. She wondered why I was calling and what had happened."

He recalled the day he had to take bad news to a member of his own congregation. The family had four sons in the Army.

"I used to visit the parents regularly. Only after the event did the mother tell me that whenever she saw me coming up the drive she always wondered what I was coming for. Then she realised she must not have this attitude, her minister was merely visiting her.

"The day came when I had to go and break the news to her. I felt I could not go alone. I asked a fellow minister to come with me. Then, after receiving a warm welcome, I had to deal a shattering blow and give her the sad news."

One Sunday evening, five minutes before a service, he was telephoned and had to go immediately to take the official news to a family, before friends who had heard it first could telephone their condolences.

Recalling incidents from his years as a chaplain he said that at 11h30 one night a wife phoned to say her husband, a regular, was threatening suicide. He had a hand grenade and threatened to pull out the pin.

"I spent 10 minutes calming him down and eventually persuaded him to give me the grenade. I was so relieved I put it in my pocket. There was pandemonium in the house with children screaming, the wife hysterical and neighbours up and wondering what was going on. Eventually I drove to another chaplain's house and handed over the grenade.

---

*Rest and Recuperation.

127

"The next morning the other chaplain said to me, 'You didn't check the pin did you?' 'No,' I said. 'Well, the split pin was closed,' he said. I went cold. The pin could easily have slipped out in my pocket. This was more evidence of God's hand upon me."

Many times the chaplain was called upon just for advice. He sometimes wondered how much help he really gave.

"In some cases I suggested that couples or families just went to church together. Some people were converted this way."

Work as an Army chaplain, he felt, was an invaluable opportunity to spread the gospel of Jesus Christ – "just by being there, showing you cared and were not so holy as not to be interested in the things they were doing..."

It was necessary however, for a chaplain to maintain his Christian principles. It was very easy to be 'one of the boys' thinking to win them over by being like them.

"They may think it good fun to see a chaplain perhaps drinking or swearing with them but, in my experience, when they are in trouble they don't like to go to 'one of the boys'. They prefer the one who is different, who has something they haven't got and can help them."

14 *Spiritual war*

"Be strong and of good courage: be not afraid, neither be thou dismayed; for the Lord thy God is with thee whithersoever thou goest."

JOSHUA 1:9

The nine metre high stone cross on a kopje on the eastern boundary of the city of Umtali is a prominent beacon on the border between Mozambique and Zimbabwe. It was erected in memory of African troops killed in World War I. Floodlit for the first time at Christmas 1974, the illuminated cross became part of another war in 1976 when rockets and mortar bombs rained on Umtali from across the border. People believed the attackers were using the cross as a sighting aid so the Mayor ordered the light to be switched off. It was not until the ceasefire, on December 31, 1979, that the light went on again.

Although men and women no longer had a golden cross shining against the blackness of the night sky before them as a physical reminder, for many the Cross of Calvary began to have real meaning. Tragedy, danger, fear, turned people to Christ. They were drawn together in adversity. Denominational differences faded. Attendances at Sunday services and prayer meetings increased. Many responded to the Gospel. Oneness in Christ was a blessing and a source of strength.

In Umtali three new churches were built and dedicated during those dark days.

Praying with the sounds of war in the background added a sense of urgency. The boom of distant mortar attacks sometimes interrupted Bible studies and church meetings and sent parents hurrying home to their children. Loud explosions from the border minefield made people jump, even in church or at prayer.

People began to matter more than things. One woman, surveying the ruins of her once lovely home after an attack, said: "They can never separate me from my Lord."

There was unity, love and caring, which enabled the people of Umtali and districts to face the death and destruction which became almost commonplace – and horrors such as the Elim massacre.*

Funerals were frequent and for ministers who had to notify next of kin of death and serious injury it was difficult. Imagine what it meant to

---

*This occurred in 1978. 12 missionaries and their children were criminally assaulted and brutally murdered by Communist terrorists.

a pastor to have a little girl say to her mother, "I don't want to go to that church because it is a funeral church."

Said one: "This was the kind of thing we never got used to. However, the counselling which followed each tragic situation did provide us with the opportunity to share Christian love, fellowship, compassion and, most of all, the Gospel."

It was during those terrible years that people learnt the true meaning and power of prayer.

In April 1978 six Umtali people, who had been meeting on a regular basis to cover special prayer needs within their own church, decided to spread the net wider. They agreed to meet every Wednesday during the lunchhour at the One Way Christian Centre to pray for the needs of the country and all its people.

After a few months they heard about a Salisbury-based Prayer Project, aimed at covering 'every centimetre of Rhodesian soil with God's Divine protection', and especially the sensitive farming areas. The idea was for small groups to pray daily for specific areas and people by name.

The tiny Umtali group felt this was just the kind of expansion they needed and they joined the Prayer Project. Two local groups immediately undertook to pray for the Inyanga area, with another group praying for Melsetter district.

As the idea spread and more people became interested, it was decided Umtali should co-ordinate the prayer commitment for the whole of Manicaland.

The work grew and with it came offers of help from all denominations. Within two months there were 17 groups covering various areas of Manicaland. More and more people became interested and wanted to help. People in the areas being prayed for learnt of the project and sent in lists of the farmers living there. Some formed their own prayer groups and there were people in Umtali praying for Chipinga, and a group in Chipinga praying for Inyanga Downs.

Contacts were made by letter with many of the farming community being upheld in prayer and some lovely, meaningful friendships developed as a result.

As one pray-er remarked: "When people start praying for each other a bond is set up that becomes quite unbreakable."

The contacts in the rural areas became a vital part of the whole organisation. They provided up-to-date lists, news of special needs and dangers and told of the wonderful answers to prayer that were experienced.

In the danger areas knowledge of the constant prayers being offered was a great morale booster and brought a sense of peace. In many places a drop in serious incidents was reported.

Then, in September 1978, it was decided in Salisbury to work with another organisation called 'Operation Esther', with a similar vision. In February 1979 the two groups became one unit.

The Esthers, originating in South Africa in mid-1978 as a group praying for their nation, were named after the Old Testament queen who interceded with the king of the Persians for the safety of the Jewish nation. Just as her prayers were wonderfully answered, so were those of the latter-day Esthers.

Beginning with three groups in Umtali in August 1978 the project expanded until there were 28, involving about 200 people, stretching from one end of Manicaland to the other. At least 800 people were being prayed for by name, as well as 'blanket groups', farms, mines, estates, schools, missions and villages.

The province was divided into 12 areas: Inyanga North, Inyanga village, Juliasdale (with Rodel, Airedale and Sanyatwe), Honde (and Mutasa), Penhalonga (including Stapleford, Imbeza, Old Umtali), Odzi, Inyazura, Cashel/Melsetter, Mid and Lower Sabi, Chipinga, Vumba/Burma Valley, Umtali, Sakubva and Dangamvura.

The prayers were never aimed *against* anyone. The terrorists were frequently remembered too, and Esthers prayed that they would turn from violence to peace and come back to restore the land, rather than destroy it. Prayers were directed at protection of all people from harm and for them to come into an awareness of God in their lives. As with Queen Esther the main objective was to accept a challenge in faith and trust and to try to yield oneself as a channel through which God could work out His purpose and plan. This was seeking for deliverance, not vengeance.

At the beginning of November 1978 two telephone chains were set up, making it possible to contact about 50 people in a very short time.

The first two numbers were widely circulated and appeared in Police Reserve offices all over the province. At any time of the day or night anyone under attack, threatened attack or facing an emergency (including serious illness) could 'phone in for immediate prayer. Many of the calls came from neighbours picking up an emergency on the *agric-alert*.

In the first three months 40 emergency calls were received, ranging from direct attacks on farms or townships, ambushes and fires to injuries, dangerous undertakings and abduction.

There were wonderful results. People reported minimal damage following severe attacks; rockets, bombs and other material that did not go off; fires just dying out ... Real miracles were recorded, angels were seen and visions received.

So many people reported escapes and incidents that can only be called miraculous. For example, there was the time when three security force vehicles 'jumped' a 1,2 m trench during an ambush; bees appeared 'out of the blue' to drive away attackers; mist suddenly descended to give protection; a whirlwind uncovered a landmine right in front of a vehicle; and all the time bullet-ridden engines continued to run until the vehicle was out of the danger area.

Perhaps most spectacular of all were the many stories (mostly authenticated) of 'soldiers in white' who appeared and frightened off attackers in moments of the direst need. Although Operation Esther did not claim credit for any of these – that can only go to God – it is noteworthy that most of the people concerned were receiving covering prayer.

Two dramatic answers came as a result of emergency calls on the telephone Prayer Chain.

One concerned a small school in an outlying area. A bush fire had been raging all day and could not be contained. At about 20h30 a call came from the school saying that the fire was now roaring down the hillside towards the school grounds and the young boarders were frightened. Please, would the Prayer Chain pray?

The chains were alerted at once, and one or two people were led to visualise a wall of light all round the school grounds, becoming an impenetrable barrier to the fire. Early next morning a call came. It said that about 30 minutes after the original alert the fire had stopped – a metre from the school boundary!

The other, even more dramatic, also concerns a fire. A call came, soon after midnight, from the Middle Sabi farming area to say that some of the wheatfields were being set on fire by terrorists. It was reaping season and the fires could have spread very quickly throughout the area. This time it was visualised that damp would descend and the wheat prove too wet to burn (at harvest time this was asking a great deal!)

The next morning the first words were: "You won't believe this, but the wheat was too wet to burn!" Very little was lost. It was mainly the stubble that burnt. As a footnote to the story, one member of the chain was not called that night. But she awoke about midnight and was 'shown' a field of burning wheat, so she prayed about it anyway, without knowing the full story until much later.

Looking back, one of the Esthers said: "One of the great blessings to come out of this prayer commitment was the way in which God moved in the hearts of so many people, not only those who received the prayers but also in the spiritual strengthening and renewal among those involved.

"Christians of all races and all denominations came together in an exciting and rewarding commitment, united in a common bond of concern for the welfare of their people and the nation. They were also united in complete trust that God would do three things if they would humble themselves and pray, namely, (1) hear their prayers (2) forgive their sins and (3) heal their land, according to His promise in II Chronicles 7:14."

Operation Esther groups also involved themselves deeply in national prayer needs, and linked up with the 'Nation at Prayer' organisation, where there was also a telephone link, on a countrywide basis, for any special emergency prayer situation.

Before the 1979 Elections, Operation Esther mounted prayer programmes all over the country to pray for a peaceful election period and a positive result. God answered. There was no bloodshed and the joy and happiness among the contending parties was miraculous.

Again, before the 1980 Election, groups and individuals prayed and fasted and met for intercession, not to ask for a specific result, but again praying for peace and harmony and that God's will and purpose might prevail. The accent was on praise to God in all things and all situations. The election result came as a shock to many, but it brought peace to a weary, wartorn country.

The aftermath of war brought a new dimension to the spiritual life of Manicaland. With the pressure lifted and the strains gone, people began to relax. Tragically, many of them took off their spiritual armour.

A clearly discernible lethargy, a kind of overpowering inertia, became evident. Congregations dwindled as people left the country. Prayer groups, Bible studies and youth groups suffered as numbers dropped. People seemed weak and weary and to have lost direction. Many wondered whether God was still in control and whether He still answered prayers.

Faithful followers of Christ now see, however, that they are still at war, fighting an even greater battle, to save souls and change men and women by spreading the gospel in the new Zimbabwe.

There is a great hunger for the Bible and the good news of Jesus Christ in many rural areas where Tribal Trust Land churches were closed and Christians had to meet clandestinely during the war. Terrible devastation took place on the mission stations. In Melsetter, for example, the damage to Rusitu Mission was estimated at $300 000, while the estimated cost of reopening Catholic mission schools and hospitals in Manicaland was put at more than $2 000 000 in 1980.

When there was a contact with the terrorists they sometimes left a message: 'Down with Smith, Muzorewa and Jesus Christ'. Many pastors and evangelists in the Tribal Trust Lands paid with their lives. They were regarded as 'agents' of Jesus Christ. During those dark days the hero in the rural areas was the common Christian man.

The Roman Catholic Bishop of Umtali, Donal Lamont, sentenced in an Umtali court for aiding terrorists, and afterwards deported, said this when he returned to Zimbabwe after Independence: "We were regarded as the enemy. We (that is the Catholic Church) articulated the grievances of the African people and as a result the security forces, when they came to any of our missions, regarded themselves as being in unfriendly territory.

"The Government 'wanted the Church to associate itself in defence of the establishment and in defence of the racist regime'. I saw that if the Church were to agree to collaborate to any extent ... we would be making a mockery of Christianity."

He said he had told his missionaries that when people came looking for food and medicine 'they were not to ask for political beliefs but merely to give'. The tragedy, in so many instances, was that the terrorists were given food and sheltered from the pursuing Security Forces who were treated as the real enemy.

NOTE: Bishop Lamont left the country voluntarily to return to his native Ireland in 1982 saying that he considered the morals of the country to have been in better hands under the Smith Government than with the present regime.

15 *The wheels keep turning*

Everything comes out of the dirt – everything comes out of the people, the everyday people as you find them and leave them, people, people, just people.

WALT WHITMAN

War brought many problems to the people who stayed at home battling to keep things running, the wheels of industry turning, and water, sewerage and roads functioning in the built-up areas. Entertainment and sport also presented challenges.

Municipal Services

Umtali City Council and the Rural Councils in Manicaland – Makoni, Tsungwesi, Inyanga, Umtali, Cashel, Melsetter and Chipinga – somehow managed to carry on even though short of staff, money and equipment. Due to the dedication of the men and women working for local government authorities there were no major breakdowns of services to the public, though some necessarily had to be curtailed. Rural councils, for instance, found they had virtually to abandon certain areas as the war intensified and people were driven from their homes. There was no point in maintaining roads that served no one. The abandoned farms, looted stores and wrecked rural industries also meant financial headaches for the councils. People were unwilling to pay taxes and licences for something that brought nothing in return.

Umtali Municipality ran literally on half staff. Army commitments effectively took up half the working year. Men serving with the Air Force Reserve were called up for two weeks every two months, while the Police Reservists were called up at weekends. During emergencies they were on call at any time. In addition, those without military commitments were involved in Civil Defence.

"All this meant an additional burden for the remaining staff," said a municipal official. "They took work home in the evenings and weekends. Procedures were streamlined to keep the day-to-day business of the Council running. The Councillors also helped by accepting these changes as routine and taking their decisions in the light of the existing circumstances."

It was a matter of pride to all that all municipal services were fully maintained throughout the war. Men working in the water section and

Looking south down Main Street, Umtali at night. The building with the Clock Tower (left) is the Magistrates' Court and opposite it the old Cecil Hotel, now Headquarters of 3 Brigade.

electricity department ran the risk of ambush and landmines when carrying out maintenance of these essential services, but they did not think about the dangers, they just got on with the job.

A shining example of dedication was given by the waterworks staff at Odzani. Living as they did in a 'hairy' area 48 km from Umtali, they were fenced into the complex, and a dusk to dawn curfew was in force. The waterworks were attacked at night and sometimes the staff were fired on during the day while carrying out their duties. But no one resigned. The men stuck to their job of supplying Umtali with water and the wives stayed with their menfolk.

The city's new sewage works at Gimboki, near the African housing estate at Dangamvura, was attacked twice, but the only damage was to a storeroom and a vehicle. The only other municipal installation to be hit was the repeater station on Cecil Kop, part of the radio link between the city and the waterworks.

One official with a 4th Battalion commitment was frequently called out of meetings to 'put on his other hat' and go off on military business. "I was attending an important meeting at 11h00 one morning when I was given a message saying there was 'a presence in Dangamvura'," he said. "I had to leave the meeting to find out what was going on. It turned out to be a wild goose chase – but that sort of thing was part of life in those days. If I went out anywhere in the evening or at weekends

136

I left my telephone number at the operations room and I always carried two radios in my car."

Commenting on the liaison between the Army, Police, Civil Defence, Air Force and Artillery, he said that all of these, and communications, "were welded into an ops room. It was a real Heath Robinson set-up, but it worked. If you were needed you just went there, no matter what you were doing or wearing." There had been so much that was worthwhile. "It deserved a better ending," he added.

The Civic Centre also became the nerve centre for the city's Civil Defence system. There were two reasons for this, firstly, because the Mayor was, by law, designated Umtali's Civil Defence Officer and, secondly, because the municipal radio network could be used as part of the communications system. As records of sewer, water and power lines were also kept in the same building, Civil Defence could easily pinpoint damage to any of these services and have repairs started quickly.

Commenting on those tough days, another municipal official said: "The minor population group (White) carried the responsibility for the total population. The whole place was kept going by fewer than 1 000 people – all of them wearing two hats – who supplied services for at least 70 000 people."

Influx problems

As the war spread on the eastern border and increased in intensity, Africans flocked from the rural areas into Sakubva and Dangamvura, the high density black townships on the outskirts of the city. Sakubva, an old township, spread over more than 400 hectares, was most affected and in the course of time its population more than doubled.

The influx consisted of blacks frightened by war, threatened by terrorists, caught in the crossfire and those whose homes, farms or business premises had been looted or destroyed by terrorists.

Children of township residents who had been sent to country schools or to help on the land were recalled when their schools were closed or destroyed by terrorist activity and threats. Teachers, also, when schools no longer existed, came to the city to seek alternative employment. Countrymen sent their wives and dependents to their brothers in town, to avoid the intimidation, torture, rape and killing being organised in the Tribal Trust Lands by terrorists.

Not only were the houses filled to bursting point but the township services, designed for a normal population, were stretched to bursting point. The number of sewer blockages rose dramatically and water consumption from communal wash-houses and taps soared. It was remarkable that fears of a major epidemic did not materialise. However, below the surface, the intensive overcrowding of houses had sociological consequences.

In the short term there was an increase in the incidence of prostitution and venereal disease. In the long term the effect of such conditions upon young and impressionable children has yet to be measured.

A continuing upward swing of unemployment over the war years provided not only a veering towards crime but also a source of recruitment to the terrorist ranks. Even schoolchildren on the brink of academic attainment, to the consternation and grief of many parents, crossed the border, either voluntarily or under terrorist compulsion. Even young adults abandoned their jobs. These included 11 municipal barmen and canteen hands who deserted to the terrorist cause in August and September 1976 with their cash floats in their pockets.

The presence of terrorists or their agents in the African townships from time to time was known, but residents, either through sympathy for their cause or because of fear, were not prepared to supply information to the authorities. A knock on the door in the small hours, followed by the threat of violence, frequently led to supplies of clothing, food and money going out to the terrorists. It is now known that a prime meeting place for them was a house in the Chisamba section of Sakubva African Township, 274 metres from the Sakubva Police Station. This must have been known to many, but fear of reprisals ensured silence.

In the latter part of 1978 terrorists enforced the virtual evacuation of Zimunya African Township, 25 km from Umtali, thus adding to the influx problems in Sakubva and Dangamvura.

In the first half of 1979 Dangamvura was attacked twice. The first attack, an attempt to bring about a Zimunya-type evacuation, was light and abortive. However, on April 8, 1979, the area was subjected to a heavy rocket, mortar and smallarms attack. Two pairs of semi-detached houses were destroyed and many others holed by shrapnel and bullets. Remarkably, there was only one fatality. The apparent object of the attack was to unsettle the black population and discourage participation in the April national elections. In this respect it was a total failure and it was to the credit of the people of Dangamvura that they stood their ground and went on to vote in large numbers.

In spite of approaches from members of the security forces, co-operation, by way of information on strangers in the township, was not readily forthcoming. Few, if any, were prepared to risk possible retribution at the hands of terrorists or 'mujibas'.

138

Before the end of the war Dangamvura came under further mortar and rocket attacks, but apart from holed houses and roofs, little damage was done and there were no fatalities until a bus was ambushed at the entrance to the township. One death resulted from this incident.

Despite the pressures of war in and around Umtali, the structure of administration in Sakubva and Dangamvura was maintained. A total of 1 790 new houses were built and new major facilities, including a polyclinic, a multi-purpose community hall, the first stage of a secondary school and a cocktail bar, were erected. Through community effort a golf course was also laid out. In the midst of war and destruction, there was life and constructive progress yet.

Entertainment

Entertainment dropped into the doldrums during the war years. The Umtali Players, an amateur theatre group, staged a few productions at the Courtauld Theatre and had some successes, despite casting difficulties due to the constant call-up of men.

Audiences were poor on the whole – the night attacks on the city kept people at home – although on one memorable occasion young ballet dancers went on with their show for an invited audience of senior citizens, only minutes after a bombardment from Mozambique.

Many of the old folk had endured far worse in the London blitz and were not going to let a few bangs spoil their enjoyment, while ballet mistress Jeanette (who later narrowly escaped death when her home was hit) inspired everyone by declaring that the show must continue.

The local Arts Council persuaded a few artistes to bring their talents from afar, but Umtali was not a popular venue. In 1974 the Council had been 'stung into activity' and gala occasions organised. Progress was maintained the following year, but 1976 saw setbacks due to the war. The Salisbury Youth Orchestra, with 41 talented youngsters, was particularly welcome in June that year, and was immediately booked for a return visit in 1977.

The Fiesta Group, which specialised in Spanish dancing and classical guitar music, made a notable visit, although the gifted pianist's reaction to the Courtauld Theatre's upright piano was almost unprintable. From the safety of Cape Town the company were 'jittery' about the local security situation and wanted to overfly the dangerous area to Chiredzi, their next stop. This was not possible, but the group was provided with a strong Police escort. They had only just left when Umtali suffered its first mortar attack.

The Arts Council undertook to sponsor the Manicaland Artists' exhibition and when the late Mr G. E. McGrath, the Council chairman, was nominated to the National Gallery board, Umtali became the 'third arm' of the Gallery, receiving regular exhibitions previously only shown in Bulawayo and Salisbury.

With the intensification of the war, Police drivers/escorts were provided for visiting artistes. They played brilliantly and provided much-needed relaxation for a city under considerable strain.

The Manicaland Society of Artists' membership dropped, and although they had visits from national artists of repute, they had to use their own resources for regular lectures and demonstrations.

Umtali potters celebrated their 25th aniversary (during the war) with the acquisition of a much larger kiln. They worked in part of an historic city building, Umtali's first hospital, now known as Kopje House, which forms part of the Umtali Museum Cultural Centre. An umbrella organisation, the Umtali Museum Scientific and Cultural Association, which includes most local societies catering for art, scientific and hobby-type interests, plans to build a Cultural Centre attached to the Museum to give a 'home' to all these groups. Fund-raising for this continued throughout the war. UMSCA also arranged an annual Expo at which the societies exhibited their work to the public. A monthly newsletter was published giving news of UMSCA activities, and keeping hobbyists in touch.

For those who preferred their entertainment at the touch of a switch, the 'goggle box',* which came to Umtali in the mid 1970's, was a must. Most people developed a compulsive neurosis for listening regularly to news bulletins on radio and TV, and the dreaded 'Combined Operations regrets to report . . .' was heard nightly with trepidation, in case a friend or neighbour had been killed.

The repeated acts of violence throughout the country became part of the daily diet of the listening and looking public.

In spite of this there was some fun, notably during the Aloe Festivals, held for the week leading up to Rhodes and Founders, the holiday weekend in July.

The festivals brought a little light relief and glamour (with an Aloe Queen competition) to a jaded city. The processions had a strong military flavour when uniformed men and women, black and white, took time off from their duties to 'show the flag' in the street parades.

Although Umtali lacked holidaymakers and tourists, the Manicaland

---

*Television.

Publicity Bureau encouraged clubs to provide entertainment for local enjoyment.

Sport

Sports teams from other centres almost ceased to visit Umtali. School teams going to play in Salisbury travelled under armed escort. Few schools made the reverse journey, and the days of hockey, swimming and rugby enthusiasts travelling by overnight train became nostalgic memories. (Night trains were stopped after a series of attacks on drivers and landmine explosions on the tracks.)

For adults, the major golf and bowls trophies were kept circulating – with the added interest of extra holes on local courses after attacks!

Wildlife Society Branch

In spite of Umtali's isolation (or perhaps because of it) the Wildlife Society branch flourished and produced an excellent small game park at Cecil Kop, the city's northern boundary.

"Conceived in dark days, this act of faith was a shining beacon that proved that, despite the indiscipline, anarchism and cynicism of our so-called civilisation, the large, but regrettably silent, majority still believes in the preservation of true values as well as the necessary material requirements," the Wildlife Society chairman said. "Had action not been taken when it was, Cecil Kop by now would have been denuded of trees and all manner of beautiful things which allow us to relax from our worldly tensions."

A society member commented: "This is one of the bright things to have gone ahead regardless of the war and faint hearts."

In the early 60's an Umtali schoolboy was ridiculed when he said that one day the Cecil Kop range would be a game park, with elephant, white rhino and many other animals there. He spent countless week-ends roaming the area and studying the terrain.

Years later, as a municipal official, his dreams became public and the 'ragging' was widespread. Notices appeared outside his gate: 'White Rhino Wanted' and 'Elephants for Sale!'

People wrote saying the idea was ridiculous. Rhino would fall off the slopes into Murambi! Zebra could only live on plains and other animals could not adjust to new environments.

But wildlife enthusiasts persevered and the dream became reality. The primary game area (about 320 hectares) is fenced. Baby elephant, white rhino, eland, tsessebe, impala, waterbuck, zebra, wildebeest, kudu, sable and ostrich live there. All have been 'imported', some from the other end of the country, being moved at night when it was cooler, though much more dangerous, to travel.

Nobody laughs about Cecil Kop now and the project gives pleasure to thousands of visitors who have come to know individual animals by sight – 'Matilda Splodge' the smallest elephant, and 'Picky', the lady rhino.

While many have helped, special credit goes to Iain and Sue who gave up every spare moment to establish the game park – surveying, clearing, fencing, building walls and advertising with art work, T-shirts and air letters, as well as encouraging others in fund-raising, morning markets, flag days and show stands.

Future plans include an environmental school camp, a reptile park and a wilderness zone.

The SPCA

War brought new problems to the dedicated members of the Umtali branch of the Society for the Prevention of Cruelty to Animals. They found themselves caring for frightened, injured animals, victims of terrorist ambushes and homestead attacks.

"We had one couple ambushed on their way to Umtali from Melsetter," an SPCA inspector said. "The wife was badly hurt and it was hours later before anyone thought about their Maltese poodle. The dog was covered in blood and we all thought it had been hurt, but it was the woman's blood." That was the first time the SPCA had anything to do with the war, the inspector added.

On another occasion horses from Chipinga being evacuated to Umtali for safety were ambushed on the way. They were abandoned in the horsebox and the SPCA had to rescue them, unhitching the box to get it out of the 'killing area'. The horses were unharmed.

The SPCA cared for three dogs wounded at Odzi when a rocket landed on the verandah of the farmhouse where they were sleeping. One of them, a bull terrier, was later put down because his nerves were shattered. "He went berserk whenever he heard a bang," the inspector said.

Sometimes SPCA personnel had to travel with the Army in a protected vehicle to collect animals from dangerous areas. Penhalonga and Melsetter were two such spots.

After a man had been killed in the Imbeza Valley the SPCA wanted to fetch his dogs. "They had been behind a security fence for 10 days

142

before we were allowed to collect them," the inspector said. "Then we became very 'pushy' about this because we knew the best time to go in after an attack was straight away. I was not really nervous. I was clenched up against the horror of the whole thing but I was not really afraid."

The inspector collected the three dogs belonging to an Imbeza Valley couple killed in a landmine blast, but two of them had to be put down.

The society was able to find homes for most of the 'orphaned' dogs, especially the big ones.

Recalling the capture of a cat which ran away after its owner was shot in the Vumba, the inspector said she had to return time after time to try to collect it.

"There is a rocky kopje above the house, and while I was up there I heard baboons coming along talking to themselves. Then I heard their alarm calls and knew something was up in the rocks. It wasn't a dog, it was terrorists lying there. I knew they were there and I was scared, but I also knew it was the last chance to get the cat." She caught him, and pussy now lives with the murdered man's widow.

The cat had been in the house during the attack with two dogs – one too deaf to hear the terrorists coming and the other, a Labrador, who ran away.

An SPCA member who went to the Imbeza Valley to collect a dog after another murder said the animal had been under the bed where his master was killed. The dog was so bewildered it had to be put down.

Dogs were also involved in the Elim Mission massacre at Eagle School. A Labrador spent all night sitting over the bodies of her murdered family. They were all killed, husband, wife and children, and it was the dog's howling that attracted the attention of the one teacher who survived. "She was in such a state we had to tranquillize her for three days afterwards," the inspector said. "She was terribly confused. We kept her for about a fortnight and then found a home for her at Penhalonga."

One dog, a pug type, was stolen from the Mission. It was put on the back of a bicycle. The inspector found it later on the edge of a Tribal Trust Land.

She said that most dogs involved in attacks were left with nervous reactions and the SPCA really had to nurse them to restore their confidence and courage.

A big problem came from Army men who picked up dogs at various places. In one instance a stray at Inyazura was given a home. It became sick after a week, was brought to the SPCA and found to be rabid.

At Grand Reef there was a dog which ran away after the base was attacked on Christmas Eve. It was missing for three months and when it was eventually found the animal had a 'massive' sore on its back with maggots crawling out of it.

"We nursed him for six weeks," the inspector said. "He was beginning to pick up when he suddenly started acting peculiarly. It was found that he had rabies. We all had to have antirabies inoculations."

One of the worst side effects of the war, the inspector felt, was the influx of rabid animals due to the breakdown in animal health control and veterinary inspections in the rural areas of Manicaland.

Libraries

The Turner Memorial Library managed to keep going, but the high price of books forced the library committee to build up stocks with paperbacks.

While the library building was untouched (the Queen's Hall next door was hit during one attack), both members and books became war casualties.

A Juliasdale family returned library books riddled with bullet holes after an attack on their farmhouse.

Another man, hiding under a bush, watched his lifework go up in flames at Inyanga when his home was burnt. His library books were burnt too.

Another Inyanga area resident saw her husband killed before her eyes. Their home was burnt (including the library books). She escaped after a terrifying, cold night in an outbuilding.

Other country members withstood attacks on their homes, among them three from Odzani. All the massacred Elim missionaries, including the children, belonged to the library.

An Imbeza Valley couple, who died in their car when it was blown up in a landmine blast, had books with them to return to the library. All were lost.

Two members were abducted. One, Tom,* was back in 1981 enjoying the library again. The other, Mr Deryck Lamb, disappeared from Cashel. His body was found months later on his farm.

There were other tragic cases, including the deaths of young men who, not long before, were junior members going to the library for help with school projects or reading Biggles and the Hardy Boys.

---

*He has now written a book on his experiences.

144

A member of the library staff, living in the Vumba, had a narrow escape when bullets were fired through her lounge window. They missed her but hit the clock. Her husband was so fast on the draw that the intruders took flight and no one was hurt. The couple had to leave their home and farm, like many others whose livelihood was gone.

Garden Clubs

Gardeners sought relaxation in the beauty of their own grounds. Umtali has some lovely plots, in tree-lined settings, and the Horticultural Society, renamed the Garden Club, arranged two shows each year.

The city's floral art groups have always been well-attended and they kept up to date with modern trends, inspired by the need to have a little beauty in the home to counteract the ugliness of war. Inevitably 'an arrangement for a troopie in hospital' (with beer nestling among the flowers and cigarettes) was a topical theme at shows.

Unfortunately, the popularity of La Rochelle, the lovely wooded National Trust property in the Imbeza Valley, bequeathed by the Courtaulds, declined. The trustees had a hard task to maintain the gardens and orchid houses with limited funds, and took to selling potted plants when the income from weekend teas failed.

A series of brutal and pointless murders by terrorists of Europeans in the neighbourhood tragically ended plans to make the former stately home a national conference centre and tourist attraction.

Nearby the Forestry Commission opened a training centre in a large house which was renovated and equipped as a school. It was close to Imbeza Forest Estate and sawmill and ran well until the white principal was murdered. The school then closed. It has since reopened to aid forest progress in Zimbabwe.

In the Vumba, blue duiker, bushbuck, Samango monkeys and wild pig, with an occasional leopard on the prowl (the spotted cat as well as the clumsy, but effective, protected Army vehicle of the same name) had the lovely botanical gardens to themselves for most of the war.

"Visitors dropped from 2 600 a month to about 20," said the curator, who stayed at his post for five years, helping the local Police Reserve and making ends meet as best he could.

The colourful gardens were kept up to standard and the staff stayed on, despite the proximity of a troubled border. Tragedy struck at Elim a few kilometres away, and Leopard Rock and Mountain Lodge hotels in the vicinity were attacked. Privately owned holiday chalets were closed through lack of custom in 1976.

But visitors are slowly returning and the National Park had campers and caravanners for the 1980 holidays.

* * *

What did the war on the home front mean to a man who has lived in Umtali for longer than most citizens?

Harry, born in Umtali in 1907, father of five, grandfather of 11, said he had no wish to repeat the memories of the bombardments the city went through. Though nothing like those when 'bigger forces collide', they were bad enough. Lying under insufficient cover hearing the bursts come nearer, would never be forgotten.

Born of a mother who, in 1896, at the age of six, left the comfort of home in Grahamstown to travel to Beira by sea, narrow-guage railway to Chimoio and wagon to Old Umtali (then a tiny pioneer village in a vast area of wild, empty bushland), he said he had seen everything from late Victorianism to the Man on the Moon.

"I have seen it all, from water-drip charcoal cooler-box (ant-free when hung) to deep freeze; from water brought in by the bucket and boiled for safety to pipes laid on all over the house; from candles and paraffin lights to any intensity of light at the flick of a switch; from a long, cold walk to an outside latrine to modern sanitation on all floors; from unbridged tracks which took three days' motoring to cover 320 km to modern transport which can cover the distance (not nearly so safely) in three hours; from donkey wagon travel to speed sufficient to throw one off the earth."

What a lifetime. It could never happen again, he said. Such tremendous progress in one lifetime! A lovely country had been built up. "It will be a tragedy if we have to watch it disintegrate. Then the majority will suffer," he said.

16 *Why?*

"For the Lord has comforted His people, and will have compassion on His afflicted."

ISAIAH 48:13

Why did this have to happen to *us*? How many times did heartbroken families ask this question during the dark days of the bush war? How does one answer that despairing cry? Christians could find comfort in God's promises, even in their sorrow, but for those who did not believe, there was just a terrible emptiness, as widows and bereaved parents asked, *Why?*

The world stopped for one Umtali family the day they were told their dearly-loved only son had been killed.

Gentle, kind, trustworthy, dependable and 'a wonderful son', brave and strong, his death left his family heartbroken.

"No words can tell the depth of sadness we feel," said his mother. "We loved him dearly and nothing eases the ache or erases those words we heard that morning ... Now all we can do is to look forward to the Lord's calling us, when we will see our Bob again."

Their boy, Robert James, was born in England in 1950. From an early age he had a strong sense of right and wrong, and being a sensitive child, 'felt' for the underdog.

At eight he went to live in Kenya with his parents, attending primary and secondary schools there and becoming deputy headboy of the Duke of York School. He was not a brilliant pupil, but he slogged at his studies and made the grade.

Circumstances forced the family to leave Kenya and at his father's insistence Bob entered Natal University in 1970 to read for a degree in geology. After a year he asked to be allowed to study for his real love, farming. He went to Gwebi Agricultural College and obtained his diploma, but in the middle of 1973 he was called up.

By now tall and well-proportioned, he was medically down-graded because of polio which he had contracted at the age of two. He had always refused to let this interfere with his life and now again refused to spend the war as a storeman. After three more medicals he was accepted by the BSA Police. He signed on for three years instead of settling for a one year call-up.

His philosophy was simple. "I love this country, and if it is worth living in it is worth fighting for," he said.

Leopard armoured vehicle.

After passing out from the Police training depot in Salisbury he was posted to Bindura in the uniform branch and was soon doing ground coverage work. He hoped to join the CID and, ultimately, Special Branch.

After a time he was transferred to CID, working with different sections, in particular the drugs section. He also spent long periods in the bush in an anti-terrorist role. In his fourth year in the BSAP he was promoted to Detective Section Officer. He married in June 1976 and had a son, David Robert.

Towards the end of the war he spent longer and longer periods in the bush, explaining: "I want to see this through to the end."

On February 15, 1979, three weeks before his 29th birthday, he was sent, with one police constable, to the scene of a terrorist atrocity. On the way back to base at about 10h10 he was ambushed by terrorists and killed.

His parents spent many anxious hours during those years, knowing a little of the dangerous work he was doing, and longing for him to come home on leave.

He worried about his father, mother and sister, especially when Umtali was attacked, but he believed that God's hand would be over his family, as indeed it was.

"Bob did not have to fight," his mother said. "He was down-graded with a weak leg and back, but he felt it was right to fight evil and Communism, which is anti-God."

Bob's story is typical of the family tragedies of those days.

When the news went round that 'The Smiths have lost their eldest' or 'The Jones' youngest has been killed in action' the community shared in the family's grief. Condolence notices from friends and neighbours flooded into the advertising department of *The Umtali Post*. Hardly a family in the city was unaffected by the death, knowing the young man from school, work, the sports field or some other connection in a tightly-knit community.

Shopping in Umtali one day in October 1978, two countrywomen had a strange premonition of disaster. Peggy, one of the women, returned to her Lowveld cotton and wheat farm, driving in convoy as usual. Her husband, Bill, a trained pilot, was on Police Reserve Air Wing call-up.

The crops were due for harvesting and Peggy chatted about this with the local farmers' harvesting committee.

For some reason, unknown then, she burst into tears. Normally she is a competent woman, with a cheerful and strong personality. At home she found a labourer 'having a quibble about the pay' with her husband, who was back home for the night.

"Is there some trouble among the labourers?" she asked.

"I don't think so. I'd feel it, sense it, if there was," he replied. "Don't worry. Let's go over and see if old Jim has finished his harvesting yet."

The next day he promised to chat to his workers and discover any trouble before he returned to flying duty. He left home as usual on his motorcycle at 05h00 for the compound.

Peggy was half asleep, half awake, when she suddenly heard 'pop-pop-pop'.

"It sounded like a noise I knew I ought to know," she said. "Then it dawned on me. I jumped into a track suit and grabbed an FN."

She had served with the WFR and was familiar with most weapons.

"As I ran past the *agric alert* I called out a warning over the radio and heard others reporting automatic fire. Someone else shouted in: 'What's going on?' Then I saw the wheat starting to burn..."

She raced into the house and realised her husband was not back from the compound. "Send a reaction stick quickly," she shouted into the *agric-alert*. A passing field reservist coming off-duty dashed over in his car and saw spent bullets near the compound.

Peggy said: "I saw several Africans there but couldn't fire as I didn't know whether they were terrorists or our own workers."

Local farmers immediately responded to the call for help and started follow-up operations. They found Bill in the wheat, badly burnt, having been fatally shot. A local pilot had already taken off to fly to the area and he landed at the airstrip. The men quickly grouped themselves into two sticks, one following the tracks while the other went further down the river.

"The Police lifted my husband's body into the plane and flew him to Chipinga Hospital. Then the pilot helped in the search. It appeared that

Kudu armoured vehicle.

150

two groups had attacked Bill as he went by on his bike. They stole his watch as well as all the farm keys."

In spite of her shock and grief, Peggy was filled with praise for her neighbours. They were 'fantastic' in their immediate offers of help, and a tremendous feeling of love from them all flowed through her. Friends were asked to tell the three children, one at Chipinga School and the other two in Umtali.

When her small daughter ran to greet her mother on coming home her first words were so significant, said Peggy. "I'm so glad Daddy was a Christian!"

"We had somehow thought that if he had to 'go' it would be through his work with the air wing, never like this, at home," said his widow. "My husband had committed himself to Christ only a few weeks previously."

This was the first bad incident for their farming area although there had been landmines and ambushes further afield.

"We had been having wonderful services for all denominations, taken by visiting clergy who themselves faced danger to visit us regularly and give us spiritual support," she said. "The prayers that were being said throughout our country at the time were incredible. We also knew that hundreds of people here and in South Africa were praying for us. It made all the difference."

The funeral was held in Umtali and was unforgettable. Friends and family came from afar and they all left 'completely uplifted'.

The neighbours feared the crops would be burnt and by an extra effort combined to help, busy as they were. With 14 harvesters working, 202 ha of wheat were reaped and Peggy's labour was kept active by friendly assistance.

"Our farm was Bill's life work. I couldn't see it fail so suddenly. There were times when I just cried and cried and couldn't stop. Once I went into the chemist's in town with tears streaming down my face and asked him for something to help. He quite understood – as everyone did.

"We decided not to sell the plane which had brought Bill so much happiness. Living so far from anywhere it had been a necessity to us, not a luxury. We shall keep the plane for the family.

"When the boys were at school and I had to decide their educational plans I thought of getting away to Salisbury. But after listening to their headmaster I re-considered. Why not stay here? Umtali is a wonderful place to be, a sympathetic city in which to re-adjust," she said.

"It's a sensitive place. People here are so intensely alive to others' tragedies. Umtali has had such a high fatality rate that we're all affected by it and I think we've learnt a lesson in compassion. As people, we've learnt to feel as deeply for others as we do for ourselves. We have a greater understanding of things spiritual. When I think of all the families we know with even greater burdens, I realise the value and strength of this real fellowship between us."

As an answer to prayer, a young man offered his services to help until she got a manager. Initially Peggy had little business sense. She knew enough about the farm to help, but not to cope with the accounts and decisions.

"I was inclined to sink into the doldrums and failed to get to grips with financial affairs. I just curled up against it. When it came to matters on the farm, which we own, one businessman said firmly: 'What do you mean, you don't know? Come, I refuse to discuss anything with you until you do!'

"Kindly, he pulled me up. I realised I *had* to respond to our situation and plan for the future."

Following her husband's death the Terrorist Victims' Relief Fund was 'fantastic'. When the death notice appeared a cheque for $450 arrived for immediate expenses. The Fund paid the funeral costs and sent a Christmas card and cash to tide her over.

The Terrorist Victims' Relief Fund scheme offered holidays to many. People who otherwise could not afford to get away found this a wonderful relief – a chance for a break until they could face the community bravely again with their plans for the future.

"Bill's death is not a bugbear anymore," said Peggy. "The children and I talk and laugh about the times we had. We don't make him out to be a paragon. But by forcing ourselves to face up to his death immediately, we spoke of it, and shared our grief together openly."

Now the children often comment thoughtfully, 'that's just what Dad would say or do'.

Peggy feels strongly that God has put her country and its people where they are for a reason. He is still in control. It was up to mankind to realise the very real strength of the satanic forces at work, to do its utmost to combat the evil, to fight back spiritually and make the necessary changes for good, before it is too late.

"Christian fellowship and commitment are invaluable at times like these," she said. "We need prayer in order to recharge our batteries and carry on for the family's sake. There are so many of us around," she said of the widows in Umtali, Chipinga, Rusape and elsewhere.

"I miss my husband's physical presence so deeply, yet I see him all

Cougar armoured vehicle.

around me, in the trees and fields, and still hear his voice. What we do and what we are in this life is only a prelude to our future spiritual life with God," said another widow.

She is carrying on with quiet courage, keeping her son and daughter cheerful and busy, educating them in the land they love, without bitterness. Her husband's life was devoted to the training of Africans. To her knowledge he had no enemies among them. A Christian, he was a gentle, nature-loving, dedicated man of the woods.

And still she wonders ... Why? Why did this have to happen?

* * *

This same question must have been asked many times by a black agricultural demonstrator, Mr John Tapera (this is not his real name) as he lay, critically injured, beside the road on Christmas Day while all the people passed by on the other side.

It was his job to teach the people in an African Tribal Area on the

153

eastern border how to grow better crops and livestock. But because he worked for the Government he was regarded as a 'sell-out' by the freedom fighters.

Late in the afternoon of Christmas Eve he was in a farmer's fields when he was called to the bus stop by some children*. Here a gang of 20 terrorists had detained a bus and called up all the people living in the vicinity.

Mr Tapera (he is in his 50's) was beaten with thick sticks in front of all the bystanders and then made to lie face down on the side of the road. Three AK bullets ripped into him. One went through his left shoulder, another shattered his left upper arm bone and the third his left thigh bone. The group moved on to another target and the bystanders disappeared, leaving the injured man on the dusty roadside.

Back home Mrs Tapera waited for her husband's return. Tomorrow was Christmas and as a deeply religious family they would be spending the day quietly together. There had been shots in the distance but there was no reason to suspect her husband was at risk. He was well liked by all the farmers.

But as night fell it was obvious something had happened. In the darkness she could only wait and pray.

Next morning – Christmas Day – she set out to look for her husband. She scoured the irrigation scheme and the bush all around. She asked neighbours. No, they did not know where he was.

On the roadside the half-conscious man lay, unable to move, with a steady rain falling and the African passers-by too frightened either to help him, call his wife or notify the Police.

On Boxing Day Mrs Tapera found her husband. He was still alive, but only just. She tried to lift him but could not. She tried to borrow a wheelbarrow to take him back home but no one dared lend her one.

He had not eaten or drunk anything for nearly 48 hours. None of the people he had helped for years would even give her a portion of maize porridge for him. What could she do?

A Good Samaritan was the only answer. God sent him, in camouflage uniform, with others, in the shape of a passing Army patrol. An emergency evacuation was arranged to Umtali Hospital. There he had two operations to reset his shattered bones, followed by an amputation of the injured leg. Because of the long interval between the brutal attack

*Obviously 'mujibas'.

154

and Mr Tapera receiving assistance, gangrene had set in. He is a cripple for life.

* * *

"All I want for Christmas is a new left leg!" declared Esnath, a bus passenger who was badly injured in a landmine explosion in a Tribal Trust Land. A passenger was killed, several others were injured.

Esnath was rescued from the wreckage and taken to the nearest clinic, shocked and in great pain. A helicopter carried her to Umtali hospital, where her most badly injured leg was amputated.

"I thank God for His kindness. I bled a lot and should have died," she said afterwards. "But luckily I still have my right leg, my accelerator foot, so that I can drive again."

Recuperating in a hospital bed she kept busy planning how to earn a living (she has two small sons), reading, receiving Get Well cards – and writing poetry.

A trained teacher, Esnath writes in English. "I prefer it, I can express myself better," she said. "The Shona vocabulary is too limited."

* * *

For reasons that were never explained, people were taken, at gunpoint, from their homes or places of work, across the border into Mozambique. Manicaland had its share of these bewildered abductees. White or black, young or old, they received varying degrees of treatment – from some occasional consideration to forced labour and sometimes death, while worried families waited anxiously for news of their missing loved ones.

Seized on his farm near Penhalonga, Tom W lived to tell an astonishing tale which was published as a humane and honest book, *Perhaps Tomorrow*.

He was made to trek in Mozambique for six months with different bands of guerillas until his release in Maputo in February 1979, after continual pressure from the 'outside'.

Also taken from the Umtali area by Communist terrorists was Eddie B, who was returned via South Africa in September 1976 after being captured by a gang of 12 terrorists on May 16 that year. They tied him up and discussed killing him or sending him 'for training'. He was met by another group who ill-treated him disgracefully. Imprisoned in Vila

Pery (now Chimoio) for two months, he was eventually taken to Maputo.

A Melsetter forester named James was taken from work but later released after months over the border. In Chipinga, Mr T vanished from a tea estate in 1978 and was later presumed dead. Mr B was captured in the Imbeza Valley. He was found buried on the estate some time later, as was Deryck, of Cashel, who was taken from his work one day. For many long months his brave wife never gave up hope of his return.

A farmer from Juliasdale, who returned after an enforced sojourn in the neighbouring country, was indignant to receive a bill from the British Government for his repatriation from Maputo! "I didn't go there of my own accord for a holiday!" he said bitterly.

Apart from sickness and physical hardships, the worst suffering was that 'we all felt neglected and forgotten'. Letters written to wives and families were never received, except one, posted in London. Mail or news from home was non-existent.

Thousands of blacks, including children, were also taken across the border against their will.

"I had been doing two trips a day over dirt roads in the Chipinga district where many buses were blown up by landmines," said one black driver, who survived three years' abduction.

"One afternoon a group of seven men carrying AK rifles, bazookas* and machine guns approached my bus," he said. "They demanded the cash bag and one stuck a gun barrel into my chest."

Then they ordered the driver to take them and the bus to Mozambique.

He refused to do any such thing. "I don't suppose anyone can understand the feeling a driver has for his bus," he explained later. "It becomes a part of you. I felt for my bus as a dog lover feels about his dog. And now they were telling me: 'We'll burn your bus!'

"We'll kill you and then burn the bus if you don't get a move on," they shouted.

With a gun pressed into his ribs he was forced to drive the bus and the seven men across the border. Then followed weeks of misery when he was imprisoned, starved and used as a driver to take Communist trainees to Tete, Beira, Chimoio and Maputo to board planes for overseas, Yugoslavia and Rumania.

He met a woman who had escaped from Dorowe refugee camp. "If they want to take you to Dorowe, refuse," she urged. "It is dreadful. It is

---

*Rocket-firing weapon.

156

Flying fortress.

a labour camp and people are dying from starvation. It would be better for you to be killed than go there."

He was in Chimoio – a heavily-armed ZANLA camp, full of ammunition – when it was attacked by Rhodesian security forces.

"That was terrible – the noise of guns firing, bombs dropping and hundreds killed," he said. "My bus was destroyed with other trucks and vehicles. I was able to hide in the bush but my eye was injured by shrapnel. Chinese doctors operated on it without anaesthetic and I felt so dizzy and ill that they sent me to Beira by ambulance. A Russian doctor there confirmed my suspicions that the Chinese doctors had spoiled my eye by cutting the nerves."

Eventually he returned to Chimoio where there was another captured bus. He transported many of the leaders until he was sent to Beira to drive an ambulance. After three years in exile he was flown back to Salisbury.

Many promises were made to him which were not fulfilled and his homecoming to his own village was not a happy one. All his livestock and possessions had been taken by the 'comrades', including his home and business. He had to start all over again by building a grass hut.

17 *Stay at Rusape or not?*

New occasions teach new duties; Time makes ancient food uncouth,
They must upward still, and onward, who would keep abreast with truth.
LOWELL

Stretched in a great semi-circle, with Umtali as the hub, are the districts making up the province of Manicaland – Makoni (Rusape), Inyanga, Melsetter and Chipinga. The people there mainly live off the land, as commercial or peasant crop farmers, foresters, coffee, tea and fruit growers. While the war was keenly felt in the city, its greatest impact was in the rural areas, where all-out efforts were made by the terrorists to force farmers from their land. In the following pages countryfolk tell their stories, beginning with Rusape, the first small town in Manicaland on the main road travelling from Salisbury, and 93 km west of Umtali in the Makoni District.

An area of wide open spaces with distant views, Rusape produces tobacco, maize, fruit and cattle. Near the town is a large dam, opened in the 1970's, which stores water for Lowveld irrigation.

Rusape farmers and their families were active, sincere Christian people trying to make a living out of the land. Years of effort, stumping out trees, clearing the bush, fencing, ploughing, discing, fertilising, had gone into creating these lands. Years of effort too went into the establishment of a happy, stable labour force with mutual trust between farmers and employees.

In spite of the economic sanctions of the 60's and 70's, imposed upon Rhodesia by a world which knew nothing of local conditions, farmers made a living from the soil, provided plenty of food for other nations, built homes for themselves and their workers and kept hoping 'Next year would be better'.

Collen and Franscina, with Lorraine (7) and Collen (5) had enjoyed a happy day and were in bed asleep when a rocket (made in some European country) hit the gable of their house on Sunday, November 21, 1976. There had been no previous homestead attacks in Rusape, so they were the first to know the shock of being awakened by a tremendous blast of noise and the confusion of automatic firing in the dark.

Collen and Franscina's first thoughts were for the children. They rushed to roll them under the beds, telling them to stay there.

They had no security fence, no *agric alert*. The 'phone rang. It was a neighbour. "We're under attack," Collen said hurriedly. The noise was devastating and the firing seemed to be reverberating around them. Collen and Franscina started firing back in a desperate attempt to frighten off the attackers.

Franscina is slim, fair-haired and fragile. "I grabbed a gun and fired through the bedroom window. Then I looked round and saw little Collen crying in the doorway opposite the window. I dropped the gun and grabbed him to push him into a safer place, when a rocket hit the house and lit up the bedroom like daylight. Bricks were falling down about us. Then little Collen shouted, "My hand!"

In the darkness I could feel his blood, sticky and warm. I wrapped my nightie round his hand and pressed his wrist to stop the bleeding. "Little Collen's been shot in the hand!" I yelled to my husband. "Sit in the passage with the children," he ordered.

Collen had 'phoned the Police to warn them and was hoping they would arrive soon. The firing stopped. Were the terrorists creeping up to the house?

"We were tense and the children shaking uncontrollably," said Franscina. "My father was in a cottage 18 m away. We didn't know if he was dead or alive and the children were upset about him. Later, when the police arrived, he came with them. He'd gone to neighbours for help.

"After an attack one's nerves remain on edge for months. As soon as darkness falls, the slightest noise makes you jump. One night a cake tin fell off the shelf with a bang and I froze, thinking, 'Here we go again'. Another night a storm was approaching and at the first clap of thunder, thinking it was a rocket or mortar, I was under the kitchen table."

Yet this slender young girl continued to stand by her husband on the farm for another three years, in spite of a second attack in August 1978.

"This time we were security fenced, with walls, an *agric-alert* and a steel sheet on little Collen's bed, where the children were trained to go if anything happened.

"I had just dished up supper when there was a sudden firing. My husband ran to shoot back through the bedroom window, pressing the *agric-alert* alarm as he ran. I told the children to get under the bed as I followed to help with the shooting. As I ran I felt something sticky under my feet. Was it blood? Had our daughter been wounded? I tried to call 'Control' on the *agric-alert* and use the 'phone but the lines had been cut. However, I found Lorraine under the bed with her plate of supper. It was gravy under my feet – not blood!

"There was a blaze outside and the compound* had been set alight. What was happening to the labourers?

"Three mortars were fired at us but fortunately they all missed. The Army were stationed nearby and heard the noise so came to our aid within half an hour.

"Next morning we found a dead man at the fence whose hands were tied behind his back and who had been badly beaten. Later we found he had been one of the attackers, punished for his lack of enthusiasm.

"Our 40 workers disappeared, except for one old man, so the months of struggle started. We had a large maize crop and no hands to reap it. There was no one to herd the cattle. We lost 110 during those months and were not paid compensation by Government as officials said our cattle had not been properly checked. We managed to find six workers from Salisbury and with help from neighbours, managed to reap part of the crop.

"To stay or not to stay? It was impossible to grow crops with labour so uncertain. We decided to stay and carry on with cattle only."

How many farmers throughout the land faced the same decision? Their operations had been completely disrupted, yet where could they go? Their capital was all invested in land and cattle. Many had been born here and could not envisage life elsewhere. How could they take families to a new land with no capital and no training in anything other than farming?

"Our teenage children grew up overnight," said June, another Rusape wife. "They had to learn how to handle weapons and counter-attack devices for their own protection and survival. Our farm borders Makoni Tribal Trust Land which was home to many bands of terrorists and we were harassed continually by cattle rustlers. Fencing was stolen, dip tanks smashed, grazing burnt.

"Our homestead was attacked on May 17, 1977, at 18h45, after the children had returned to boarding school. My husband Philip had been working all day reaping maize with the labourers and I had been spring-cleaning the kitchen. I had been at the stables attending the horses and was returning when I saw some of the black girls from the compound coming from the bush with baskets and a bucket. When they saw me they ran to the compound, which was very strange behaviour.

"Later when Philip came home I told him, but he thought they'd probably been picking caterpillars off the trees for food. It was cold and

---

*Collection of farm labourers' dwellings.

160

he was in a hurry to fetch firewood. It was fortunate that he turned the truck round and came and went on the same road. Later we found that 15 terrorists were waiting to ambush him at the main entrance, and they had been fed by the maids.

"Philip came back on the same road. We had just sat down that evening when there was a loud explosion as the first rocket hit the gable. It was followed by automatic fire and more explosions all round the house. It happened so quickly. One moment we were relaxed by the fire, the next the air exploded around us. We made a dash for our weapons. Philip fired through the windows and I joined him after giving the alarm. It only lasted 15 minutes but seemed to carry on forever. It was such a relief when the Support Unit* arrived and scattered the terrorists. We could only thank God that we had come out of it alive and we know that He was with us throughout the attack. We had been bombarded with RPG 11's,† five different types of grenades and with AK 47 assault rifles and SKS‡ rifles. Our labourers and domestic workers had fled.

"We had the house repaired and carried on with three men but it was months before others came asking for work. Friends and neighbours helped us reap the maize crop and during the holidays the children, with five labourers, helped shell and pack 3 000 bags of maize. We left the potatoes in the ground as we just could not cope."

Roy, a young bachelor farmer, was attacked in May 1978. "I went out to check my tobacco barns at about 20h30. I was still curing, due to the drought, and had just returned when that dreaded, always expected, concentrated gunfire started. Almost immediately the lights went out. I could see hundreds of red and white tracers coming towards me and, at the last second, curving up over the roof.

"I fumbled about in the dark, found the *agric-alert* button and told them I was under attack. I couldn't believe it! A loud explosion shook me into reality and I dashed outside behind the blast wall to return fire.

"I could hear terrified screaming coming from the African labourers' quarters. I prayed quietly for our protection. There was another bang and a fire was burning behind the house.

"The *agric* was calling me so I ran back inside to answer, right into my cook who had come inside for protection! During a lull in the firing the

---

*Police Support Unit.
†Rhodesian-made semi-automatic sub machinegun.
‡All Communist-made weapons.

most terrible abuse was being hurled at me by the gang. My ammunition was running low. Where was the reaction stick? My army training came back to me. *Conserve ammunition. Fire low at night. Look for a target. Don't fire wildly.* I only had half a mag left so I got my 9 mm LDP, when suddenly the firing stopped. A deadly hush! I couldn't bear the silence so I fired a few shots and then all hell was let loose again. It seemed an eternity since I'd pressed the alarm. No firing seemed to be coming from the black guard in the compound. He was probably dead. (It later appeared he had run with the labourers, cleared the high security fence without thinking and made an escape.) There were more shots, then total quiet. Suddenly I heard the sound of motor engines coming. Relief was on its way. Out of 60 labourers only eight remained to work. None were injured, but they were all badly shaken."

Marty and Jennifer were preparing for a New Year's Eve dance when they were attacked by about 25 armed men on December 30, 1979.

"I had just hung out my evening dress for the next night's dance when we were alerted by a 'ping' on the corrugated iron roof," said Jennifer. "Luckily for us one of the men had fired prematurely. We reacted quickly, turning off the lights, sounding the alarm, just as they opened fire on us.

"The terrorists were well armed, and well oiled – for they had been drinking in the compound. Our attack lasted 30 minutes.

"The roof was peppered with holes. Thank goodness it didn't rain till it was repaired! My evening dress got a bullet right through it while other bullets went through my wardrobe, ruining many dresses.

"Help arrived in an hour. Our labourers had been terrorised and all their watches stolen as well as a large TV set. When the Army arrived they followed the tracks but nothing was ever found – not even the TV."

As in other areas Rusape farmers lost hundreds of cattle, all traced back to the Tribal Trust Lands.

"We were losing cattle continuously throughout the war," said June. "They were driven off at night and disposed of without trace. Once a cow came back home with a large axe wound on her hip and almost hamstrung on one hind foot. It was sad to know these lovely animals were being hacked to pieces."

Rusape farmers also had their share of road ambushes. June's husband and Collen were kept busy reacting to sudden attacks. "We felt the ambushes were often set up especially to get these two men as they were so often first on the scene," said June.

"When neighbours were attacked late one night we heard the alarm and my husband and son Andrew arranged to go immediately, meeting

A member of the Security Forces stands in a hole in the road caused when a boosted landmine blew up a vehicle loaded with Africans. A number were killed. The incident happened in the Rusape area.

Collen on the way. They left in our small truck, transferred to Collen's mine-proofed vehicle, and continued up the road and ran into an ambush from which they were lucky to escape alive. Andrew returned fire over the tail gate of the truck while Collen battled to keep the vehicle moving as a front tyre was shot out. They halted a few hundred

163

metres up the road and took cover in the bush. There were 15 terrorists waiting for them while another 15 were attacking the neighbours.

"It was a night of tension for us all. Franscina (Collen's wife) was at home with her father and little children and I was with our two, while the men were stranded in an ambush and the neighbours under attack."

"Collen kept me informed by radio," Franscina said. "We knew what was happening. We kept in contact and I reported to the Police that the men were in a clump of rocks waiting for the Army. They all went to help the neighbours and no one was injured."

Why, in so many accounts of attacks and ambushes, did the Army take so long to come? For this reason many farmers took matters into their own hands with their own reaction sticks, reaching the scenes in minutes, although they risked their lives to do so.

Contacts or sightings of terrorists would be reported and the Army would promise to arrive at first light. "This meant 07h30 to them – much too late to be effective," said one Police Reserve patrol.

A black pupil from St Augustine's mission, after Independence, told how he and others had crossed the border. "We were told by women in a certain area that the Security Forces always arrived at 08h00 and left at 18h00 so we went through before they arrived."

Roy was told by security forces that he would be attacked again, so a 'clandestine stick' was sent to his farm. It was not a happy Saturday evening but he was comforted by the thought of extra help nearby. Unfortunately this all-black stick got hold of beer and in a drunken state attacked the compound! The neighbours must have thought Roy was drunk when they heard him report on the *agric alert* that he was under attack from 'friendly forces'!

August 20, 1979 was a terrible day for Rusape.

"That was the day I found Peter Bassett killed in an ambush," said Paul. "We lost a fine friend and neighbour, a zealous member of our Police Reserve stick."

"As if this was not enough, the same night another neighbour, Gerald, had his barns and tobacco set alight," said Roy. "Then three weeks later, another ambush, another death. Mr Helgard Muller was killed on his way to the railway station to load tobacco at 14h30. Three of us decided to try and catch these murderers.

"We knew more or less which route the terrorists would take, past a long low range of kopjes with a river in front. We thought of an ideal place to set an ambush and at the foothills Ken stopped to decide where to hide our vehicle. As he braked and we were getting out, bullets started flying. It was like one of those first rain and hail storms of the

164

season. The terrorists were all round us, firing from 45 m away. A bullet grazed Gert's cheek. We huddled against the truck while Ken radioed for help, then picked up his shotgun to fire when a bullet splayed open the barrel. A grenade landed near and exploded, throwing sand in our faces. We were a concentrated group so I ran to a rock and fired from there. Fortunately this attack did not last long. God had certainly stood over us as three good shottists could have annihilated us."

Sandy, Paul's young wife, played a valuable role on radio duties as well as becoming the area 'medic', passing on her first-aid knowledge to local wives to prepare them for emergencies. Her reassuring voice gave many Rusape people courage when they were in danger and she was relaying reports.

"Farming became almost a secondary occupation," said her husband. "Our stick was called out most days from August 1979. At night I put on tape all the work for the next few days, what to do if it rained, or if a tractor broke down, and Sandy conveyed the orders."

Did Sandy mind being left alone at night on the farm? "We had militia and Guard Force. One became accustomed to the life and it was only when we went to Salisbury that we realised the difference – no *agric-alert*, no weapons by the bed, no gates to lock ... but we were rarely away from the farm as it was so vulnerable to attack. We were behind locked gates at 17h00 or 18h00. People were reluctant to stay overnight and even a day visit meant risking a landmine or ambush."

Life revolved around the *agric-alert* with its roll-calls and nerve-wracking incidents. The worst was when one heard of attacks and wanted to go to help. Then the silence was worrying, as neighbours wondered what was happening.

The Rusape 'freedom fighters' chopped out hectares of maize and tobacco, burnt out valuable grazing, destroyed tobacco barns and dip tanks and set fire to abandoned houses. But Rusape had courageous and selfless people who acknowledged that the war had brought them together and they praised God for bringing so many of them through safely. They protected themselves and each other from vicious assaults but felt no bitterness or hatred. Many black soldiers had stood with them and white farmers had risked their own lives to save their labourers. What more can one ask than that a man give his life for his friends?

18 *Attacks at Odzi*

We struggled through the dongas
We strove against the height
Until the further stars stooped down
To mock us in the fight.

KINGSLEY FAIRBRIDGE

Thirty kilometres west of Umtali lies the Odzi farming area, named after the river Odzi, a tributary of the Sabi. The name 'Odzi' stems from the Shona 'hodza', meaning 'rotten bodies'. In the days before civilisation reached this part of Africa, the river rose in flood during the rainy season and washed drowned bodies down where they stuck on the rocks.

Bush-covered hills and rocky kopjes form a varied landscape with ranges of blue mountains on the horizon. Each farm is the result of hard pioneering work, wrestling with the elements, for the climate is hot in summer with devastating storms and hail, and cold and dry with hard-hitting frost in winter.

In the 1960's the farms were mostly well-established with farm schools for labourers' children and farm stores for the convenience of workers. The labourers, well-housed and fed, with their children being educated nearby, were happy. At weekends there would be beer parties and the Saturday night drums beat out the invitations to attend.

But soon there were rumours that what had happened in the countries to the north was going to happen here. By the early 1970's most Rhodesians knew they were facing an invasion by Communist terrorists. The rumours became facts – but Rhodesians, both black and white, were perhaps too busy to take them seriously.

In the Tribal Trust Lands, however, the rumours grew into commands and the Africans knew fear. Reserved for those who were still untouched by civilisation and could only live according to their natural tribal ways, the Tribal Trust Lands were havens of refuge. After working and earning money in a European community, doing unfamiliar jobs, dressed in unfamiliar clothes and living at a pace far removed from old tribal ways in the bush, many Africans returned to their kraals to rest, some never wishing to live again at the speed required in such a community. They sat in the sun outside their hut doors in peace, until fear came. It came in the form of murder and rape, of torture and intimidation.

"You are a sell-out. You work for the white man," came the accusations.

Quietly, giving no reasons, driven by fear, the wives and children from the farms began leaving the compounds to return to the Tribal Trust Lands. But fear followed them.

"Your husband is working for the white man. He is a sell-out. If he does not return, you and your children will be killed," came the threats. Messages were sent to tractor drivers, mechanics, boss boys and labourers on the farms, who went home to investigate. Without work they soon had no money, so the men drifted back to the farms leaving their families in the villages. By 1976 the farm schools were closing down as there were too few pupils.

It was in October that year that Nigel and Margaret were attacked at their homestead. The peace was shattered. The atmosphere changed. It was war at last and theirs was the first house attack in the Odzi area. The next month Vic and Dinkie's home was hit by smallarms fire. Rockets which went too high over the roof failed to cause damage.

On Christmas Eve Odzi had its first ambush when a couple were opening a gate near Condo farm and both were wounded.

On Boxing Day Jean and Ben had their traditional open-day house party, but for the first time friends and family were urged to leave at 16h00. The roads were no longer safe. Stories of terrorist attacks and ambushes were coming in from all over the country. Many farmers had already erected security fences round their homesteads. Some were adding alarms and outside lights, while yet others were still thinking about it. The Government was subsidising these precautions and many farmers fenced their compounds too, to protect their labourers.

That same Boxing Night, Ernest and Rosemary, next door to Ben and Jean, were attacked with rockets, mortars and smallarms fire. Ben and Jean listened helplessly to the terrible sounds while the neighbourhood heard the reports on *agric-alert* and prayed for the couple.

Three attacks in three months. Life at Odzi was becoming 'grim'. No-one drove after dark unnecessarily and weapons were carried in cars. All tried to continue as usual but fear stalked the quiet countryside.

The small stores which provided labourers with luxuries, extra food and clothes, were robbed regularly by armed terrorists who shot the African caretakers and made off with the goods.

One night in April 1977, Richard and Heather were asleep on their farm. It was 23h45 when they were woken by a terrific explosion. Richard jumped out of bed, grabbing his rifle. Heather sounded the alarm on the *agric-alert*.

"There was automatic fire, then another explosion and the lights went out," said Heather. "I rushed to get my baby, Philip. A bullet went through my dressing-gown as I ran down the passage. The bedcovers had caught fire. Three rockets went over, one hit the house and the thatched roof caught fire. Some bullets went right through the walls. They were a new kind provided by some European country, we were told later.

"As the electricity had been hit there was no pump, therefore no water. Richard was on the roof trying to prevent the fire spreading on the thatch. I was so afraid the terrorists would fire at him as he was easily seen in the moonlight.

"They'd cut the hosepipes so Richard couldn't use water anyway. He slashed away at the thatch with the kitchen knife!

"They'd cut our security fence and hidden in the summer house in the garden, walking right past our bedroom window to reach their positions for attack.

"The thatched roof was fortunately wet, so it didn't burn too quickly. We rushed to take our valuables outside and thought the fire would get worse as it crawled through the thatch, constantly coming out in different places.

"The police at Odzi were so comforting on the *agric-alert* but it was an hour before a Lynx plane came with a flare*. We were scrabbling about in the dark, losing the gun and the torch. Our African maid was so terrified she was unable to hold the baby. I put my arms round her to comfort her, but she'd quite lost control of herself.

"Richard saw the barns go up in flames. Our attack lasted only five or ten minutes and the tobacco bales were in front of the barns so the terrorists couldn't get in. They poured petrol on the bales and then set fire to them. Later we found they'd been to our farm store previously and stolen everything they wanted. Then they'd burnt the store down. They left a letter: 'Dear Sir, Why no bully beef? Please in future keep bully beef in your store.'

"The Security Forces were wonderful. In spite of the power lines they flew in by helicopter and landed in a nearby field. Others came in Land Rovers. The pilot of the Lynx had been circling round and his flare had frightened off the terrorists, I'm sure.

"The neighbours' pump was working so the men passed buckets of

---

*Flares were dropped and floated above the 'scene' lighting the whole area and usually frightened off the terrorists.

water by a human chain and eventually put out the fire. The front bedroom was badly damaged. One man fell through the roof and broke his ankle. He was a stick leader and he lay on the lawn, giving orders.

"The Army personnel arrived next morning, the trackers going out at 06h00. All our labourers were waiting at the farm office, upset and sympathetic. But we discovered later that the suspects who had helped the terrorists to set up the attack were two foremen who had been retired on pension. A son of one of them had been educated and sent to a British university at our expense.

"The attack was terrifying but the psychological effect afterwards was even worse. For months I imagined shapes in the dark and was unable to sleep. At night I was mostly on the verge of giving up, but the next morning I'd open the window to see and hear the birds and decide to try another day.

"Naturally it affected our relationship with the workers. We no longer felt able to trust them and talk freely. Part of our former life had died."

In 1977 many Odzi farm stores were burned down. Vic and Dinkie's house was burned and in August Chrissie and Maanse were attacked. Chrissie said:

"It was early evening and we were in the sitting-room. I had gone to the bedroom to change my skirt for slacks as it was cold. I turned off the light in the bedroom and the terrorists must have been watching and thought we'd gone to bed. A few minutes later we were under attack and the bedroom was badly hit.

"There was a huge explosion and the whole house vibrated. This was the first we knew of the presence of terrorists. Maanse grabbed his FN. Then there was smallarms fire. I crawled to the *agric-alert* to give the alarm and then another rocket hit the house. I crawled to the bedroom and there was an enormous hole in the wall. A rocket had gone right through the bed, skimming the skirt I'd changed and hitting the opposite wall. I wriggled round keeping my head below that hole until I reached the ammunition. I filled the FN magazine and crawled via the bathroom to my husband who was by now in need of the bullets.

"Then a third rocket hit the verandah wall and knocked Maanse over. There was shrapnel in his chest and head. I cleaned the cement out of his eyes and there was dust, plaster and cement everywhere. My own eyes were filled with dust. A mirror in one of the rooms was broken and the last blast lifted the whole roof. Next day we found 30 broken window panes.

"Our brother and sister-in-law, Deinke and Helena, had radioed that they were coming and very bravely arrived within half an hour of the

169

attack. Maanse had to go to the gate to let them in – a hairy experience as terrorists might have been waiting to shoot as they drove up."

Four months later they were attacked again, the day before Christmas Eve. Chrissie said: "All our family were with us but some felt uneasy that night. At about 21h00 we were all going to bed when there was a loud bang. My young sister shouted, 'It's them!' I sent everyone into the passage, the safest place. The children were pushed under beds and lights switched off as we alerted Odzi police.

"Then we heard smallarms and rocket fire. The terrorists were shooting cattle in the kraal near the dip. More than 30 cattle were just shot and left. The rest stampeded. Nine were wounded. What a waste of good stock!

"Later we found the terrorists had murdered our black herdsman. They put a dog chain round his neck, tied his hands behind his back and then shot him. They put a log across the road to make us stop and see his body. He had been born on our farm and we were fond of him, so it was a terrible shock to see him – his teeth smashed in by a gun butt, kick marks all over his body, then shot in the back..."

Chrissie and Maanse had 650 cattle taken out of the 800 they possessed, while Jean and Ben narrowly missed being ambushed at their cattle dip.

Perhaps no one who has not suffered it can really know the frustration and heartache that comes from seeing a herd of beautiful cattle (built up over years of careful breeding, feeding and tending), maimed, killed or stolen. The farmers in this area would wake up to find large numbers of their cattle gone. Fences were cut, sometimes within a few hundred metres of the homestead. Security Force stocktheft teams went out but tracks were lost as soon as they entered the Tribal Trust Lands. Morning after morning, week after week, farmers woke to fewer cattle in their herds. This was their capital – it was like watching the money being burnt by the bank.

It was in October 1978 that Jean and Ben heard their dogs barking all night. "Next morning we found we were the only two human beings left on the farm. All our labourers had fled in the night. The compound was a pathetic sight. Hut doors were standing open, clothes, food and other possessions were lying about, obviously dropped as the owners fled in tremendous haste, running in all directions.

"Our neighbours, Bert and Sally and their son Dave had also lost their labourers. Dave found 14 acres of tobacco had been slashed in the land. There was nothing to do but get on with the hundreds of chores – cows to milk, chickens to feed, sheep to be let out and so on. We buckled down and did our best, and we had plenty of laughs in spite of it all. Friends and neighbours were so wonderfully helpful and comforting that it made the battle worthwile. On dipping day, friends came on horseback and we rounded up and dipped our remaining cattle.

"Later, friends came to help us plant our crop for which the lands were all ready. On November 29, 21 tractors arrived with all the necessary equipment and our lands were disced, fertilised and planted."

One well-known Odzi family had come up to Rhodesia and settled in the Marandellas area in 1894. The father had served (at 16) as a Scout in the 1896 Rebellion. In 1913 he bought the farm near the Sabi River where his son, Coen, was brought up. A typical born Rhodesian, Coen knew the bush like the back of his hand and spoke Shona as fluently as the young blacks on the farms.

When Coen took over the family farm he worked hard to improve the stock and make a good living for his wife and family. It was not easy as the farm was in a remote area with no near neighbours. Coen, being part of the soil and knowing the local population well, sensed the infiltration of terrorists, the intimidation of the people and the stirring-up of racial feelings by trained agents, at an early date.

One night in October 1976, a small black lad was leaving the homestead rather late and Blondie, Coen's son, went to open the security gate for him. There was a noise in the bushes outside. The boy shouted: "Who's there?"

"We want the whites," said a voice.

"What do you want to do with them?" the lad asked, and then turned and fled back to Blondie for safety. The tracks of five terrorists were found the next morning.

This was the start of the troubles for the Sabi farmers in the Odzi area. "Then the labourers started leaving," said Coen.

"Cattle rustling went on all the time. We lost over 500, stolen and shot. There seemed to be nothing one could do. One was not allowed to follow the rustlers to try and get cattle back, or mete out punishment to the cattle thieves. The Security Forces never appeared to follow-up with any real enthusiasm or determination. Their efforts were weak. When I tried to follow cattle thieves myself I only got into trouble with the authorities. I believe it was the Government that broke the farmers in the end. They would not allow us to do anything to help ourselves. At times it appeared they were on the side of the enemy."

There were many attempts to harass this particular family and in March 1976 the houses in which Coen and his son Fritz and their families lived, were attacked with rockets and mortars.

171

"Thirty bombs were hurled at us and the attack lasted over an hour," said Coen. "Our son's wife, Marie, managed to get the baby out of the cot just before it was damaged with shrapnel. Our other son, Blondie, had nothing on when the attack started! He was so busy retaliating that he never realised he was naked until much later. After attacking our houses the terrorists went 274 m to our cattle pens and shot and killed 40 animals, our whole Friesland herd. Others they wounded and left bellowing in pain."

Four months later Coen, his wife Ruby and their little grandson were travelling between their two farms when their vehicle hit a landmine, placed at the same point where several ambushes had taken place. Friends who saw the wreck later, said it was a miracle anyone got out alive. It had overturned and landed on Coen's arm. Two blacks sitting in the back were killed. Another had a dislocated hip and fractured arm. The truck was loaded with potatoes which may have cushioned the blast and saved the lives of Coen, Ruby and the little boy.

"I was trapped under the truck, twisted up in the metal," said Coen. "I didn't hear the blast. I heard my wife shout, 'Oh God!' then heard the dreadful sound of metal creaking, groaning and cracking. The engine was still running and I was afraid the whole vehicle might burst into flames. Ruby could not get me out alone so she went for help. Our grandson was unharmed. I can still see one big tear rolling down his little cheek. Coenie and Blondie had heard the blast and came quickly to our aid.

"The terrorists were always writing me letters. After they attacked the house they wrote, saying 'The attack on your house is because you sent Grey's Scouts into Maranke Tribal Trust Land...' In later letters they asked for $600. Then just before we hit the landmine they warned me that if I had not paid within 14 days they'd be after me. 'We are after you now,' a letter said. About 14 days later we hit the mine."

Three months later, at the same spot, Blondie was ambushed. "It was a good place because it afforded them an ideal escape route. One of us took milk 100 km into Umtali every second day. Blondie had always felt he'd be ambushed there, and then it happened. He drove right through and it was a miracle he was not killed because one terrorist was lying in a drain only 2,7 m from the road. Luckily the terrorist used a live round to fire a rifle grenade and it exploded in his face.

"I was about one km behind Blondie and drove on for 800 m before two of my labourers came rushing up to say they had heard firing from where they were cutting firewood. So we followed Blondie's tracks. He'd taken the road to the other farm where he knew his brother was working. My son Robert and I found Blondie where the vehicle had finally packed up.

"This was the worst part of the war – the awful feeling, 'What am I going to see when I get there?' Blondie was in an open field, with a smile on his face although he'd been shot in the arm and in the right eye. He lost the eye. He was pretty badly hurt and spent a long time in hospital. There were three labourers with him, one of whom had been with me in the landmine incident and badly injured. He was again wounded."

A stick of Odzi Police Reservists cleared the road for the Sabi farmers every morning, starting from the police station at 06h00 and travelling the entire circuit. Sometimes a Pookie* would go ahead to clear the road. The 'milk run' (so called in many areas because it cleared the roads early for the farmers to take their milk to town), was ambushed four times, and all at the same spot.

After harassing the labour force, terrorists killed Coen's tractor driver, Tom McKelvie, who was a Coloured man whom the terrorists wanted to join them. He refused to go, so they came especially one morning at 06h00 and murdered him. They burnt out the tractor he was driving and destroyed the irrigation unit.

Unfortunately the Police Support Unit only reached the farm at 08h00 and found a letter saying: 'By now you'll be on our tracks. Try and catch us if you can!' Of course, once the tracks reached the Tribal Trust Land they were obliterated by many other footprints, cattle and goat tracks.

"We buried Tom McKelvie on the farm. A letter was found on a dead terrorist's body left there by the 'comrades'. It said: 'Blacks were told not to side with the enemy and we must teach them a lesson now.' With the labour intimidated, herdsmen gone, a tractor driver killed, it became impossible to farm," concluded Coen.

He and his sons, however, were attacked yet again, and when a house on one of their farms was left unguarded, it was ransacked, stripped and destroyed to a useless ruin.

"We had to leave in the end. As we moved out, assisted by Police, we ran into an ambush and I heard rude words shouted, then: 'Dutchman, you've had it now!' We were lucky to get out alive as they continually ambushed the roads but we changed our routes and times frequently."

Although the family had to leave they showed tremendous courage and their brave stand, their persistence in carrying on as long as pos-

---

*A special vehicle used for detecting landmines.

sible, despite all they suffered, earned the respect of the Odzi community.

Maanse and Chrissie, mentioned earlier, had lived on their farm for 22 years. Originally wild bush, they built it up into a beautiful farm and homestead, taking 20 years to pay for the land. By 1976 they had completed payment and took over the title deeds. In 1978 they came to the heartbreaking decision to leave their farm. Maanse had been born on the next door farm which his parents had built up from nothing.

Just before they left Maanse went down to the lands one evening with his son. They stopped to look at the tomato crop before driving on in the Land Rover. This saved their lives. A black herdsman and three Guard Force men were walking ahead and saw some terrorists lying in ambush. Their appearance frightened the attackers who let off the rockets they had ready for the farmers. The herdsman and Guard Force ran off and Maanse was warned. Later they found the rockets set up facing a large antheap where Maanse always turned his Land Rover.

Chrissie heard the explosions at home. So many Odzi farming wives sympathised. To have one's heart turn over, to pray desperately for one's husband and son, was now a familiar experience.

The couple were packing up to move nearer Umtali when they returned to their old home to find terrorists had tried to burn it down. The beautiful Aga stove lay in pieces, 90 bags of maize had been burnt, the refrigerator, gas cylinders and pantry shelves had been destroyed as well as the tomato land. January and February 1979 were sad months for the Odzi people.

On January 6, Jean and Ben had a quiet Saturday morning. Their nextdoor neighbour, Rosemary, called at midday on her way home from work. Jean and Rosemary were old schoolfriends and spent half an hour chatting before Rosemary set off home along the last stretch of road she always hated and called 'Ambush Alley'.

"I believe she knew something was going to happen there sooner or later," said Jean. "She was in high spirits, looking forward to an afternoon game of bowls at the club, then two weeks' leave. Six minutes after she left there was a horrific explosion. We knew it was on the road and she was the only one there. We grabbed first-aid boxes and rushed off with our hearts pounding with fear. It was a boosted mine and all we can say is 'Thank God – she did not know what hit her'. Gone was a wonderful friend and neighbour, and the bravest girl I've known."

The whole district heard the explosion and later they heard Ernie, Rosemary's husband, report the incident on the *agric-alert* with great courage and in a calm manner.

Rosemary's family suffered tragically in the terrorist war. Her brother Ken was murdered by terrorists in Chipinga and her cousins had been killed in an ambush.

Another couple who had a night of horror were Ian and Barbara, who returned home on January 28, 1979, after taking their daughter back to boarding school. To them it appeared a normal evening. Little did they know that a gang had forced their labourers out of the compound and used them to slash and destroy 10,5 ha of tobacco. They then set fire to the tobacco barns. Ian had checked on the barns earlier but he and Barbara were asleep when seven barns went up in flames.

At 01h15 they woke to the sound of hail on the roof – a hail of bullets. It was hot and Barbara was under a sheet in her birthday suit. She jumped out of bed to report the attack on the *agric-alert* while Ian raced to the window to return fire and drive the terrorists off. A bullet from the attack position struck a window frame and shrapnel cut through Ian's eye. The force of the contact knocked him to his knees.

"He came down the passage," said Barbara, "and I helped him tie a towel round his head to stop the bleeding. Then he returned to the window to carry on firing. It was strange to have no clothes on, but every time I crawled to the bedroom to fetch my nightie an explosion or bullets would send me scuttling back to a safer area. I got the first aid pad from the spare bedroom and bandaged it on Ian's head, answered the Police calls, and fetched the Uzi* for Ian as his FN had jammed. The Uzi was jammed as well! Someone had dropped the magazine and bent it. The shotgun was also jammed. Fortunately Ian had a pistol in good working order.

"I was still crawling round in the dark, determined to get my nightie. Bullets had been coming in through the door near the 'phone but when it rang Ian answered it. Luckily he was kneeling, but a bullet caught his arm.

"He went from window to window firing his pistol to make sure the terrorists had all gone. Then I propped him up with a pillow in the passage. When the Police came Ian had to go out to open the gate for them – a nasty moment, but the chopper landed outside the door and after the Police had set up a drip for Ian, who had lost a lot of blood, they took him to hospital. He lost his good eye. The other has never had 100 per cent vision. He went to Salisbury for an operation to remove the

---

*Israeli type machine gun.

eye and shrapnel from the socket, but we were back on the farm within a week."

Jean continued the tale of Odzi events. "By 1979 we had the use of a Leopard to clear our road every morning. Ben called it the Dawn Patrol. I had enjoyed it but since Rosemary's death I went with deep fear in my heart. On March 3, Ernie 'phoned to tell us not to leave. He was coming through on his way to a Police Reserve training day, so we said we'd wait for him. Just before 07h00 there was an almighty noise – automatic firing and rockets. We knew he'd run into an ambush and our hearts stood still as we prayed.

"Thank goodness Ernie managed to keep going in spite of several hits on his vehicle, one of which wounded him. As usual, Security Forces followed the tracks of the terrorists but found they led back into the Tribal Trust Lands where they were lost in a myriad other tracks."

Jean and Ben were attacked again on March 23, but in spite of the damage and danger, and loss of stock, with tremendous courage and persistence, they battled on. Their third attack came the following month.

"Ben was recovering from pneumonia," said Jean. "We had our children home from boarding school and my sister-in-law had come to stay with us – for a rest! It was 23h40 and we woke with the most dreadful explosion. A 3.5 British-made rocket had hit the verandah. It ripped the iron off the roof and blasted out three doors. This time we were not sure from which side we were being attacked. The noise was appalling. They were sending mortars and automatic fire as well. Ben and our son fired back and our daughters re-loaded the magazines. No one panicked but it was a very frightening experience. When it was over and we saw the damage we realised how lucky we had been. Once again we just had to clear and patch up the mess.

"In our second attack two of our favourite dogs had been killed and four were badly wounded. Besides the three attacks, two more land-mines were found on our road.

"Why did we battle on?

"Where else could we go? This was our home. Rhodesians have lived here for four or five generations.

"I worried about the effect the war was having on our children. No more could they ride around or go for picnics. They worried about us while they were at boarding school. We were told once that the children were being watched by terrorists from their OP* on a hill only 180 m

---

*Observation Post.

away from the farm tennis court where they were playing. There have been times when I have felt sick with fear but then I would think of people worse off than ourselves.

"What kept us going was the wonderful encouragement we had from friends and neighbours, and a determination to hold what was rightfully ours, land which we had built up."

Even a cursory glance at the facts of the war in the countryside shows the number of times people were 'lucky' or 'saved from certain death'. There is no doubt that the majority of Rhodesian farmers were Christian, and the prayers of their families and friends were so often answered.

It was clear by 1979 that the Communist terrorists were being helped and trained to a higher degree of efficiency. Earlier their firing was inaccurate, but now their attacks were better organised – and far more deadly.

19 Bullets fly at Inyanga

"Bind us together Lord; bind us together Lord,
Bind us together with love."

PSALM 121

By day the four-star Montclair hotel dining-room looks out over green terraced lawns and bright flowerbeds to the lovely Inyanga hills and valleys.

On the evening of May 2, 1978, darkness had fallen and the curtains were drawn. The guests were enjoying choosing dinner from an excellent menu. It was 19h50.

Suddenly two armed black men in blue denims and caps appeared in the doorway. They held up the wine waiter with his tray of glasses then sprang into the dining-room and sprayed the guests at their tables with AK bullets. One woman was shot through the head and fell to the floor.

The two men moved down the long room firing as they went. The receptionist, Betty, was shot dead at her table. The assistant manager got a bullet through his thigh. Screams, shouts and the sound of shattering glass as 15 more terrorists poured bullets into the room through the French windows, mingled with cries, sobs, the crash of breaking china, several American voices praying out loud and the staccato barking of guns with bangs from grenades and rockets.

The curtains hung in frayed tatters. Cups and glasses lay shattered on the carpet. Some guests sat paralysed. Others crouched under their tables while more gathered round the injured. One woman had a broken shoulder. A man had a heart attack.

"I was under the table," said the hotel owner, Ann. "A grenade dropped 30 cm from me. Thank God it did not explode." When her husband died in 1975 she had decided to carry on alone at the hotel.

"There was a second attack a year later, also at night. Again they attacked from the garden side of the hotel and did a fair amount of damage. But it was the third attack in November 1979 that was the worst.

"I was woken at 01h10 by a dreadful noise. I could hear terrorists talking outside my window, then a rocket landed in the room. Another landed in the room next door. Bullets seemed to be flying everywhere, and later 137 bullet marks were found in my room. I rolled off the bed and it shunted over the floor and penned me in. I was hemmed in between the bed and the wall and couldn't move. My door was locked but I could hear the staff in the passage. They couldn't open my door and were busy looking after the injured anyway. They thought I'd been killed. Then a tracer bullet set fire to the bed. I shouted but nobody heard me above the din, until at last a voice said, 'She's alive after all!' A woman croupier from the casino shot the lock off my door and let me out."

For a woman of 74 these were unnerving times and with hardly any visitors to the hotel, she had to sell.

Across the road from the Montclair, in Juliasdale, stands an attractive little church built of local stone – a monument to the spirit of Inyanga people. Contributing in cash and kind, the community built it as a place of Christian worship for black and white residents. After years of combined effort the Church of the Good Samaritan was dedicated on February 20, 1977. The secretary of the Church Association, Alicia, wrote: "This is a dream come true. People have said they considered it an odd time to build a church with all the uncertainties that face our country.

"Inyanga people believe that many of the best things are done in the worst times, and they are proud to have shown faith in their beliefs, and in the future of their country."

The worst times were still to come, but members were to feel that their church had drawn them closer together, and closer to God. Who was to know on that happy Dedication Day, presided over by six clergymen of different denominations and attended by the late President and Mrs John Wrathall, that it was to be the last day for Charles and Gwen Ward?

Their house was found the following day destroyed by fire. Their car was burnt out in the garage, but their bodies were nowhere to be seen. It was only four days later that their corpses were dragged up from the bottom of their dam, encased in chicken wire and weighted down with rocks.

During 1977 life began to change for the people of Inyanga. As early as 1976 terrorists infiltrating from Mozambique had begun intimidating the African people in the Tribal Trust Lands, especially in Nyamaropa to the north, and the Honde Valley. One fateful night a score of black men, women and children in a tea estate compound near the border were lined up and shot. This was a warning to all other labourers to leave their jobs.

"I remember the feeling of the war starting in 1976," another Ann said. "I was a WFR on duty at Selborne when the first terrorist was wounded in the area and captured for interrogation. The Police, Army and Special Branch all wanted him at once. I drove three times a week to radio duty and was given an Uzi for protection. I was aware there could be landmines or an ambush on the roads, and then a friend's house was set alight by the first rocket and the first landmine was seen and uplifted."

Agric-alert sets were installed, WFR and Police Reservists were called up, convoys were started, canteens were opened, Op Turkey* was initiated and Civil Defence came into operation in Inyanga.

Inyanga district covers an extensive area including Inyanga Downs, south of the downs, and the farms on the west nearer Rusape. There are deciduous fruit orchards, potato lands, cattle pastures and large tea estates as well as forest plantations of wattle and pine.

For Civil Defence purposes the area was divided into zones and cells, with chairmen, members and leaders, each leader dedicated to keeping in touch with his own area, trying to meet needs and helping people stay on the land. It was their job to know all about everybody, their alarm and security devices, positions of fences and safe areas, where keys were kept, the number of dogs at a homestead, even the health of all concerned. Regular meetings were held to keep the civilian population 'in the picture'.

Richard and Ann, with a fruit farm adjoining a Tribal Trust Land west of Inyanga, were soon aware of a change of atmosphere among their labourers.

"We used girls from the Tribal Trust Lands for fruit picking," Ann said. "The work was easy and a welcome source of income for them. They were keen to come and we were never short of willing hands.

"My husband created a team spirit with them by discussing what to plant each season. 'Shall it be brussels sprouts, or potatoes?' he'd ask. Often their male relatives would thank us for giving the women work and for the handsome bonuses they earned. Richard never mechanised or even bought a tractor because he wanted to help the women by providing as much work as possible.

"In 1977 we began losing labourers. In December the girls were singing political songs instead of the usual Christmas carols as they worked. Then all the young girls left. The woman in charge, their spokesman, who had never missed a day's work, just disappeared. There had been two murders in the area – a headman and his son had

---

*Op Turkey – an order restricting the amount of maize meal Africans could possess at any one time to try to prevent the terrorists from being too easily fed by the locals. Op Turkey was tried in all areas of the country.

been killed by terrorists and one body was found on the path they used. They never spoke of these things – they just failed to come to work.

"By January 1978 we had only 12 older women left. The foreman's wife was their leader and although they came to help us with the winter crop, this woman worked slowly and influenced the others.

"We were conscious now of the presence of terrorists. It was something one felt all the time. One evening, just before Easter, I went to my bedroom to refer to the Bible – to learn how to pray for the terrorists. Suddenly there was a tremendous explosion, then more, like giant fireworks. These were RPG 12's* and rifle grenades.

"My first reaction was anger and I reached for my pistol, nicknamed 'Plink' because it was so small. 'Plonk' was another, slightly bigger, but out of reach. I ran to a window and shot out of it. 'Plink', it went, and jammed!

"I never felt any fear and I knew Richard was safe. I ran to the sitting-room where he and the *agric-alert* were. What a sight met my eyes! Dust and plaster fell everywhere and the lights were still on. A light bulb was swinging over Richard's head. The curtains were dangling in disarray at the windows. Richard, suffering from shock, had forgotten to switch the lights off and was looking at me over his spectacles as he reloaded his rifle. A rocket had exploded just above his head as he was sitting by the radio, reading. The loudspeaker was above him so it was a miracle his hearing was not damaged.

"I grabbed the *agric-alert* and tried to raise the Police by pushing the alarm button. 'Confirm you're testing alarm', came a voice from Control.

"No, this is Lima Mike 415. The terrorists are attacking us!

"'Confirm you're testing alarm.'

"No! We're under attack!" Neighbours on the same network took it up and the Member-in-Charge came on the air. Gently he told me I had my finger on the red alarm button instead of the green speaker button.

"The terrorists had come noiselessly over the soft, mulched land ready for the brussels sprouts.

"'Is there any evidence of the terrorists coming into your homestead area?' the Member-in-Charge asked, and suddenly I was aware of the danger – we had no fence and they could be only a stone's throw away. Fortunately they came no nearer and the attack was soon over. When the Army stick arrived about an hour later, they were so tired from another scene that they fell into their beds. Luckily none of our children

---

*Rockets fired from Rocket Projectile Guns.

were at home. We cleared up the debris and shattered glass and our daughter Elaine 'phoned us from Cape Town half an hour after the attack. She had a feeling something was happening. I told her the only target properly hit was our car and I had shot it with 'Plink'. But later we found it was terrorist bullets which did the damage and not my poor aim after all."

Later Richard and Ann moved to Umtali to work as it was impossible to carry on farming without labourers. They returned to Inyanga during the fruit-picking season and stayed with neighbours near their other fruit farm, but it was impossible to find workers to help them pick their peaches, plums and nectarines.

"Eventually one African said he'd get all his family to come," said Ann. "The terrorists were continually intimidating the people but this man said he'd pay the terrorists to let his family do the job.

"One evening, from a neighbour's house, we saw fire in the labourers' compound. When the Security Forces came they found our foreman on the road, shot, after having both arms broken. Richard had a struggle to get any labourers at all, but nine workers stayed with us for the fruit season. The roads were dangerous with constant landmines and ambushes so we decided to turn a dip-tank into a safe place on one of our two farms as there was no house. We built up the walls to firing level and had pine logs for a roof. We camped there daily, returning each evening to our kind neighbours."

The little church of the Good Samaritan was used for memorials of many friends killed through terrorist action. Clergymen braved the roads to take services as usual. True to their Christian convictions, they were unarmed and there were no convoys on Sundays.

"Once we got a fright when a priest failed to arrive," Alicia said. "His truck had been commandeered by terrorists as he was setting out, so we muddled through with a lay service and anxious hearts. From the church windows we could see where a farmer had been killed previously. It became a familiar, sorry sight to see FN's propped along the church walls and Uzis lying on the benches or on the organ top. At the 'hottest' time we had Police Reservists doing a 360 degree patrol around the church grounds during services."

There were eventually many memorial plaques as well as a Garden of Remembrance at the new church. Alicia wrote regular newsletters to keep up the morale. She spent much time and loving thought producing them for members of this Juliasdale congregation. Each was filled with inspiring thoughts and Christian concern for all in the district as well as local news, comforting thoughts, quotations to inspire bravery, determination and persistence, congratulations and loving tributes. They played a great part in keeping the people of Inyanga closely knit, with a high level of courage and morale.

The year 1978 began with the death of Dick Williams, a beloved and respected member of the community, killed by terrorists in February, and ended in December with the death of David Garlay at the hands of terrorists. The March 1979 newsletter paid tribute to two African constables, Nyadute and Chambuko, killed in a contact with terrorists. "They were fine policemen whose loss to Inyanga Police will be keenly felt."

Christopher was killed at Claremont Estates and Manfred was killed in action. He had made the pews for The Good Samaritan. Bill and Sheila Swift were ambushed and shot when 360 bullets were fired into their car. They had been building their home with their own hands and hoping it would be completed before their daughter's wedding.

Maurice was also killed, a man who was always a wonderful example of service to others. "His contribution to *agric-alert* problems in time, effort and mileage could never be repaid, nor his unobtrusive, constant acts of kindness. He refused to leave for a safer haven because he had a job to do for us – the people of Inyanga," said the newsletter. "Truly, 'Greater love has no man than this, that a man lay down his life for his friends'. Maurice lived on the edge of a valley in a prefabricated home impossible to defend. He was shot while reading a newspaper in his sitting-room one evening on returning from tea with friends."

Molly (83) lived alone, bravely and independently at the caravan park with no transport and no security fence. "I'll not be frightened. I've got my own weapon. I'll squirt Zeb oven cleaner over any attackers. That'll fix 'em!" But she was shot through the leg as she lay in bed. Her voice was very calm as she made her report the next day on *agric alert* – but she died on the way to Umtali Hospital.

Ray was so badly wounded in an ambush on Christmas Day, 1979, that he took many months to recover. "We in Inyanga have so much for which to be grateful to Ray and his stick. He is a dedicated leader, patrolling his area ceaselessly, and we are certain many of us owe our safety to his vigilance," said the newsletter. "Last year he served 149 days on a 42-day commitment."

People were drawn closer together by prayer and nobody slept when others were under attack. They were all praying for the afflicted ones.

People were courageous, calm, comforting each other, and Operation Esther, mentioned fully in chapter 14, also embraced the people of Inyanga. The prayer grapevine was quicker than one could imagine and very little happened at Inyanga that was not immediately upheld by loving prayer groups in Salisbury, Umtali, Rusape and Marandellas.

John and Jennie bore witness to the strength of this support. No family could have given a finer example of courage and faith over a long period of harrassment. They lived in the Downs area of Inyanga where many farms and estates border on Mozambique and were in the forefront of the Inyanga 'war'.

"After having farmed leased land," Jennie said, "in 1975 we became the proud possessors of our own place. With little capital we put in our first crop and lived in a tin hut for 14 months while brick by brick and cent by cent we built our house, which is still only half finished, but what fun! Bathing under the stars with piping hot water from a Rhodesian boiler, and often getting cold showers from above through the grass hut that served as a bathroom..."

"Then came the rumblings and talk of war. It was another year full of Police Reserve work for both of us, security fences went up and John had his first contact. We were aware of the menace but thought it couldn't happen to us, yet we were the first to be attacked – on New Year's Day 1978 at 23h00.

"We've been struck by lightning!" was John's comment, but it was terrorists.

"We couldn't find the FN, we hadn't put clothes out, we couldn't find our shoes. We crawled to the children to get them on the floor. Belinda (6) said firmly: 'I'm tired. God is looking after me.' She climbed back into bed and slept through it all. Next morning we realised how God had protected us, for Nicky found three AK rifles and many unfired mortar bombs. The terrorists had mortared themselves because the soil was wet and they had no base plate. I remember a left-over Christmas pudding in the pantry had bullets in it," said Jenny.

"A second miracle happened two weeks later when John and his friend Brian were ambushed. I was on radio duty at the time. There were shots behind John's head, three bullets passing either side of his neck and above his head. He hid behind the Land Rover and Brian jumped out right into the terrorists' range. A rocket hit the rock John was making for, just as he changed his mind and ran back to the vehicle.

"They chased the terrorists for six hours, bullets flying, but the only injury was John's broken ribs from throwing himself down on a rock.

"Night after night I'd lie in bed shaking with fear until I read something comforting from the Bible and fell asleep at last. But there were happy times too. One night the children were at home for the school holidays and we all went to bed horrified at the news of the Viscount disaster. We had not heard the result and prayed hard for the passengers. Young Sandy said she had a feeling 'the terrorists were coming'. Sure enough at 23h00 there were tremendous explosions, screams from the children's room, and more bullets. 'I've been shot!' Sandy called.

"You can't have been if you're talking like that," her father said.

"'Bricks and plaster were falling on me, that's why I thought I'd been shot,' she recalled.

"Three miracles happened that night," said Jennie. "Firstly Nicky was away playing tennis in Bulawayo and her bed was ripped with bullets. Secondly, we had made, only two days before, a 'snivel hole' through which the children could crawl from their bedroom to the bathroom. There was no other way they could get out of their room without going outside. This escape route saved their lives.

"The battle raged for what seemed like hours but in fact was only 25 minutes. John was firing out of the window and called for more ammunition. I got the bag of heavy, unbreakable plastic but couldn't open it. I tried urgently to break the bag with my teeth but the plastic was too strong. I prayed for help and, groping around in the dark, suddenly found my sewing scissors close at hand – a real miracle as they're always in the drawer of my sewing machine.

"A great explosion came from the garage – our brand-new 504 car, only half paid for, was hit. A fire broke out and car and garage burnt to a cinder. This prevented John going to his usual firing position. In the morning, when we found this place riddled with bullet holes, we realised that here too, God had protected us.

"I could hardly walk the next morning. I'd been crawling so long on hands and knees they were sore. The children sang hymns to stop shivering during the attack, and John's hand was blistered from the hot FN. When we took the children back to school, matron said the girls' dresses were torn. The suitcases had been packed ready and bullets must have ripped into them."

John and Jennie were attacked a third time and their labourers were included in the onslaught. Their workers fled and after eight weeks with no help, it became impossible to carry on farming. They left for a while, returned to try to lift their crop, and John was badly injured in a landmine incident.

"The Army commander, the District Commissioner and the doctor allowed me to fly in the helicopter with John," said Jennie. "He was seriously injured. I remember taking off, surrounded by troopies at the Army camp all wishing us luck, and flying over our magnificent country

185

with two young pilots at the controls. They were wonderful. They came down in terrorist-infested country to adjust John's drip and cover him with blankets, then took us right to the Andrew Fleming hospital in Salisbury.

"I was aghast at what the war had done to so many of our men, but I'm still proud and thankful to be part of our country's lifeblood, happy to be back on our farm, both of us whole and healthy, determined to face the future with confidence and love for all Zimbabweans."

*   *   *

The Inyanga Downs, like the Juliasdale area, has a church and hotel. Troutbeck Inn stands amid pine-covered mountains, with lawns sloping down to a lake stocked with trout.

It was on July 22, 1978 at 22h00 that Troutbeck was attacked, the terrorists firing at the hotel from the other side of the lake. Tourists became reluctant to visit Inyanga and the hotel had a struggle to keep going. The manager and his staff had identified themselves with the district and shared its troubles. When husbands were away on Security Force duties, wives were given free accommodation. When people lost their homes they were welcomed into Troutbeck as into a private home. So when in February 1979, all the African staff were intimidated by terrorists and left the hotel, the people of the Downs came to help. Some served behind the bar, some made beds, others washed up in the kitchen.

"The hotel was full of guests," said Wendy. "The catering manager did the cooking himself because the chefs had gone. He worked with the radio full on in the kitchen. We all helped out for a week until a skeleton staff came to keep the hotel running. It was like a lifeline to us and we all used to lunch at Troutbeck every Sunday to give support."

Peter and Jane lived in a wood and stone house on the border. They also lived at the edge of danger for years.

Their house was used as a Police radio relay base from 1960 and Jane was in charge in those early days. When terrorist infiltration from Mozambique increased, a radio room was built and men were stationed near their home. The radio work had become too much for one person.

In 1966 Jane opened a weaving centre where black women learnt the art over the years. She also ran a farm store. Peter's main crop was seed potatoes and he kept cattle and sheep. What courage is required to remain calm in the face of approaching war, when your farm borders enemy territory? Peter and Jane had the necessary courage and although they were attacked in their home twice, they endured, and are still there.

"Our first attack on Christmas Day, 1978, was a total surprise. All our family were with us, plus boyfriends, and when the rockets and mortars hit, there were deafening explosions. All the windows shattered and the roof was damaged. Bullets came into the bedrooms over the beds. Someone knew the layout," said Jane.

"One sniper fired constantly at the window under the stairs, knowing Peter was there. Our four black Guard Force members were very good. The attack lasted only 10 minutes and then we all cleared up the mess, determined to celebrate Christmas Day as usual."

Charles had been living alone at his own home. "One night I was suddenly woken by shots striking the wall behind my head," he said. "Plaster was falling everywhere. My loaded rifle was by my bed, so I raised the alarm and then fired out of different windows downstairs, hoping 'they' would think there were several people indoors.

"I was just nipping upstairs to shoot from a window there when I changed my mind and came down to fire at where I thought they were positioned. A moment later, and I'd have been killed. A rocket came through the roof just where I'd been standing on the stairs. It exploded and set the house alight. It was a furious fire so I began retreating in front of it to the other end of the house. Fortunately no doors were locked so I came to a stop outside the kitchen door in the angle of a buttress. I was concerned but not frightened, only furiously angry, determined to get two or three of them before they got me. I had my favourite, most trusted weapon, a .303 rifle I'd bought in Quetta in 1918 for 3/6."

Charles crouched waiting for over an hour, his house burning behind him. Surely the prayer call-up was in action! The terrorists never came. Did they imagine the solitary old man had died in the flames? The Army was 32 km away and arrived more than an hour later.

"My night clothes and rifle were all I had left," said Charles. "Everything else was destroyed." So he went to live with Bill and was there for the Christmas 'do'. The following day, December 28, the Inyanga Downs Orchards houses were attacked but fortunately the occupants were all away.

"It is miraculous and only thanks to God that none of our immediate community in the isolated Inyanga Downs area was killed," said Deirdre, one of the wives.

"One night in February 1979, we had gone to sleep to the sound of our dogs barking. 'Mombies',* my husband murmured, but suddenly there were explosions, gunfire, flashes round the bedroom ceiling and all hell let loose. It was a hot night and our blankets lay on the floor covering the *agric-alert* and all our equipment. We scrabbled around in the dark and I reported on the *agric-alert* that this time it was us. We crawled around dragging our assorted weapons with explosions rocking the house and bits of masonry and dust everywhere.

"Twenty-two mortars had been fired within our garden. A couple had hit home in the shed area, causing little damage, but we both felt much humbled by this miraculous escape."

Later they had 'Bright Lights', an assortment of vigilante-type men, to help defend their property. One day a couple decided to go to town. They were to catch the Pookie† and Army lorry returning from escort duties. It was wet and misty. Deirdre's husband Anthony drove to the sheds for petrol.

"The stillness was shattered by the rattle of gunfire and explosions, so close, I thought they were shooting my husband. I rushed into the house for my pistol and heard the radio reporting that it was the Army escort on the way to us. The Pookie took the brunt of the attack but the driver bailed out unhurt. The labourers were uninjured."

There were two more attacks on this homestead that year, but mercifully the children of the family were away.

Bill and Charles, as well as Peter and Jane, were again attacked.

"We were expecting this one," said Jane. "I sensed an ominous atmosphere when I returned home after a few days away. Our cook (for 17 years) requested immediate leave. 'I must go by February 1,' he insisted. We had a party arranged for February 2 but he could not wait. This was unlike him and it made me suspicious. That weekend half the labourers disappeared – before receiving their salaries. I was in the store when the terrorists came in, walking through, buying goods as they went.

"Our labourers surrounded me and the Guard Force stood nearby in protection but I was scared. The terrorists left but I was convinced an attack was imminent.

"It did not come till Friday, February 9, and it was terrible. We had an 82 m mortar hit us. It landed at the top of the stairs and the house just blew to bits. Thank goodness the children were not at home as they

---

*Shona word for cattle.
†Special vehicle used for detecting landmines.

could not have survived the first blast. Shrapnel went right through Louise's bed. She usually arrived home on a Friday but had decided to come on Saturday instead.

"Twenty-three more mortar bombs landed within our fenced area. The terrorists seemed well trained this time and fired accurately. Our Land Rover was blown up and the noise and mess was incredible. Peter retaliated from his firing position and the whole area was riddled with bullets, but the sandbags saved him. The sniper was there again – just one man aiming directly at Peter. Later we found seven perfectly polished 'doppies' outside where the sniper had stood.

"The animals suffered. We had five Alsatian dogs (now nervous of bangs) and we couldn't find my cat. He eventually appeared from between the ceiling and the roof. The horses kicked down the poles and escaped from their stables. We had to search for them as well as the cows. Only the sheep stayed – silly things!

"It seemed the African storekeeper had been feeding the terrorists and our African maid (with us for 10 years) had given information to our attackers – where the *agric-alert* was kept, Peter's firing position and so on. I had a letter from her the other day asking if I was well!

"With the compound burnt and labour gone, Peter tried unsuccessfully to recruit more. Eventually the RNFU* recruited for three farms locally, and 160 labourers came from Rusape, Umtali and Salisbury. The ACC† and Rural Council arranged their accommodation at Inyanga village as they refused to live on the farms. Council tipper trucks would bring the labourers at 09h00 and fetch them at 15h30. We had to pay all expenses – very costly. To prevent others getting free lifts the labourers were issued with tickets, blue for one farm, red for another, yellow for the third.

"One morning," said Sue, another Downs farmer's wife, "the labourers were late arriving. The Army usually escorted the lorry to the farm boundary where the Guard Force took over. We were standing wondering what had held them up when we saw the lorry arrive. Just as it started up to move again there was a tremendous explosion. To our horror we saw black bodies being flung into the air. We rushed for first-aid kits and went to the scene, most apprehensive as to what we might find. There were terrible injuries. It was such a dismal, sad, tragic scene – the survivors with dusty, begrimed faces shuffling towards the farm to work; the crying babies, the wailing old men.

---

*Rhodesia National Farmers' Union.
†Area Co-ordinating Committee.

"We had radioed for help and two helicopters flew in. Meanwhile we had to swallow our nausea, calm our nerves and give first aid. How thankful we were for our training. I remember encouraging a young soldier as he gave a drip, then I had to splint a leg which was almost crushed to pulp and extremely swollen. One black woman's pelvis was blown forward. She wanted her baby. The yelling infant, with wet nappy, was handed to a fresh-faced white technician who sat next to the mother all the way to hospital with the baby on his lap. I remember him alighting from the helicopter with the baby under one arm and his FN under the other."

One of the busiest at casevac scenes was Wendy, who was an active WFR and medic. She and her husband, Robin, farmed in the Downs area.

"The blowing up of the lorry carrying labour happened a week after I'd passed out as a PATU medic," said Wendy. "I heard the bang and guessed it was a mine. After reporting to the Police that I was on my way and asking them to advise the hospital, my husband and I ran to the scene. There were 37 casualties, 10 of which were serious."

Wendy later attended a course for instructors in Salisbury (many Inyanga people later became PATU medics under her instruction).

She showed such ability she was enrolled for a five-week medic course at Llewellin Barracks in Bulawayo. Of the 69 SF personnel on the course two WFR tied in second place with 92 per cent and Wendy was one of them. She also won the 'Best Medic' cup – the first time it had been won by a woman.

"I was on permanent 24-hour call-up duty."

There was an abortive attack on Inyanga village in 1979 at a time when the Red Cross ambulance had been stolen by terrorists to ferry supplies and the Army had set an ambush to catch them.

As a district, the farmers were drawn closer together by the constant danger and necessity to keep alert. "We were like one family," Alicia commented. "We knew who was hard of hearing, who had gone to town for the day, who expected visitors for the weekend. Even our vocabulary changed. A child summoned by his mother to 'Get out of the bath now' replied, 'I'm only reading you strength two!'"

Close bonds existed between many blacks and whites. One cook came to warn his employers of an impending attack by terrorists. He did not want to run and leave his employers to be killed. Many domestic workers felt as close to the family for whom they worked, as to be part of them.

"We're off!" this particular cook cried, rushing into the sitting-room.

190

"Come with me into the bush!" The couple for whom he worked did not go with him but they appreciated his concern. They understood his flight. He'd been part of their family for years.

A young white girl was alone in the house when her parents were out. She had the radio on rather loudly while washing her hair. The programme was a serial and a woman was screaming. The black gardener heard this from his quarters and thought his employer's daughter was being assaulted. He came running to save her. The family were touched and grateful for his bravery.

When the war ended Alicia wrote: *Return to Normality* to sum up the wonderful spirit of Inyanga people.

"What is normality? For Inyanga it is the sudden, almost traumatic ending of an era of vigilance, night fear and restricted movement. No one who has not borne 'the heat and burden of the day' can begin to understand what these simple words mean. Mothers and wives know only too well. Weapon-carrying, a hateful practice, especially for women, can be thankfully discontinued and yet one feels naked.

"It often struck me, during the bad years, that there was a measure of underlying trust between the races (despite what mischievous propaganda might say), that no African in our community ever showed or had reason to feel the slightest fear or anxiety at the presence of all these weapons, knowing they were for his protection too.

"In smaller ways, normality means things like sleeping without one ear alert; without finger poised for *agric-alert* button. It means no more buckets of water at the ready, no weapons covered against falling masonry which could jam them, no eiderdowns handy to wrap children against shrapnel, no bundle of dark, warm clothing at the end of the bed. No more do we hear the dreaded call 'We're under attack!'; the instant, aching prayers, the comforting words from Control: 'Keep your head down dearie, Crusader* is on the way.'

"And the relief in the Tribal Trust Lands must be even greater. One does not need to spell it out to know what it must have been like to be sandwiched, unarmed, uninformed, bewildered, between the Security Forces and the gunpoint demands of the guerillas, to be deprived of vital bus communications, of schools, hospitals and clinics.

"Thank God the fighting is over. Let us not, however, relax the tremendous community efforts which prevailed during the war. I recall being heartened and moved during the 'bad' days by an evening 'phone call.

---

*Term for Army used in radio messages.

"It was from a Police Reserve colleague with whom I had worked all day. She called to see if I was 'home safe' and then she said: 'I am just going to sit quietly and read Psalm 121. Will you join me?'

"These are the incidents which live on, the deep comradeship which need not be lost. It is up to us.

"*Bind us together, Lord; bind us together, Lord,*
With cords that cannot be broken.
Bind us together, Lord; bind us together, Lord,
Bind us together with love."

20 *Penhalonga hopes for the best*

Not unto us a fertile heritage,
Nor any wealth of comfort idly won,
But only this – a land of toil and stress,
Where utter needs calls utter effort forth,
Until of babe and stripling comes the Man.

KINGSLEY FAIRBRIDGE

"We had our amusing moments," recalled a Penhalonga forester who, with his staff, escaped death when nine landmines were found on different occasions at his border estate in Imbeza Valley.

Life was never dull for him or his wife, and they were delighted to be the first recipients of the original thousand dollar bounty handed over by Government for spotting and reporting landmines. They promptly handed the money to Tsanga Lodge convalescent centre for the troopies.

Shot at in ambush, bombarded by rockets and rifle grenades, harassed by arsonists, blown up in landmine incidents, Reg was philosophical: "We had a job to do, and we just stuck to it."

While on fire-duty in June 1978 he was travelling from his home to the office in a Land Rover when he saw a disturbance of soil in the road ahead. He avoided it and carried on beyond the spot, then returned on foot to examine it. He found a TM 46, and summoned the local reserve stick on the Police channel on his vehicle. They came out in their clattering Hyena*. It was a tricky position, as Reg was on the far side of the mine and the Police Reservists in their transport were bowling merrily along towards him.

"I signalled madly, pointed into the road between us and then covered my ears in pantomime gesture, to warn them to stop before they hit it."

It struck them all as comic at the time, and later the Engineers lifted it before it did any damage. This was the first of nine mines found in the forest over the years. Two exploded and blew up vehicles and their occupants. One forest ranger had slight injuries and Reg suffered headache, ear damage and shock.

Imbeza estate had 2 428 ha under forest with a force of 350 labourers,

---

*A type of protected vehicle.

including sawmill workers. Originally a third of them lived in Mozambique where part of the forest estate lay, but the Frelimo government refused the company permission to continue working there.

Like many of their neighbours, the couple served with the Police Reserve, giving up much of their leisure time and never knowing when danger lay around the corner.

"We never kept a journal, but things were happening all the time," said Reg. "We needed an eye on the road for mines, an eye on the side for ambushes, and one in the back of our heads for smoke from possible fires." Their work – his wife was a devoted Public Health nurse – necessitated carrying arms and having armed escorts, but their constant motto was: 'Hope for the best, expect the worst – and keep your nose clean.'

Once Reg was shot at from over the border during an early morning incident when his Police Reserve stick was on reconnaissance and ran into an ambush. They were separated from their vehicle and after radioing for help, managed to rescue it, under covering fire from a chopper force, and 'beat it back to base'.

"I remember one shooting incident when the Army was called out and after visiting the spot they retired to our house to drink tea. All day Frelimo poured rounds into the area as though ammunition was going out of fashion, but no one was hurt," he said.

"Then there were three days of bombardment from 'over the border' when Frelimo objected to the presence of our men laying down the protective minefield. As a result, 20 fires were started in the valuable trees. All the neighbouring estates sent out fire teams to help us beat out the blaze. We lost 40,5 ha of pine only as it was November and rain had fallen."

Driving home from work in a light protected vehicle Reg hit a landmine in his own driveway but escaped with slight injuries. Although it had been decided that the men over the border were responsible, there was no doubt they had plenty of support from locals in the compounds.

Theft from the forest estate store was so frequent that after 10 break-ins the staff lost count. Twice the sawmill was damaged by rockets and smallarms fire, and six mules were killed by the 'freedom fighters' from Mozambique, who also shot at passing planes. A black foreman from the sawmill was executed after a 'trial' by terror, and his mother was also murdered.

An Umtali schoolboy who lived in the valley was locked up in his own house by terrorists and his possessions were stolen, but he managed to effect a brave and lucky escape.

After his own home had been attacked heavily during a night on-slaught which they miraculously survived, Reg, the indomitable for-ester, had the sad task later of identifying the body of a young white forester, abducted and found dead on the estate within 100 m of a compound.

Penhalonga is a small mining village 20 km north of Umtali, within walking distance of the Mozambique border. Despite the goldmines' waste dumps, it is a lovely sylvan centre for a Police station, post office, trading stores and garage. One of the most beautifully situated mining villages on the continent, it has always been associated with the pro-gress of the earliest Rhodesian pioneers and their descendants.

It has the first established Anglican church in the country. A small, historic, tin-roofed building on stilts, it is a quiet landmark in a grassy corner near the main road to forest estates and Tribal Trust Lands on the way to Inyanga.

The village thrived in earlier days then suffered a depression in the 40's till the mines re-opened with modern technology (and the in-creased price of gold) in the early 70's.

It was a warm day in October 1975 when the first shot was fired near Penhalonga. A Police patrol investigating minor crimes on the border was shot at by Frelimo and a constable abducted.

The Member-in-Charge and his deputy returned to base and called up the reservists to man the control room. Numerous pots of tea were made in the hastily-organised 'phone and radio centre while the men discussed the day's excitement.

"This is it!" they said. "From now on, things will be hotting up." The local Women's Field Reservists brushed up their office drill and stood by for a detailed roster of call-up periods which lasted for several years. The Police Reservists cleaned the barrels of their guns at home and said farewell to regular golf, tennis or sailing weekends. Then followed a series of tragedies.

Charlie and his wife Nora were shot and injured in an ambush beyond Lake Alexander when returning to their home in a distant forest one Sunday afternoon.

A well-known forester, John, was killed on the verandah of his home one Saturday evening, in his wife's presence, by an unknown gunman.

A medical doctor whose Odzani homestead was at 'the end of the line' from Penhalonga village, defended himself at night against a rocket and mortar attack on his house. Later a landmine was lifted near his home. That night the Police Reserve stick on duty at the Police station rushed to his aid and found 'every man jack at his road-end, armed and uniformed, ready to join in the defence of a friend'.

A great spirit of neighbourliness was being built up under stress and strain of war.

Zengeni, the lovely double-storeyed home of Lady Jacqueline Wilson and the late Sir Ian (former Speaker of the Federal Assembly and a local MP) was attacked several times by Frelimo, whose armed post on the border was practically in Lady Wilson's back garden. Although Rhodesian born and bred she was later forced to abandon everything and leave for Britain.

Driving along the border road was a hair-raising experience for herself and her family as well as the local Police and reservists. They were only 100 m from the heavily-armed men. Once a zealous reservist, sitting on the cab of his vehicle, was thrown into the ditch when a wheel hit an unseen culvert. (A fallen tree across the road had blocked their way.) Face down in the mud, with his rifle askew beside him, he expected to be shot immediately by Frelimo as a sitting target. But the Mozambiquans simply roared with laughter, and tension was eased immediately.

Later an elderly European suffering from cancer was attacked at his home and a fruit-farming couple in their 70's were beaten up and threatened during an armed robbery. Another forester was ambushed on several occasions and Police sticks escorting convoys were attacked on lonely stretches of road.

The water-purification works at Lake Alexander were attacked twice in sabotage attempts to cut off the water supply to Umtali. Power lines were cut on many occasions in the area.

There was a heavy attack on Savillen Estate where Elizabeth and Bernard had a shocking experience. They returned home from a visit to town one night to find several massacred employees in their compound. Bernard was later attacked in the bush and escaped from a hail of bullets.

The Old Umtali farms which came within the Penhalonga Police area were the first to be threatened, with the O'Donovan's home being attacked and burnt. Reg, a leading farmer, suffered two attacks with burnt compounds, labourers beaten up and the house fired on, while cattle were repeatedly stolen and driven across the borders of the Tribal Trust Lands. His wife had the terrifying experience of lying down in the garden one night for 10 minutes while attackers fired over her head with her husband retaliating from the house, not knowing where she was. There were two teenagers at home at the time and the house was riddled with bullets.

Foreign journalists were taken to the scene of a horrible massacre at the farm of Ilsa and Marius when several labourers were shot and their huts burnt. A white woman doctor, a neighbour, went straight over to help the wounded, braving terrorists, landmines and a possible ambush, to give medical help and comfort the bereaved and dying. For years most of her work was among the black population and she won a medal for gallantry.

The African village beerhall near Penhalonga was robbed by armed invaders on many occasions and farm stores throughout the district were broken into and ransacked. A Polish princess and her mother survived a heavy attack on their home when they returned from Umtali one teatime. Morning, noon or night, the terrorists attacked defenceless people but fled as soon as anyone returned fire, or Security Forces were on their way.

When Kukwanisa, the thriving farm school for Africans in the Inyanga Road area (built by the Courtauld Trust many years ago for training black peasant farmers and potential farm managers), was attacked and destroyed, many local benefactors who had concerned themselves with the scheme, became disgusted.

Loud bangs frequently disturbed the peace of Penhalonga, otherwise a tranquil village, and they were not always due to mining operations. The protective minefield laid along the border to prevent large-scale incursions from Mozambique claimed a few lives, animal or otherwise. Once a rare lion detonated a landmine and was found dead near a local farm. It was said that the terrorists deliberately drove cattle through the minefield to clear the way.

A brutal murder took place on the main Penhalonga road at St Augustine's mission turn-off when a passing white mining couple were returning from Umtali at 22h00 and were blasted by rockets fired at their car. The woman was killed instantly and her husband injured.

Young Ian was shot and killed when he and his wife returned home one night to the estate they bravely tried to administer during the war.

The Imbeza Valley murders before Christmas 1979 shocked the village community as never before. A quiet, peacable, Coloured man, Mr Wright, was chopped to death at his home in a secluded spot. Guthrie Hall, a Christian gentleman of long standing in the neighbourhood, was next to be axed in his bed. Pat and Dennis Tapping, a well-known Police Reserve couple on an Imbeza smallholding, were killed by a boosted landmine in their car early one Monday morning on their way to work. Shortly afterwards Ivor Harvey and Don Brown were killed at work at Nyabara Forest Training School and La Rochelle respectively.

A brave and spirited horsewoman and former WFR, Rosalie Lucke-raft, was murdered by a large gang who attacked her early one Monday morning at her home where she was frequently alone, guarding her horses and her husband's smallholding from attack and destruction.

In the final stages of the war a local farmer and butcher found several of his cattle dead and others wounded near the main Penhalonga Road. The petrol station at Christmas Pass was set alight at night to the horror of the widow living alone above the pumps. She woke to see flames shooting up past her bedroom window.

Intimidation on the estates was rife during both general elections and strikes and labour unrest became common. Most policemen and reservists had narrow escapes from death.

"We were checking out a hut in Odzani and moved on to another nearby," said a stick leader. "As we moved in, a group of 50 terrorists moved quickly out into hiding – and we were a five-man stick. It could have been fatal."

One particular Land Rover, the 'Moon Buggy', became historic for its frequent involvement in drama. It was bought by the stick concerned and is still going strong.

"Some 90 men and women in our area served loyally with the Reserve and many had trained since the mid 50's," said Stick leader Jimmy. At the opening of the WVS canteen (the first in Manicaland), he said the village was truly a 'community' because of its new involvement in the service of others.

"We knew the attacks would be on the soft targets – lonely people, isolated homes, the elderly. I think the presence of our reaction sticks did much to help landowners stay put."

Some in Penhalonga said other farmers were 'paying the terrorists to leave them alone'. A few saw gross inefficiency on the part of soldiers when contacts were reported and 'the wrong people', the innocent, got killed by mistake. There was also a large proportion of unnecessary wounded and dead through careless handling of weapons or in vehicle accidents and in cross-fire.

What was it like to be an ordinary housewife in Penhalonga during the war? There were times when the grief and sorrow must have become almost unbearable. Heartfelt sympathy went out to the white women whose husbands had been abducted.

It was a bitter occasion when, after the so-called cease-fire in December 1979, Ted was murdered at about midday on the main Penhalonga road near the Country Club when he was driving to visit his wife in hospital. She had been badly hurt when they were ambushed some months previously. (The entire world was shocked when three members of the International Committee of the Red Cross (one a local African employee) were murdered as their white, Red Cross flagged vehicle passed through the Honde Valley, where they were taking supplies to beleaguered villagers.)

"We lived on a 'runway' 6 km from the border and twice the local store was robbed," a Penhalonga forester said. "I looked after 5 261 ha of pine plantations and once had to extinguish seven fires in one night, but these were things we had to live with."

One week in four he spent in the bush on Police Reserve patrol or on standby duty at the Police station while his wife and children stayed with friends. Their two baby girls have been brought up in this atmosphere of fighting and fear.

"How do you die if you don't get shot?" asked their six-year-old curiously.

The wife ran a kitchen dry-goods store for the benefit of the labourers as well as a daily clinic, dealing with everything from simple spots to maternity cases. A trained nurse, she was appalled at the malnutrition prevalent in the Tribal Trust Lands, and the general debilitation of health and family life as the result of black husbands and fathers abandoning their homes or being forced away for guerilla training.

Keen nurse though she is, she resists the post-war political instruction that all must join the Zimbabwe Nurses' Association. "Not on your life! Politics has nothing to do with nursing," she insists.

She saw the decline of work at the Well-baby clinic, the family planning centre and in public health routines. She also saw the local homecraft club burned down. In spite of efforts to continue these services, they were rarely appreciated, except by old women who walked many kilometres to get the aid they knew they needed.

"We of the white community *did* try, in spite of what subsequent anti-colonial propaganda says," she commented. "We were not all that bad. But they were so much against us. We could never win. But what the 'tsotsis'* want is not what the older people want.

"We thought we were fighting for an ideal, to help the people overcome savagery and the Middle Ages outlook which was dragging them down. But what of the future? Will it be any better for them? I was a

---

*Muggers or young town layabouts.

VSO for 18 months in Malawi and it was hard work, but we felt we were beginning to uplift the women there and guide them to a better way of life.

"In spite of everything, my husband and I want to stay, although only five white families out of 30 still remain here."

She, like many others, knew the missions were giving no help to the Security Forces in their battle against terrorism and she felt this encouraged the murderers.

"Here was a case where we felt religion had been misused. Religious principles were wrongly attributed to the terrorists and the missionaries, to cover up evil and support their anti-government stand."

The couple felt strongly that a Communist government brought in by the power of the gun was wrong. A moderate government elected by gradual process through the ballot box (and still retaining the high standard the European had introduced and wanted to extend for all), would have been better for all races.

There was a great need for change, but it was coming slowly and could have come peacefully.

"Our children will read the 'new history' which indicates that anything white was wrong and misdirected, and this is not the truth. The Europeans have completed their epic in history and this must be told fairly, for future generations to judge for themselves."

"When I am asked by my family in South Africa, what it was like during the terrorist war, I am very wary," said another young forestry wife.

"I would not like them to know how my husband and I narrowly escaped death on two occasions. As a South African, married to a Rhodesian, I arrived fully aware of the war situation but never dreamt it would affect us. We lived in a remote spot on the eastern border but until 1978 it was not an operational area. The only times it affected me was when my husband was on frequent call-ups and it became very lonely."

But one night in April 1978 the newly-weds had a rude awakening.

It was misty with a fine drizzle. They had a friend staying, so turned in later than usual. Shortly after switching off the electric light generator they heard the dogs barking. They turned over and told them to be quiet.

"That was our saving grace, not getting up to check their barking. Soon all hell broke loose outside and automatic fire was directed through our bedroom window. It came from the front lawn, 3 m from the bedroom. I don't remember much after that, just rolling off the bed onto the floor and lying in a mess of glass and cement. My husband pressed the alarm on the *agric-alert* but by then all firing had stopped. We spent the next hour sitting in the passage drinking wine to calm our shattered nerves!

"Our security guards arrived soon after. The fence had been cut with pliers pinched from our toolshed up the road, and the 'phone lines were cut. Had we stood up when the dogs barked we would have been shot at point blank range."

A year later they were driving home after shopping in Umtali and rounded a corner to see fire by the road. Not thinking, they slowed down for a closer look.

"The next minute a rocket exploded in front of the car and we drove through dust and debris over the hole with heavy automatic fire pouring down on us. It seemed ages before we were out of the line of bullets, as the terrorists had chosen a good ambush site, but again we were lucky and our car was not even scratched."

These are only two incidents out of hundreds that occurred, but it failed to dissuade the young couple from staying on. They pray their children may never have to live in fear at night as they did. To hear a dog bark or an owl hoot might mean *they* were coming again, and with others they shared countless sleepless nights.

"We feel strongly for this beautiful country and her future. We remember the good times and hope to remain here," they both said.

"My nightmare memory was the anguish of trying to pull on clothes over my wet body while automatic fire was too close for comfort. I had been luxuriating in a hot bath when the attack started," said another Penhalonga wife.

"Our servant was banging on the door yelling that we were being shot at. It was early one morning, payday, and Frelimo attacked the nearby farm office, hoping to get the moneybags before the payout started. The Mozambique border was less than a kilometre away and the minefield not yet established.

"Our young farmer and his elderly uncle were in the office, and the younger man went to the front door to speak to an employee. He was suddenly confronted by three armed Frelimo advancing up the steps. He threw himself from the doorway just as a volley of AK automatic fire hailed in at pointblank range. He dashed out at the back to save his three-year-old son playing in the Land Rover close by.

"An African employee had grabbed the child and run to an outbuilding where the little boy was safely hiding behind an oildrum.

"Meanwhile the elderly uncle reached for his FN which fell behind

201

the filing cabinet. He quickly retrieved it and was able to fire shots after the fleeing Frelimo. With their back-up group there were 14 who continued to fire at the office from a nearby forest, until the helicopter arrived to pick up the only casualty, one employee wounded in cross-fire."

Once the elderly uncle was surrounded by six Frelimo with a bayonet pressed into his stomach. He told them firmly to get back to their own side of the border before they were seen by the Security Forces. After a heated argument and the timely intervention of an employee, the soldiers retreated, arguing that they would kill him if he did not stop Rhodesian forces patrolling the Rhodesian side of the border.

They were told emphatically by this brave and well-known son of a pioneer, "You patrol your side. We will continue to patrol ours."

Another incident on the same property had a sad conclusion.

"One morning a faithful house servant of 30 years was missing," said the family.

"He was a religious man who neither drank nor smoked and being away from work without permission was quite out of character. Inquiries brought no response and the Police were notified. Eventually a shallow grave was found where both man and wife were buried after being cruelly beheaded.

"Apparently the couple, with a large family to support, had refused to pay the monthly levy to the terrorists. One night, in front of everyone in the compound, the terrorists had killed them 'as an example to others'. Four small children were left in their home. Their mother, before being led away for execution, had whispered to the eldest (a nine-year-old) to take his three brothers and sisters to an older sister nearby. Everyone in the compound was too afraid to be seen feeding or helping the children in any way, and the youngsters were too afraid to report what had happened. The four toddlers were seen walking down the road, hand-in-hand, and were later claimed by a relative."

So the mourning in the neighbourhood continued, with sympathy between black and white unbounded.

European children knew it was dangerous to wander outside their security fences and they were drilled in procedure should their home be attacked. Most four-year-olds and upwards knew how to use their *agric-alert*. They were taught to press the alarm, tell the operator who they were, their *agric-alert* number, and what was happening, in case their parents had been wounded. Most children could give their map reference. They were encouraged to practise under supervision and as soon as they were strong enough, most knew how to re-load magazines. "Can my little brother have a go now?" was a frequent plea.

"My great-nephew was only six when he told me how to behave in a Leopard, our armoured vehicle," said a Penhalonga great-aunt.

"I took him to school each day and he solemnly strapped himself in and gave me a detailed lesson on the intricate working of the armament panel. In ambush, his part would be to fire the left side and rear cannons, while I would fire the right and front, he said. 'You will need me to help you because you will have to drive like fury.'

"He added: 'And don't fire each cannon more than once because you never know – there might be a second ambush round the next corner, when we'll need the second shots!'"

In the Odzani district of Penhalonga it was tragic to see how many people had started farming from scratch under adverse conditions, often living in tents to plant fruit trees, build a home and develop smallholdings, only to be driven out later, said Myra.

"The war drew us together as a community and with the *agric-alert* we all knew instantly of trouble nearby. Our main concern was to help our neighbours."

Myra is a woman who spent years helping African women to develop clubs for homecraft skills, encouraging their shows, sports days, first-aid classes, clinics and hospital training. She felt strongly that the white woman's influence had been 'fantastic' in raising the standards of village life.

She had many African women friends and now finds they are too embarrassed to speak to her in public because of the intimidation to which they have been subjected.

After all the Imbeza Valley murders in December 1979, which were believed to be part of a pincer movement to encircle Umtali, many harsh comments were made about St Augustine's mission, close to the village, which had never been attacked (as other missions were) and which had frequently been visited by terrorists to talk to pupils and obtain medical treatment.

St Augustine's clergy were responsible for taking the services and ministering to a small congregation of whites at St Michael's and All Angels in Penhalonga, of whom a high proportion were killed or wounded by violence.

People asked each other, if these terrorists were responsible for the brutalities in the area, why did an Anglican mission tolerate their presence? The tension increased when the head of the mission publicly supported ZANU (PF) in the national press.

When some of the men responsible for the killings were caught and brought to trial they were allowed to go free under the then Governor (Soames') amnesty. Countless others were pardoned later under the Independence amnesty.

A high proportion of ministers in the new Zimbabwe Government in 1980 were former St Augustine's pupils who went to 'progressive socialist' countries for terrorist training.

21 *Vumba peace shattered*

"In your distress, say to God, 'My Father, I do not understand You, but I trust You' and then you will experience His help."

VUMBA PRAISE PLAQUE

The Vumba Mountains – Mountains of the Mist – lie south of Umtali, and from the city this lovely range of wooded hills is frequently clothed in cloud. The Vumba is home to hundreds of Umtali workers and was a favourite holiday spot for thousands of visitors before the war.

The road from Umtali rises steeply to Cloudlands, the highest point. Here the tar changes to gravel at a left fork which starts the lovely, circular drive down Essex Road, through the Burma Valley and back through Zimunya Tribal Trust Lands. Many Vumba homes have a view across rolling hills to Chicamba Dam in Mozambique.

The varying climatic conditions support the production of widely differing crops – coffee, cotton, bananas and Burley tobacco can all be seen from the road, and there are many delightfully situated hotels and chalets, as well as the Vumba National Park.

Into this scene of natural peace and tranquillity came, in 1978, ugliness and brutality, with the Elim massacre. 'Elim' is now a word that will live forever in the memories of those who love the Vumba.

The world was shocked when 13 white people, innocent missionaries, their wives and young children, were brutally assaulted and murdered on June 23, 1978, a night of unspeakable horror at Elim Mission which had taken over the former Eagle preparatory school in the Vumba, several kilometres from Umtali.

They were teachers who had given their salaries voluntarily to pay for the education and welfare of their 250 African pupils. Their reward? Their mutilated bodies were found on a cold Saturday morning at a scene of abomination.

There had been previous trouble when two busloads of Elim pupils had been blown up by a landmine at their former school north of Inyanga. Then the mission was re-established in the Vumba with local help, for their own safety, or so they believed.

A local landowner happened to call at the mission that Saturday morning.

"When I arrived to check that all was well, I found the school under Police control. I was advised to leave at once. No-one would speak about what had happened. On the sports field I noticed a number of pieces of different coloured canvas. I returned home and my wife told me she had heard there had been a massacre and all the white people there had been killed in the night. The women had been criminally assaulted and then murdered. The children and men were beaten and stabbed to death – a most ghastly and barbarous affair."

The funeral service was held in the Queen's Hall, Umtali, when the grief of the relatives was shared by 500 mourners and thousands more throughout the Christian world. The missionaries were from Britain. Security forces later tracked down and killed two of the band of 21 terrorists responsible. A diary was found describing the attack and admitting their guilt.

Many Vumba residents were old-established, well-known families, who loved their land, looked after their labourers well and saw no reason to leave, despite the tactics used to frighten them away.

At Leopard Rock Hotel the management had a smile and welcome for guests soon after the building was badly damaged by bullet and shrapnel holes in an attack in January 1978. A rocket went through a main bedroom window, luckily without fatal results as it was unoccupied. The assault came from below the front lawn, where visitors would sit in the sun with their tea and drinks. But the hotel never closed. The managers carried on, thankful that the main road to their area was at last to be tarred, minimising the risk of mines.

Another hotel manager and his wife had a nightmare experience.

"My husband and I were managing Mountain Lodge in February 1979," said Joyce. "One day at about 20h00 a large gang of armed men arrived. We were alone as guests were few and far between in those days. People were afraid to holiday in the Vumba and our servants and waiters had gone off duty.

"The intruders seemed casual and happy. They had taken our keys and got my husband's gun. Then they tied our arms and legs to the beds and sprayed us with gunfire. How did the bullets miss us? I simply don't know! I saw my husband roll off onto the floor and thought he was dead.

"I was feigning death, so the men thought we were both done for and left the room. I could hear them helping themselves to drinks in the bar.

"I managed to untie my legs and hands to loosen my husband. I dragged him out of the window, thinking we could hide below the front terrace. As I approached the edge I found a gang there waiting for us, so I ran back dragging my husband through the window again into the bedroom.

"While the gang were in the other rooms I went to the bar, hoping to

206

'phone or use the *agric-alert* but this had been destroyed and the 'phone wire cut. I thought of an extension which might still be working and crawled on hands and knees, hoping *they* would not see or hear. I could still hear them! I found an extension intact – praise be! – so I dialled the Police.

"We're under attack!" I whispered. "The terrorists are here. Please come quickly!"

"Who's speaking?" a ponderous voice asked.

"It's Mountain Lodge Hotel. This is Joyce..."

"How do you spell it?" the policeman asked!

"I threw down the phone in despair. What could I do? The men would soon return and if they found us alive... Then there was the sound of a vehicle coming. The men fled. The local Police Reserve stick had heard the shooting and come to help."

The intruders turned out to be a mob of 'pseudo-terrorists', some with green painted wooden 'guns' and fir-cones resembling grenades. They were later caught and brought to justice.

One of The Wattle Company's coffee estates was heavily attacked one night and the factory put out of production for some time. Staff 'blooded their weapons' one morning after following a section of terrorists across the border. They found the enemy asleep and shot them up. Four were killed.

Some of the Vumba incidents were most unhappy occasions.

"One evening in 1979 we heard a gigantic explosion outside our house," said a housewife. "We immediately reported it on *agric-alert* and were told 'Don't worry. We know about it.' So we went to bed and anxiously awaited the morning to hear what had happened.

"At 06h00 we knew the worst. A curfew was in force and no one was supposed to go out after 18h00. We had warned our two servants of this and they were very good about it, except on this occasion. Apparently there was some stolen buck meat being sold in the neighbourhood and they risked the curfew to go down the road to buy it. The path below us was reckoned to be a well-known terrorist route, though we had never come across anything suspicious. But the Army or local militia (we never knew which, it may be both) decided to plant a claymore mine there in the hope of catching terrorists. We ourselves used to walk along this path every day with our dogs but never knew anything of this.

"Our two servants, one an excellent domestic who had been with us for 10 years, and the other our gardener for 15 years, 'caught it' when returning with the meat. This was the explosion we heard. They were left lying on the path all night with a couple of militia sitting behind some rocks nearby, believing them to be terrorists. Our house-servant tried to drag himself along the road to us, but his legs were badly shattered and he bled to death."

Vumba folk, although so near the Mozambique border, were angered by 'scare stories' going round Umtali in March 1976, and maintained that their area was as safe as anywhere, and far more beautiful and peaceful. Special 'Save The Hotels' tours were started by the Manicaland Publicity Director, with transport provided, to alleviate the petrol rationing problem. Although none of the hotels closed, they suffered a sharp loss of normal tourist trade, except at public holiday weekends when Rhodesians came in force and packed out the accommodation available.

Many vacant properties were bought and occupied, in defiance of 'the troubles' and one resident, who had his three-year-old 'dream house' and collection of antiques burnt to the ground while he was on call-up, set to and rebuilt again.

* * *

"What's a picnic?" asked the children of the Burma Valley during the war. They had never had the opportunity of enjoying this delightful type of open-air eating-out. Their parents were too busy defending home and farmlands, and the local bush could easily have been a hiding place for armed gangs.

The Burma Valley (so called because of its heat and humidity) lies 48 km from Umtali, bounded on the east by Mozambique, the west by Zimunya Tribal Trust Land, the north by the main Vumba ridge (over which one must pass to reach town), and the south by the Himalaya range. It is a hot, fertile valley, originally pioneered by the Vorster and Steyn families, who rode over on horseback more than 60 years ago to buy land there for farming tobacco, cotton, citrus, bananas, vegetables and other crops.

Dense, sub-tropical forest covered the area and there were no roads. More families moved in and through sheer hard work and perseverance, built up successful estates. It became a small, close-knit community and numbered 17 farmers when the troubles started. They soon realised they must rely on their own resources for survival. The forces of law and order were stationed too far away for any to arrive quickly enough if danger arose. If the farmers lost one of their number it would make all the rest more vulnerable.

First-aid classes, target practice, radio procedure and 'children's hour' on the *agric-alert* became the order of the day. Homesteads were fenced, lights and alarms installed under the strict supervision of a committee appointed to study the best methods. Compounds were consolidated and fenced, and where possible intercom systems were arranged between homesteads and compounds.

All seemed peaceful until one morning before Christmas 1976 when a farmer riding a motorcycle near the border noticed tracks on the main road leading west. By this time nobody moved at night as there were, as yet, no mine-protected vehicles.

He called on a neighbour and together they followed the tracks, which seemed to confirm that 50 heavily laden people had passed this way.

Six other farmers were called and together they followed the 'spoor' up the escarpment leading out of the valley. Near the top of the mountain the tracks veered off the road.

In the bush they walked into a resting-camp of about 100 terrorists. Luckily none of the farmers was injured in the contact. In follow-up operations large quantities of arms were captured. The valley knew without doubt that the war had started.

Quickly everyone acquired mine-protected vehicles and convoys were organised for mutual support in travelling to and from Umtali.

The main Burma Valley road was 'swept' for mines every morning with the co-operation of the Ministry of Internal Affairs which had set up a base in the nearby Tribal Trust Land. Escorts were arranged for the many heavy vehicles moving produce out of the valley. But more positive action was needed, the residents felt. The local Area Co-ordinating Committee commandeered an empty homestead and, with financial contributions from all, they were able to employ a full-time security guard. He was assisted by members of the Guard Force and a Leopard was bought out of community funds.

The Police provided suitable radio equipment for the team. They planned random night ambushes and had several successes, but the main object was to let every resident know that in the event of an attack there would be a standby team to re-act immediately.

"There were a few false alarms but no one minded," said a farmer. "It was good training for all. Terrorists attacks on compounds soon frightened away the labourers involved and several farmers had their labourers abducted. One man found himself with four living souls left on his farm and was almost out of business. But his son, from the northern part of the country, recruited a new labour force for him. When compounds were burnt by intruders, they were rebuilt within days as a result of community effort in supplying timber and thatching material."

During this time there was constant danger from mines in the road through the Tribal Trust Land. Due to careful surveillance many of these were lifted before they caused harm. Then came the ambushes on the steep winding road down the mountain into the valley.

Several banana trucks were attacked and set alight. A trip to town became a nightmare, but only one farmer who had left Umtali ahead of the convoy came under fire and he was uninjured.

Two of the farmers owned aircraft and were attached to the Police Reserve Air Wing. They were away on duty frequently, but the night Leopard Rock Hotel was attacked, one was at home. When the alarm came, he was airborne in less than 15 minutes and there is no doubt that his flight over the scene brought the attack to a speedy end.

Two simultaneous homestead attacks were staged near the Mozambique border, with rockets and mortars being launched from within that country. Considerable damage was done but no one was hurt. Next morning a farmer driving his protected vehicle past one of these homesteads hit a landmine. He escaped with minor leg scratches but the vehicle was 'written off'. At a full medical check-up his doctor was amazed he did not complain of earache. On examining his ears he was astounded at the amount of wax in them. He offered to clean them out but the farmer refused vehemently. That wax had saved his eardrums from being damaged!

Most of the community were Police Reservists and frequently posted elsewhere, but as things warmed up in the valley they were relieved of these duties. Many of the women without small children continued to operate the *agric-alert* control panel in Umtali and served on radio duty at Grand Reef JOC.

"It seems a long time ago now," said a farmer's wife. "Many incidents have faded from memory. There is no doubt that the determination of our community to stand firm and organise our own defences, without relying on outside help, resulted in us all being here when hostilities ceased. We were lucky to have those who assumed real and determined leadership and made it their business to ensure that all played their part to the best of their capabilties."

Following the war's end, properties were bought in the Burma Valley by progressive farmers and this strengthened the community's determination to stay and play their part in the years to come.

* * *

210

Tourists travelling the Eastern Highlands from Umtali south to Melsetter might choose to take the Cashel Road, forking to the left after the Umvumvumvu Bridge – a lonely, rocky, winding route with lovely views and large stretches of isolated farmland, all pioneered at the beginning of the century by the Steyns and other families. But the 'liberation campaign' spelt tragedy and sudden drama for the white community there.

With both shoulders smashed by terrorist bullets, his left arm immobilised, his spectacles shaved off by a bullet that missed his eyebrows by a centimetre, and with blood streaming down his body, the Reverend Jim, an American farming missionary, sat on top of an anthill in Cashel in the baking November heat of 1979 and wondered 'if his end was nigh'.

"When I heard the familiar accents of a Nebraska doctor in the rescue team, I guessed I'd died and gone to Heaven," he joked when he left Umtali Hospital after six weeks' treatment. He had survived a double ambush near his home but his staunch African foreman was killed 1½ km away and found only two weeks later.

The African Police sergeant in the Rev Jim's vehicle had fired off two magazines at their attackers before he collapsed in the early morning skirmish.

Mrs Jim told how she heard blasts that shook the house as grenades hit her husband's truck. She sounded the alarm and prayed alone for two hours for her husband's safety. When security forces told her he had been found alive but injured, she ran to kiss the Bible with tears in her eyes.

"We survived so many incidents, including landmines, but now all our cattle, 400 head, have been stolen. We were advised to leave but were reluctant to do so."

Jim always went about his work armed 'against the thugs, murderers and butchers supported by the World Council of Churches and the British and American governments', he said, earning the title 'the fighting missionary'. Both ambushes that day were set up to kill him and his wife and staff, but he believes that only by God's grace are the couple alive today.

He was first attacked that morning by a group of 35 terrorists who disabled him. He drove on and was fired at again by another 15 hidden in the bush. In severe pain, with a punctured tyre, he drove on another 7 km with the African sergeant unconscious beside him.

Jim stopped and found his lookout post on the anthill. Later, a group of Africans approached and he, half-blinded by blood, asked the leader to put up his gun and identify himself. With heartfelt relief, he found it was a Police team looking for their wounded sergeant.

"I watched spotter planes flying overhead several times before the 'chopper' arrived with medical help. A helicopter also flew into our homestead to protect my wife and we were later re-united in hospital. I intend to continue defending myself, my family, my property and my country," he said at the time.

An American reporter once asked him: "Do you always carry a gun?" He answered: "Do I always wear pants?"

Many of the mission's labour force disappeared when this incident occurred, but the missionaries returned to arrange a Christian burial for their foreman on behalf of his family. Before coming to Rhodesia in 1972 the couple had worked in Zaire and were familiar with terror campaigns there.

"Don't give up," they urged the Umtali public. "Don't surrender. We shall keep on fighting." This was the message they took back to America to the Baptist Church for which they work, when they went on holiday.

In spite of this type of brave determination, the white population of Cashel, numbering 50, dwindled to five, in five years.

The first farmhouse attacked belonged to Chris and the couple were completely unprepared. Rifles were locked away and at the first crack of gunfire and rockets, the farmer shouted: "Where are my takkies?"* It was 01h00 on Good Friday morning, 1976. As soon as the farmer retaliated, the gang of 14 terrorists fled, leaving bullet-holes in the roof and water-tank, and half a large bag of spent cartridges lying around, plus the usual landmine in the road.

One afternoon two years later while Chris was cutting cattle feed with his tractor, eight men fired on him from 30 m away. He jumped off the tractor and rolled out of the way of the cutting knife. The tractor curved away and stopped against a tree. Chris was shot three times and died that evening on his way to hospital. He was a former deacon of the Dutch Reformed Church.

Two neighbours, Jopie and Sok, were killed in December 1977 when they were ambushed on their return from Umtali and stripped of their belongings.

A white woman living alone was the last to leave the western section of Cashel. She endured two house attacks and an ambush which she

---

*Tennis shoes.

drove through with her damaged car and then walked 8 km to a neighbour and safety. She never packed to leave and the Police almost had to remove her by force for her own sake.

An elder of the church who was fencing his land prayed to his Heavenly Father during a brutal ordeal with a gang of men, led by one with an AK who stole his clothing, food and gun and boasted that he and his pals had killed many Europeans. The church elder was eventually allowed to go free after a day of threats and violence.

Visitors to all these glorious parts of the country have always envied the residents the sunshine and the servants. There has been much shadow between the sunshine, and workers are fewer and less trusted than in former times. Households are adapting to many changes and villagers who once fled from the area are returning to re-build homes and gardens after years of neglect.

22 *Shadows fall at Melsetter*

"How blessed is the man that walketh not in the counsel of the ungodly"
PSALM 1:1

On Saturday evening, July 4, 1964, Mr Petrus Oberholzer, his wife Johanna Elizabeth and their little daughter, aged three, were driving in their kombi from Umtali to their home at Silverstreams, Melsetter, where he worked for The Wattle Company.

The road curves through mountains and winds its way along valleys and over river bridges. Fear did not stalk the highways then. Motorists drove freely in a friendly atmosphere through all parts of the country. No one, not even the Police, carried arms.

Three-quarters of the way home, at Biriwiri, 30 km from Melsetter, the Oberholzers saw large rocks across the road, blocking the way. Mr Oberholzer stopped and got out to remove the obstruction and was met with a hail of stones. As he tried to climb back into the vehicle a man ran up and stabbed him, again and again. Somehow he managed to climb back into the vehicle.

"Then," Mrs Oberholzer said afterwards, "they threw petrol over us." She pleaded with her husband to drive on. Somehow, with failing strength, he crashed the kombi over the rocks. A short distance further on the vehicle overturned.

The attackers returned, smashed the windscreen and again tried to set fire to the kombi. They threw matches to set the petrol alight, but there was too much blood ... only the dry grass burned.

The providential arrival of a car saved the mother and daughter, as the killers ran off. Mr Oberholzer was dead.

This was the first terrorist attack in the country and herald of things to come.

Petrus Oberholzer was murdered because he had a white skin. His killers were a ZANU group, known as the 'Crocodile Group'. Notes were found making their purpose plain ... 'Crocodile Group will kill all white men in Zimbabwe. Confrontation.'

In the manhunt that followed, two of the gang of four were subsequently caught, tried and hanged. A third man was later arrested and imprisoned.

In years to come the horror of that night of murder was to be repeated many times in the Melsetter district. Looking back it is obvious that the shadows of war were even then beginning to fall on a lovely land.

In August 1964 the ZANU president issued a circular telling his people to prepare to fight in the event of UDI; to withdraw money from banks, refuse to pay taxes, take children out of schools, store up food and prepare their weapons... During that same period the Government confirmed that saboteurs trained in Red China had infiltrated the country.

The scene changes to another Saturday, 13 years later.

In the tiny, beautiful mountain village of Melsetter it began as just another ordinary Saturday. Like others when there was no farmers' meeting and no Women's Institute, everyone gossiped in the Post Office, the butchery and bakery or at the kiosk next to the garage while they waited for the farmer to bring the milk.

But that particular Saturday, October 1, 1977, soon turned into a nightmare as the news went round of the death of two Forestry Commission employees, Claude and Bradley. They had been killed the evening before when the motorcycle they were riding was ambushed in Tarka Forest.

This double tragedy, the day after the ghastly murder of a 6½-month-old white baby, bayoneted to death on the verandah of her parents' home on an estate between Melsetter and Chipinga, left the people feeling stunned and sick. No one's heart was in their gardening or game of bowls that afternoon.

That evening, soon after the 19h45 radio news bulletin and the official communique confirming the two Melsetter deaths, the telephone rang.

"Please pray," said the woman's voice. "We're terribly worried about the Viljoens. They haven't got home yet."

How do you explain the feelings that sweep over you at such a message: the heavy heart, the sinking feeling in the stomach? The prayers of one fearful human being seem so inadequate. But you get down on your knees and pray. Then telephone a minister in Salisbury, a friend of the couple in danger, and ask for more prayer support.

"Lord please ... no more horror. We can't take any more, Lord, we're weak and frightened."

Between the prayers more telephone calls. How can one think about going to bed until there is news, one way or another?

Finally it comes. Ken and Ann Viljoen were ambushed about two kilometres from their house on Crystal Creek Farm as they were driving home from a visit to their son. The gang that killed the couple also burned down their farmhouse. Neighbours saw the glow from the burning building and gave the alarm.

They were well-loved residents of the district, and their deaths finally brought home to everyone the grim fact that war had come to Melsetter. Death could be lurking anywhere: in the vast pine forests that clothed the hillsides; on the pretty, winding country roads; in an orchard, a coffee plantation, the cattle kraal or on your own doorstep.

Sunday brought more drama. It was decided to evacuate the white staff of Rusitu Mission – a big school, hospital, Bible school and bookshop complex in Ngorima Tribal Trust Land, close to the Mozambique border.

Billets were hastily arranged and, tired and tense, the two men and three women missionaries of the Africa Evangelical Fellowship were driven into the village under armed escort. They had been given 2½ hours in which to pack up and move out, but this undoubtedly saved their lives. Lorries brought their personal possessions, mission records and other property into Melsetter later that week and storage space had to be found for all this.

Terrorists had been infiltrating Ngorima since early 1976, building up their 'safe areas'* and undermining authority as they did so. Schools, unsupervised because of the dangers involved in visiting them, were used for Communist indoctrination purposes and as terrorist training camps.

The only Government 'presence' in Ngorima was a handful of District Assistants at a protected base. They were armed (with .303 rifles), but they had no vehicles.

Travelling in the Tribal Trust Lands in unprotected vehicles was highly dangerous, but no suitable vehicles were available (due to economic shortages under sanctions imposed against Rhodesia by the West), and Internal Affairs ceased effective patrolling of these areas. The shortage of staff forced the closure of the Ngorima base; another at Chikukwa (bordering the Chimanimani National Park) was dismantled and both Tribal Trust Lands were abandoned by Internal Affairs. Patrolling in the Muusha and Mutambara Tribal Trust Lands was so infrequent as to be virtually ineffective.

Melsetter itself and the farming and forest areas were thus surrounded by vast tracts of what came to be called 'terrorist territory'.

There are only three roads out of Melsetter. One, the scenic route to Cashel, running along the Mozambique border most of the way, is gravel-surfaced and, at that time, was highly suspect. The second, branching off at Skyline, connects with the Chipinga-Birchenough

---

*Villages intimidated into feeding and housing terrorists and not reporting their presence.

Bridge road at Waterfall outside Chipinga; and the third, also from Skyline, travels through Muusha Tribal Trust Land, part of the Cashel farming area and Mutambara Tribal Trust Land to connect with the main Umtali-Birchenough Bridge road at Wengesi. Both these roads are tarmacadam.

Thrice-weekly convoys for civilian cars were started in November 1976, run by the Melsetter Police Reserve. Initially, when the Police were short of both men and vehicles, Internal Affairs helped with the escort.

At the convoy assembly point in Umtali near the Teachers' College it was the convoy commander's duty to brief newcomers on convoy rules:

- The convoy will travel at a safe speed. The speed will be governed by the speed of the slowest vehicle which will be the first civilian vehicle in the convoy.
- At all times distances between vehicles must be maintained. Care must be taken not to bunch up or overextend. A minimum distance of 100 m and a maximum distance of 200 m is to be maintained.
- No vehicle is permitted to leave its allotted position, except where a vehicle is branching off onto a side road.
- Should there be a vehicle breakdown the convoy will stop with distances maintained and maximum alertness exercised by all concerned. Should the vehicle in question not be immediately repairable, then it will be abandoned with or without its passengers.
- It is most important to maintain distances. If you bunch up you are an easy collective target. You will not be left behind. There is an escort vehicle behind you.
- If your vehicle is fired upon then drive as fast as you can on the tarred surface out of the 'killing zone'. Do not leave the road. Do not stop. Drivers do not return fire but concentrate on getting the vehicle away from the immediate scene.
- If a vehicle or vehicles in front of you is fired at, stop, get out and get under cover in the ditch, behind a bush, etc. Do not mill around in the middle of the road trying to see what is happening! Stay put until the convoy commander gives further instructions. The road must be left clear for the rear escort to come up to the scene.
- Those who have driven through the area concerned should stop

1,5 km or so further on to reassemble the convoy. Give assistance where required.

- Should it be necessary to stop and take cover do *not* indulge in indiscriminate firing. Should you see a terrorist, then fire, but do not fire just for the sake of it. (The escort may mistake you for a target, or, unbeknown to you, the escort might have taken to the bush.)

Drivers were told to use their rear-view mirrors and make sure that the vehicle behind was following. If it stopped, so did everyone else. If it fell too far behind the vehicle in front had to slow down. The trouble was, not everyone kept to the rules. An unsuspecting driver might find himself all alone, the front of the convoy having disappeared and the rear stopped out of sight round one of the many corners. What to do – keep on ... stop ... reverse?

Then there were the 'togetherness drivers', the chaps who sat on your tail, a couple of meters behind, for the whole journey.

Besides the official rules, motorists had other things to remember too. "Keep clear of cow 'pats'," they were told at security briefings. "Watch out for patches in the tar. These could hide mines. Look out for stones in the road, or heaped beside it. If you are travelling through a Tribal Trust Land and see no activity be extra alert. The terrorists are there."

Drivers were told to keep their fuel tanks full in case the convoy had to go the long way round (via Chipinga) because of blown bridges; and to carry medical packs and water in their vehicles.

Large convoys at the beginning and end of school terms were guarded by extra escorts and sometimes a spotter plane as well.

The Melsetter convoy eventually gained a reputation for being quite a 'hairy' one because there were so many ideal ambush sites. One section was called ambush alley and everyone was geared up for it. The attacks were usually made there. The convoy was attacked a number of times, and although several civilians were injured, no one was killed. The convoys continued until April 1980.

When they stopped, Melsetter folk felt they had lost an old friend. The convoy provided an invaluable public service. People could get urgent medicines quickly, obtain spare parts for machinery, send items for mending, have money banked, letters posted and find lifts. They brought out newspapers and shopping and carried people, parcels and produce into Umtali.

Only a handful of stores were still in business, in Melsetter village and on the big estates. Others had closed because they were constantly robbed or were shut by Martial Law order as they were being used by terrorists to obtain clothing or to store weapons and ammunition.

Late one night in 1977 a woman living near the Melsetter Post Office was woken by the sound of her dogs barking frantically at the bottom of the garden. Then came the rattle of automatic fire. Thinking an attack had begun she rolled out of bed and crawled to the 'safe area'* in the passage nearby, waiting with pounding heart for the next burst. But nothing came.

Next morning it was discovered that the firing came from an armed group 'persuading' the manager of a general dealer's shop two doors away to open up. They virtually cleared the stock of clothing and blankets, which were carried across the Mozambique border. One of the bullets gouged a Post Office letterbox door; others hit the wall of a block of bedrooms at the Chimanimani Hotel. This was the second robbery at the same store, which closed soon afterwards.

Near the end of October that same year more firing was heard in the village early one evening.

Marge tells the story: "Soon after closing my shop I drove home. I had an African employee in the car with me. I was near the garage (her house stands on a large wooded plot on the outskirts of the village) when four men stepped into the drive, pointed guns at me and ordered me to stop."

They demanded her keys. Then the men, all young, interrogated Marge, who is a widow, asking her where she was born and similar questions. They spoke in English.

"I prayed," she said. "I asked God's help to say the right thing, to give the correct replies."

After what seemed like hours of questioning, Marge managed to distract their attention and run. Inside the house, she slammed the door and sounded her warning siren. Then she fired at the men. The noise roused the village, and the men fled with the Security Forces after them. The intruders took her keys with them.

Brigadier Tom Davison paid public tribute to Marge's presence of mind when he visited Melsetter to address residents later that week.

A Police Reserve stick went on follow-up operations towards the border where the magnificent Chimanimani mountains tower like a rampart. But a golden summer's day soon turned dark as the news went round the village the next day of the death of three of the Reservists,

---

*Safe because surrounded by walls and reinforced by sandbags or timber.

Peter Hanson, manager of Charleswood Estate; Harrald Holstenburg and Robin Hunt, both employed at Charter. The date was October 20, 1977, and eight people had been killed in 21 days.

Melsetter knew the chips were down. In this deadly gamble one error, relaxation of vigilance for a moment, could mean death.

The Civil Defence Committee, chaired by the District Commissioner, with representatives from various parts of the district including Cashel, held a special meeting to review the situation.

It was believed that in some cases the terrorists had been after pay, and it was suggested that employers should try to make alternative arrangements for pay. The memory of the payroll robbery at Skyline only two years before was very fresh. It was the start of the shooting war in Melsetter and resulted in the death of Field Reservist Colin Young. He was killed on the Ndima Road when a Police Reserve stick set up a road check point in response to a call to try to stop the armed men who had held up a mobile bank at Skyline, where Mike, the orchard manager, was waiting to collect Gwendingwe wages. The vehicle stopped and the African tellers opened the cash box at the back. As Mike turned to return to his own vehicle an armed man stepped from behind some scrub and opened fire. In the first burst Mike fell, wounded. The tellers and Mike's two Alsatians were also wounded.

The robber approached Mike, said: "You're not dead yet," and fired another shot through his shoulder. He took the wages, then returned to the bank vehicle, shot the locks off the boxes, packed thousands of dollars into haversacks and made off into the bush with his assistant.

Mike crawled to his car, somehow climbed in, and blood flowing from wounds in his stomach and shoulder, drove down the mountainside to Charter office and raised the alarm. The entire Police Reserve in Melsetter was called up as it was believed the robber would probably make for the Mozambique border.

Colin Young's death on April 29, 1975, was No 1 on the Melsetter Roll of Honour. Field Reservist Hunt's on October 20, 1977, was No 15. Three Cashel men were killed in December and the year drew to an end with the loss of Lt. Mark Langeman on the border serving with the Army.

By this time *agric-alert* testing was being done daily at 06h00. On estates and farms there was never any peace from the continual radio, *agric-alert* and telephone, and always some worry. Comms* became part of everyday life.

---

*Communications

Attention also turned to protective measures, such as the Adams grenade* for homestead protection and various home-made cannons that could be fitted to civilian vehicles. Martin, the District Commissioner, made up little pieces of piping as cannons, packed them with black powder and shot, and wired them so that the driver could press a button in his vehicle and fire either side.

Because people were being ambushed and killed or blown up by land mines, vehicles took on all sorts of strange 'new looks' as they were armoured, bullet- and mineproofed. The heavy armour plating on Land Rover doors made them very difficult to open, and the weight pulled the unwary out of the vehicle when they opened the door.

There was also the problem of living in a fenced area all the time, of being locked in, having to be extra careful about keys and remembering to close gates.

Clinics were told that they must keep bulk stocks of medicine in secure places, while an urgent request went in for 'Bright Lights' to guard those most vulnerable. The estates were told that they should consider setting up some form of militia.

The Civil Defence Committee had a key role in Melsetter from 1976 to the end of the war.

At its monthly meetings reports on the security situation were given by JOC representatives from Chipinga (Army, Special Branch and Police details). Zone leaders were told of the incidents that had occurred, which groups of terrorists were involved and the number of Communist terrorists known to have infiltrated each area.

Over the months definite patterns appeared. To be told that a certain group was in the farming area or operating on an estate meant *trouble* and very often a run of deaths in ambushes or homestead attacks.

It was the duty of zone leaders to tell the people living in their areas what was going on and be the link, through the Civil Defence Committee, between residents and JOC. Fine in theory, but the system didn't always work and then the fur flew at a subsequent meeting.

This happened after the Viljoen murders, when Denis, brother-in-law of the dead couple, and a coffee farmer in the Nyahodi valley, slammed the 'co-operation' that had neglected to tell one of his neighbours, as well as the Member-in-Charge of Melsetter Police and the District Commissioner, that a curfew had been imposed in a particular area. As someone said bitterly: "If a Police Reserve patrol unknowingly had gone into that curfew area..."

---

*Explosive device detonated by the householder.

It was incidents like these and the lame excuses put forward to explain away the slip-ups that made people angry. Melsetter's isolation and the tension under which people lived – there was always some part of the district on orange or red alert* – reinforced the feeling that they had been forgotten by the rest of the country. And people came out with their grouses, as a certain Brigadier from Thrasher, several politicians and others well remember after meetings they held in Melsetter.

Towards the end of 1977 a small executive was set up to receive complaints and suggestions so that concerted action could be taken instead of various people pulling strings independently – often in opposite directions. Some felt that this committee was usurping the functions of the Civil Defence Committee, but, as the District Commissioner explained, the object was to have closer liaison between the Police, Army, Internal Affairs and Civil Defence.

This was the nucleus of the Area Co-ordinating Committee which came into being some months later, despite official opposition. It was the first ACC in the country. Denis was appointed the Co-ordinator for Melsetter district on June 10, 1978. He and his wife, Pene, had moved from their coffee farm into a rented house in the village. As Area Co-ordinator, Denis reigned from a new control room hastily built at the Police Camp, but the job was no sinecure. He had to try to sort out problems at local level; receive moans, suggestions and requests; calm the nervous, smooth ruffled feathers, and always produce the goods – whether it was escorts for the RMS† lorry or local ambulance, protective screens for windows, grants for militia, walkie-talkie radios or booby traps.

In 1978, in a determined effort to drive farmers from their land, the terrorists tried to cut the lines of communication by making the main road to Umtali unusable.

Innumerable attacks were made on heavy transport vehicles. Many were burnt (12 in December 1977, nine in April 1978), so heavy vehicle convoys were introduced. They travelled via Chipinga, adding greatly to the cost, but without these convoys Melsetter would have been cut off from essential supplies, including fuel. At the same time all bus services stopped. Commercial travellers stopped coming and deliveries by some companies ceased. Even ministers of religion no longer came

---

*The alerts were: *Orange* – be prepared, an incident has occurred; *red* – full alert, subversive elements in the area; *black* – specific area is target of insurgent forces; *green* – return to normal.
†(Railway) Road Motor Service.

to Melsetter. The place had a name for being 'unhealthy' and people just weren't prepared to take the risk. But this was difficult for the locals to swallow. Melsetter folk felt that they were staying and playing a part, putting up with hardship, while others were not prepared even to visit.

Melsetter supplies the biggest percentage of sawn timber to meet the country's needs and that timber had to be kept moving. The Government and the Security Forces could not provide special convoys for the timber lorries so Border Timbers recruited its own mercenary force. They were all heavily armed with machine guns and it was quite a sight to see the six big lorries with their 20 tonne loads of timber leaving Charter every morning and evening. The convoys were attacked a number of times but these 'hot run' drivers always got through. Some were wounded. Later some joined the estate staff. They were even able to laugh about some of the incidents, blown-up bridges or rocket and machine gun attacks on them. They were quite remarkable men.

Statistics for four years of war in Melsetter tell their own grim story. European family units on estates in 1976 totalled 150 and on farms 45. In 1978 the numbers were 62 on estates and eight on farms. A total of 35 whites were killed in the four years (15 in 1977 and 13 in 1978). Reported black deaths totalled 119. Numerous others were not reported. At the height of the war in 1978, 24 homesteads and 68 vehicles were destroyed (the totals for the four years were 28 homes and 89 vehicles). From 1976 to 1979 there were 662 terrorist attacks, 144 vehicle ambushes, 105 landmines and 317 other incidents, while a total of 2 746 head of stock was stolen.

The total number of incidents in 1978 was the third highest for any part of the country. Melsetter is only a small district so it is obvious that the terrorists made a concerted effort to stop it functioning. They almost succeeded.

The chairman of the Melsetter Landowners' and Farmers' Association, reporting on the security situation in 1978 said: "... it appears that if Communist terrorists want to get a particular person, there is not much chance of them failing ... they appear to have lost no confidence in their ability to operate successfully.

"The manpower situation appears to be deteriorating further in that Bright Lights are becoming fewer – it should be noted that if there are no Bright Lights for the school there is a strong possibility of parents keeping their children away.

"Apart from actual murders, incidents such as the destruction of Tarka Sawmill reduce our European population still further by reason of consequential transfers.

"There has been no success against terrorists... while we are well aware of the virtual impossibility of preventing this type of situation arising with our current resources and the difficulties of eradicating infiltration, once achieved, it must be emphasised that the degree of risk to rural dwellers and their families is now at an unacceptable level."

And the secretary of a Government ministry wrote to another ministry: "Conditions of living in the whole of the Melsetter-Chipinga area have deteriorated to such an extent through the activities of terrorists that many of the residents are losing heart and leaving the district.

"Already out of 25 names on a directional notice board on one of the crossroads near Melsetter, 22 have left and the three remaining stalwarts are in two minds about staying on. The attitude of mind of the people is governed by the extraordinary success which terrorists have in the area. Farm houses have been attacked and burnt down, deaths have occurred in family after family either through these attacks or in ambushes while travelling to and from their farms. Convoys are no longer safe..."

As one man put it: "We've had all sorts of people here – the Air Force, RLI, the Selous Scouts, SAS, dogs – and all of them accepted that conditions favoured the opposition more than the Security Forces."

23 *The cost of survival*

Therefore get wisdom: and with all thy getting get understanding.

PROVERBS IV:7

The fact that Melsetter managed to survive was mainly due to the large forestry companies remaining in production (though in the middle of 1978 two of the major estates had no labourers at all). This was done at great cost – security fencing, militia, protected vehicles, radios and the special timber convoys to Umtali.

"Working conditions were very difficult," said one estate manager. "It was difficult for the labourers. They were intimidated constantly. The opposition forces visited the compounds at night and were fed at the point of a gun. Usually they went out with the workers in the morning and when far enough away told them to abandon the vehicle. It was then set alight by firing shots, and occasionally rockets, at the fuel tank.

"We lost a tremendous amount of equipment, tractors and lorries, flatdecks and power saws. Thousands of dollars worth were lost. The labourers were intimidated and did not know which way to turn. We fenced off villages and compounds but foremen and bossboys were shot and company houses burnt down."

Sometimes there were quick, fleeting contacts in the forests when the foresters ran into the terrorists by surprise. Sometimes foresters were ambushed and got away with it. On other occasions they did not.

Fire towers are part of the normal life of a forestry estate and are usually manned. When a fire is first sighted it is reported and bearings are given.

"Without realising it, the fire tower lookout on several occasions reported fires which we in the Police Reserve realised came from a particular farm," the estate manager said. "When we got the bearing we realised what it meant. Things like that made it very difficult for people in Melsetter, particularly people living in the forest."

If there were contacts between the Security Forces and the terrorists, or when they attacked a homestead, fires usually started and the forester would have to put them out.

"It was very, very difficult because more often than not the labourers were terrified. They didn't want to go out to a fire without weapons when they could hear the sound of rockets and mortars and the thudding of AK's but we had some very brave chaps who put out fires," he said.

At one estate a terrorist leader, unbeknown to the forestry staff, had been killed and was lying in the grass surrounded by rockets, hand grenades and other paraphernalia. Flames were all around. "We put them out and next morning discovered the body and realised what would have happened if the flames had caught up with all the ammunition and hand grenades lying around him." Another forester recalled the day one of the estate drivers came into his office 'looking like a zombie'. I said, 'What's the matter?' and he replied, 'My entire family has been killed – my wife and five children.' It was a landmine blast involving the Security Forces. They thought they had run into an ambush and in the ensuing firing the family had all been killed.

Eventually the terrorists began to think the fire towers were too valuable to the estates and not only reported fires but also their presence in an area. This did not happen, but they believed so, because whenever there was a fire there was an immediate reaction, and the reaction was usually accompanied by an Army or PR stick.

At last the terrorists went to the fire towers and said 'Out' to the people manning them. "In the last few years we had to bring in complete outsiders and offer them a large wage just to sit in the towers, but it paid off because we were able to keep the towers manned," the manager said.

An estate manager tells of an interview he was having with a man who wanted a job in the Melsetter area. "As I was talking to him a message came through that a group of terrorists had passed within 100 to 200 metres of our house. I leapt to my feet and asked the man if he could use an FN and we tore off to try to intercept the group. I left him and went to see if my wife was all right. Then I had a report that there was a fire. A different group of terrorists had started a fire by shooting at some of our guards. I did not have to tell that man how bad the security situation was and he actually took the job – whether it was because he enjoyed the adventure of the interview, I never really found out."

Mid-1978, Civil Defence told Melsetter residents that as the level of terrorist activity remained high they must keep arms and ammunition readily available at all times; practise regularly with firearms; keep emergency petrol available; check first-aid kits, torches, emergency lighting and fire extinguishers; rehearse home attack drills with children; check emergency food and water supplies; brief and drill visitors; leave the last bath water in the bath with a plastic bucket nearby; and never to follow a rigid pattern because routine can kill. Farmers were already accustomed to keeping two days' food, clothing and bedding and their vital documents at hand, in case of sudden evacuation.

And still the deaths continued. Rifleman Johannes Vorster was killed with the Army in January, Chris was shot on his farm at Cashel in April and Herbert, of Lemon Kop, was ambushed 12 days later. On May 15, Charles Olivey was killed by a landmine. Charles received a message to say that his home on Sawerombi West had been partially burnt down and he was given special leave from the Army to go back and see the extent of the damage. He called at the Police Camp to pick up one of his employees who was being interrogated, with others, by the SB.* Charles asked if he could take the one man with him, and off they drove. Charles drove his car to the spot where he always parked. A landmine had been planted there and Charles died. His employee died beside him. When the remaining employees were told of the deaths they said: "That was very foolish. He was the one who told the terrorists it was the best place to put the landmine because the boss always parked in that place."

On June 6, 1978, a group of 102 terrorists, with a great variety of weapons, made a determined attack on the Melsetter Police Camp.

At Charter Estate, John and Marigold were watching a World War II documentary on the TV. There were sounds of gunfire. John sprang to his feet and rushed outside and Marigold asked what was the matter. "Melsetter's under attack," he replied. "No, it's the TV," Marigold said. But when they switched off the sounds were in Melsetter.

A village resident recalls that she had just made a hot drink and was walking back to the lounge to listen to the 22h00 news when she heard distant 'thunder'.

"I remember thinking 'that's odd, thunder in June', when I heard the sound of smallarms fire and realised we were being attacked.

"I put the lights off and ran to the safe area in the passage – still carrying the drink – and lay down with my weapons, first-aid case, a rucksack containing spare kit, and two frightened dogs, waiting for the bullets and bombs to come. And all the time a man's voice went on and on, monotonously. I had forgotten to switch off the radio!"

A house on a hilltop overlooking the Police Camp, occupied by Johnnie and Sheelagh, was rocketted and damaged, but no one was hurt. The couple had been blown up by a landmine at their farm not long before and had moved into the village, only to be attacked there.

---

*Special Branch.

The incident however, led to the establishment of a more or less permanent Army presence in the area. Before that the Army came and went and had very little success, unlike the Support Unit operating in Mutambara Tribal Trust Land, which was much more successful. It was transferred soon after, however.

Six more Melsetter residents were murdered before the end of 1978. Eugene Swanepoel and Jeanette Douglas were ambushed on August 22 while driving back to the village from the sawmill at Rocklands where they had been inspecting a new house. The manager of Charleswood Estate, Robert Leslie Smallman, was shot coming into the village early on the morning of September 11. This was followed, two days later, by the deaths of two old and well-loved residents of the district, Jim and Helen Syme. They were murdered in their rambling, thatched farmhouse on Deysbrook, which was then set alight. Jim had had a distinguished career with the Colonial Office in West Africa before coming to Rhodesia to farm. He was an Oxford rowing blue and his oar had pride of place in their lounge.

Once again the little stone church of St George-in-the-Mountains, built under the direction of John Olivey who served with distinction in the Long Range Desert Group in World War II, was packed for their funeral.

There had been so many funerals in Melsetter in the past 12 months that people were almost getting used to them, a situation that prompted one man to say that Melsetter cemetery had more people in it than the village!

On October 4, Guy Walton, a former Colonel in the Royal Marines, was murdered at Stronachavie, a remote farm overlooking the Rusitu valley, where he had lived alone. Many efforts had been made to get him to move to somewhere safer, but he refused to leave his home.

In August, James Black, a Forestry Commission employee, was abducted from Martin Forest and taken into Mozambique.

By the end of 1978, terrorist forces were in virtual control of all the Tribal Trust Lands. In the farming areas heavy casualties had been suffered and the major forestry companies were almost at a standstill. Melsetter and Cashel Rural Councils were unable to carry out road maintenance in the farming areas. Only a handful of farmers remained at Cashel, with all the white farmers gone from the land bordering the Melsetter-Cashel main road. Chiefs Ngorima and Muusha had left their areas to live in Umtali and Melsetter respectively, while Chief Ndima had been killed by crossfire in a contact.

Typical of the nightmarish situation was the extraordinary thing that

228

happened on Charter Estate. At the beginning of one week one or two black men started asking if they could leave because they wanted 'to build a new hut'. The second day the one or two became 10 or 20.

"We were suddenly aware that there was complete panic or else massive intimidation had got at our labour force," said one of the estate staff.

"By Saturday Charter Estate had been drained of 700 to 800 employees, their wives and children. Entire villages were quite deserted. Dogs had never been allowed on the estates, so there were no stray dogs, but there were cats wandering round with no food. An uncanny silence settled over the place.

"At night white staff were extra careful. We were apprehensive and wondered what was going to happen to us. Everyone had gone. We heard birds and other sounds during the day that one never normally heard. Every machine in the carpenter's shop and the sawmill was stopped because there were no workers.

"But the estate team saw this as just another challenge. The whites took over the jobs that needed to be done, like manning the office switchboard. We all took turns. You had a man who might normally be a section manager or forester becoming a telephone operator. The accountant made the tea."

The exodus began in the last week of September and by October, the height of the fire season, there was no one left on the estate.

The timber convoys to Umtali were kept running. Near Charter sawmill there are great storage sheds, all packed with timber, and when the lorries came in they were loaded by electric cranes, operated by the staff. The estate manager was one of them. If there were fires the foresters drove the fire tenders. And there were fires, started by vehicles being set alight.

To keep people busy the white team got together in the central area of Charter and built themselves a swimming pool. The front end loader dug the hole and everyone offloaded the lorries carrying the building materials.

After three months the labourers started drifting back, looking very sheepish.

"In retrospect it was a blessing in disguise, for when the men started to come back we were able to sort the sheep from the goats."

In September 1979 came a new tactic to close down the area. This was the starting of forest fires. In the first few years of the war the terrorists valued the forests and did not set fire to them because they thought they would inherit the timber. But in the last months fires were deliberately lit. They were very serious (showing that the terrorists were now under stress from Security Forces).

The whole of Gwendingwe was set alight one night. The fire was put out over a 24-hour period with very little loss, but all forms of fire-fighting had to be used, including aircraft.

A week later Charter was set alight, starting with Zaaiplaats, and then over the hill to neighbouring Thornton.

"We went out to the fire in the morning and the place was a raging inferno. It took two days to put out. We had everyone helping – the District Commissioner, National Parks, our neighbours and aircraft giving us progress reports," said the Charter manager.

Up to that time firefighters had been going out at night, but in this instance they had been warned – and there was truth in the warning – that the fires were being set to get firefighters trapped where the opposition could wipe them out.

"Sending in civilians to put out a fire, knowing that if they went in they were going to be shot, was not a decision I was prepared to take," he said. "So we let the fire burn for the remaining hours of darkness. By the time dawn broke the extent of the fire which had been lit made it a major disaster in the area. We lost half of Thornton Forest Estate." Altogether 5 000 ha of timber was burnt.

Undoubtedly one of the highlights of those years was the coming of television. After many promises and long delays, the new TV mast to serve Melsetter and Chipinga was finally erected on Gwendingwe, the highest point in the district. People went shopping for sets and aerials and the village switched on to civilisation.

Although the programmes and the reception weren't all that good, those who could receive TV had lots of laughs. They also felt that at long last someone had acknowledged that Melsetter existed!

For those in the hollows who couldn't receive TV, there was still the radio, with the Voice of Zimbabwe from Maputo coming over loud and clear to add interest to the listening, or the BBC, Radio South Africa and a host of other overseas stations all clearer and easier to pick up than Salisbury.

The spirit of the people was remarkable and visitors couldn't help noticing it. Salisbury people said they came to Melsetter to get rid of their depression. "Coming here is a tonic, it bucks you up," they said.

The success of the fire-fighting operations however, highlighted the very close co-operation between the forest companies, Intaff, Police and the ACC, in controlling what could have been a disastrous situation.

At this stage it was apparent that the local populace was thoroughly fed up with the war. The tribesmen could help neither side, for fear of retaliation from the other side. Due to lack of transport and the closing of stores there was no trade, and people were living from hand to mouth. Black employees on farms and estates lived in constant fear of attacks and ambushes and also had to hand over some of their wages to the terrorists for 'protection'. Measures such as 'Operation Turkey', the curfew and martial law regulations affected everyone's daily life. Farms and estates were functioning, but making virtually no profit, machinery and equipment was run down and there were insufficient tradesmen available. Little wonder then that people longed for peace.

However, people laughed and grew closer together in adversity and most were determined not to give up. The Women's Institute, the Garden Club, MOTHs and the farmers' association continued to meet, although the numbers dwindled. An art and craft club remained active; there were hobbies exhibitions, flower shows, slide shows and first-aid demonstrations and practices. On the open days tea and lunch was provided by the W.I. and these became popular social gatherings for the whole community.

Visiting speakers, brought by convoy, talked on a number of interesting subjects. However, one intrepid speaker, from Rusape, often travelled alone to garden club meetings in Umtali, Odzi, Chipinga, Melsetter and Inyanga. She had a dummy soldier in the passenger seat of her car. 'He' was made of pillows, wore camouflage uniform and hat, and had a realistic 'gun' sticking out of his window. It was made from a broom handle. "It's very important to keep garden clubs going," Dorfie used to say – "it keeps up morale – and I'm fine with my 'soldier escort'!"

---

*Women's Institute.

24 Evil comes to Chipinga

Here, in a large and a sunlit land,
I will lay my hand in my neighbour's hand,
Here will we join against our foes.

RUDYARD KIPLING

The order came early in 1976. "Set up a radio control room. The war has started in Chipinga!" It was January 31 and the first landmine incident had occurred on Jersey Tea Estate near the Mozambique border.

Ernest, a leading citizen, worked with hardly a break for 58 hours until he had organised an efficient centre. Rosters were arranged and 24-hour watches were started on the Police radios and *agric-alert* systems. By February 3 every farmer had been told that terrorists had infiltrated into Chipinga district and that the *agric-alert* was ready for people to make immediate contact with the Police in emergency.

It was difficult to believe that the beautiful rolling, grassy hills, the tree-covered gwashas*, the orderly plantations of tea and coffee bushes could hide troublemakers. Born in the area, part of the soil, Chipinga residents had never before felt the need for firearms. Suddenly the whole atmosphere changed – evil had crept in.

Botha and Charlotte set off one evening to visit friends with their three sons. Near their homestead was a grid with 30 cattle standing in front of it. How were they to know the animals had been driven there for a purpose? As Botha slowed down, a shot rang out. A bullet hit his left front wheel, flattening the tyre, but he bumped on over the grid. How was he to know that waiting in the ditch ahead were 11 armed men spread at regular intervals over 73 m, their AK's aimed at the car?

Bullets whizzed around the family, shattering glass, thudding into metal. The 21-month-old baby had a bullet through his bottom. Charlotte had seven bullets through her legs. The car radiator was hit and water poured out. Botha forced the car on for another three kilometres before it ground to a halt. Two bullets had just missed his head, hitting the roof. Both front windows were smashed. Luckily they were now only 180 m from Botha's brother's house so Botha was able to run for help, while Charlotte, wounded, waited with her children, expecting the attackers to appear at any moment.

---

*Thicket of trees in the fold of a hill.

She and her baby were flown to Salisbury later and it was a miracle that the family survived, as 330 spent cartridges were picked up. One bullet penetrated the boot of the car, burying itself in a suitcase and stopping against a copy of the New Testament.

This was the first terrorist ambush in the district – the war had started in earnest for Chipinga. The date – March 6, 1976.

Three months later Louis and his wife were driving in the Lusitu Valley, 32 km from Chipinga with three daughters and a friend, Shirley. The four girls were enjoying an outing from school. Just beyond Lusitu bridge the car hit a landmine. Two of the girls were blown high into a tree 27 m away. One remained caught there while the other fell right through. Both were killed. Louis' wife's neck was broken and she died instantly. Two weeks later the third girl died in hospital. Shirley lost both her legs.

What was gained by laying landmines indiscriminately and killing innocent schoolgirls?

Landmines were also killing African civilians. Claude had a fleet of African passenger buses operating throughout the district. The first bus-landmine incident was in 1976. Another five were blown up during the following years. How many black passengers were killed or injured?

Buses in fact became somewhat unpopular. After one bus had been held up by terrorists, then burnt, and another hi-jacked into Mozambique, Claude found his business deteriorating. The cost of repairing the damage was crippling, the Government was not able to pay out sufficient (if any) compensation, and the cost of fuel was rising steadily. But he kept four or five buses on the roads throughout the war years.

The cabs were sandbagged but in spite of this one driver was shot. The pattern was for several armed men to hold up a bus at gunpoint, order the passengers out, then force the driver and conductor to hand over the cash. If the driver refused he risked being shot. Often the bus would be set alight and the passengers sent home on foot or made to walk across the border to become 'freedom fighters'.

"My drivers showed great courage," said Claude. "Without them, the bus service could not have continued."

His business included haulage and here too he lost heavily. Two vital vehicles were blown up by landmines and one was held up and burnt. But goods transport kept going and Claude's vehicles played an essential part in keeping commerce, industry and farming viable in Chipinga.

Country stores were burnt and robbed, and storekeepers killed and abducted. Storeowners like Hans and Ernest lost stock frequently for they could not afford to erect security fences, lights, alarms and screens on all the stores. Each owner concentrated on one or two which were stoutly guarded and protected.

Care had to be taken when installing automatic protective devices so they could not be set off inadvertently by customers. One of Ernest's stores had lights, alarms, screens, sirens and a double fence with mines laid between. With any less protection it would have been impossible to keep the store open. Black storekeepers also needed courage to remain in business.

Kathleen and Fred required a special brand of courage too. They lived at the small post beyond Mount Selinda on the Mozambique border where Fred was the Customs and Immigration official and where there were only three other houses.

This small post was attacked six or seven times. The attacks were mainly during daylight, so Fred coped, with two Bright Lights and a PR stick, while Kathleen was at work. She became accustomed to extra men around for meals. "Sometimes there were 12 sleeping in the house."

As district nurse for a local tea estate, Kathleen visited Jersey, Zona, Ratelshoek and New Year's Gift estates, spending a day at each, with morning clinics and afternoon homecraft clubs for black employees. She organised annual shows with prizes for classes in cooking, sewing, embroidery, knitting and crochet.

Medical attention for the Africans was free on the estates and Kathleen held Well-baby clinics with vaccinations and injections against smallpox, diphtheria, TB and polio, plus free ante- and post-natal care.

In June the border post was closed and they went to live in Chipinga, but Frelimo gave them a parting shot.

"Fred had gone ahead with the office papers and I was left to see all our belongings onto the lorry. Everything was on the lawn waiting to be loaded when – bang! A Frelimo rocket landed close by, then another and another. 'Just let me get my things away safely!' I shouted angrily, more concerned about the furniture than anything else. Several rockets landed, but missed."

Kathleen continued her nursing duties, driving over dangerous roads from Chipinga. She went over a landmine twice without detonating it while on a journey to attend to African children whose legs had been blown up by anti-personnel mines placed by the terrorists between the tea-bushes for the pickers. The mine was detonated later that day by an Army vehicle.

The District Commissioner arranged for Kathleen to have an escort and the company provided a white mine-proofed Land Rover with a

Kathleen with her mine-proofed Landrover ambulance at the scene of a Chipinga landmine blast.

red cross. "On the advice of friends and for my own safety I tried altering my rigid timetable but my black patients had to know when to expect me for their various treatments so I returned to the usual times and days."

Her quiet courage and devotion to duty, as well as the enthusiastic part she played in all Chipinga activities, were rewarded in 1979 when she received the MSM.*

"For us the war started in 1974 with hit-and-run attacks and thefts of cattle," said a young Chipinga widow from a border farm. "Our labourers were always in danger and were attacked frequently, especially when bush-clearing to make firebreaks on our boundaries."

Gradually her whole lifestyle changed. Security Force personnel came to camp near her home. With typical Rhodesian hospitality she welcomed them all, dispensing meals and providing hot baths. "Once there were 59 men living around us. It was a constant mealtime with nightly queues waiting to 'phone their wives, many of whom came to stay too.

"We had two small children and when my third was due I dreaded going into labour in front of all these men! Chipinga Hospital was

---

*Meritorious Service Medal.

kilometres away and my husband could not have taken me in by night, risking landmines and ambushes.

"Some of the troopies became good friends and many were real characters. One used his FN like a guitar and sang to the others. A crowd camped near the sawmill and one day, on a visit, one came rushing out to tell my husband not to bring me along. They were gambling, using clothes as forfeits and quite a few were in the 'all-together'."

Last stop Chipinga! One of the convoy escort vehicles ready to leave Umtali on the two hour drive to Chipinga.

One night she was alone while her husband went on the track of stock thieves.

"I was stepping into the bath when there was a loud explosion. I didn't know whether to carry on, get dressed, run, or what! I draped a towel round and ran to look out at the back – nothing. So I ran to the front – still nothing. Perhaps the men had a contact and the noise was the firing. The waiting was terrible. I heard men shouting my name and

236

just knew my husband was hurt. They called me again so I ran to open the gates. By now I was in my nightie and pulled a gown round me.

"Is my husband hurt?"

"Sorry ma'am. We shouldn't have frightened you. No, he's O.K. We've had a contact. Can you drive us to the main road to meet the Police?"

"With my sleeping babies in the car, I drove them to the main road. The worst part was driving home alone and letting myself in at the security gates with only my .22 pistol – and I knew terrorists lay in wait at the gates as well as laying landmines there too.

"Most Sundays we were fired on in our garden and had to race indoors. The children were marvellous. They just packed up their toys and came in.

"My husband was fixing up the dip kraal on the next farm one day when his labourers shouted at him. 'Boss! You're being fired at!' On the bulldozer he couldn't hear a thing. He just carried on till he felt bullets zooming past his nose and looking round, saw all his workers on the ground. He had to leave the 'dozer and run downhill to the tractor. The labourers jumped on the trailer and by the time he got them to safety their black faces were grey with fear. Troops came to guard him so that he could finish the job, even though terrorists crept up close and fired rockets at him. One burst very near to us and we still have the pieces. At cattle dipping, one of us counted the stock while the other stood guard with the gun.

"Tsetse Control sent labourers to cut a firebreak. They were fired at constantly from across the border and refused to continue. Rhodesian Air Force men were guarding the labourers then, so my husband suggested that he and they should blacken their hands and faces, dress up in overalls and take guns and ammunition to work, as well as hoes. The Air Force agreed and they went out early to work on the firebreak till 10h00. The first shots were fired. They hoed on till more terrorists appeared. Then the 'labourers' threw down their hoes, picked up their guns and a full scale war went on for three hours with Security Forces joining in. After this the Tsetse Control unit finished the firebreak without trouble."

Then came the terrible day she and her three small sons will never forget.

"My husband was working in the sawmill. I'd gone past with a friend and waved to him to come up for mid-morning tea. He nodded, but never came. He didn't come for lunch either but I thought he must be busy elsewhere as I could no longer hear him in the mill. In the afternoon some black women came, screaming and crying.

"'Whatever's the matter?' I cried, rushing out.

"'Lo boss! Lo boss!' they sobbed, tearing their hair and their clothes.

"'What's wrong? Where's the boss?' I shouted, fear gripping me. I thought 'He's been working on the bulldozer and it's fallen on him. I must run and get him out. Perhaps he's badly hurt...'

"I tried to ask the women, using my hands wildly as my knowledge of their language failed. But they howled and cried, 'Lo boss ena efeli' – 'The boss is dead!'

"'No. He's just hurt. I must get him out!' I rushed inside for a gun. Then I thought: 'Maybe it's a terrorist trap? How can I leave the babies? They might be in danger – yet I must go and help my husband.'

"Then people came and told me my husband was dead. He had been killed by terrorists soon after I'd seen him at the sawmill. His body was found lying there – so near the house ... and I never knew. The shots must have been drowned by the noise of the mill and the sound of my friend's Land Rover. I could feel myself losing consciousness, so I walked down the passage banging my arms against the walls to keep myself from fainting. My arms were black and blue for days afterwards. But I was determined to stay on the farm for his sake.

"One night I was alone with the baby and two African guards when terrorists attacked. A Chipinga man heard my *agric-alert* report and came immediately with Army personnel as he knew the way.

"The children and I stayed for seven months after this, sometimes on our own, sometimes with the Bright Lights or two African guards. In the end the Security Forces urged me to leave and said I was being selfish, endangering men's lives to protect me. They asked me to sign a paper taking responsibility for my children's lives but I did not feel able to do this, so I had to move into Chipinga and find a job."

This young woman's experience was typical of the tactics used to drive white farmers off their land. Farming operations in Chipinga depend largely on hand labour so the terrorists did their best to frighten workers away as well.

"Three of my foremen were abducted and killed near our house," said Jack. "We found two skeletons after the war ended. The third was beaten to death with sticks in the African quarters. I went to the compound early one morning to ask where he was but nobody knew. I went to his house and found his battered body, covered with a blanket. Everyone in the compound must have heard the killing, yet nobody reported it. His wife and children were sitting weeping. No one came to

238

comfort or help them, or help me move the body. They were terrified. These head workers who were killed had been outspoken in their anti-terrorist views."

Jack and his wife Elaine had lived on their farm which adjoins Mutema Tribal Trust Land for more than 20 years. Besides the theft of many livestock, the murder of their foremen and the loss of labourers, they also suffered the abduction of many key workers which disrupted progress on their irrigated crops. Meat was stolen from their butchery in daylight hours. One day, a letter wrapped round an AK bullet was found on the verandah of the butchery. No one would touch it, except Jack, to whom it was addressed.

The letter, well written and in good English, asked him to join the terrorists and pay a certain sum each month. He was to reply via the housemaid. Later it was found she had been secretly feeding the terrorists.

A second letter said the consequences would be fatal if he did not pay up. A detailed list of all farm activities giving exact times and places showed how closely the terrorists had been watching them and their Bright Lights. "We know all your movements. We have the topography of your farm too. If you want to stay, you must pay, and then you can have your farm after the war."

The third letter gave Jack three days in which to get rid of the Bright Lights, Guard Force and any other Security Force on the farm. If he did not do so, he would suffer the consequences on the third day. Jack reported this, as he had the others, and on the third day Security Forces in helicopters saw the band of terrorists approach the farm. Although surrounded and fired on the group escaped, to return in revenge on January 6, 1977.

It was 20h45 and a lovely, cloudless night. Jack and Elaine remarked on the beauty of the rising moon as they played bridge with Jack's parents. It had been bright moonlight when a neighbouring store had been burnt down.

This night there was no sound or shadow to warn them that 14 terrorists were creeping up to their firing positions. Suddenly a rocket hit a tree outside with an earsplitting explosion. A window shattered. The Bright Light standing on the verandah was knocked down by the blast. The house was bombarded with rockets, mortars and smallarms fire, all from one side. The wires of the electric generator were cut and the homestead damaged. While the other three had dropped their bridge cards to scatter over the sitting-room floor at the sounds, Jack's

239

mother still held her hand of 13 cards intact two hours later! No one was injured, although that night three dairy cows were killed.

Fences were cut, reservoirs damaged, cattle stolen, workers killed, abducted and threatened, yet still Jack and Elaine carried on, and Jack's parents, both over 80, stayed with them, while a nephew, Roy, arrived to assist.

Two months later Roy was badly injured by a landmine explosion at the homestead gate. After he returned to the farm from hospital he was ambushed. Fifteen terrorists were waiting for Roy when he was told people wanted to buy tomatoes. They wounded him badly in several places. He feigned death and was conscious of them stripping off his watch and other valuables. Then came the sound of a tractor. The terrorists fled and Roy was helped to the house. Dr Bob, who was indefatigable in his hospital and district duties, arrived in record time to save Roy's life but Jack's father was so shocked he had a stroke and died shortly afterwards. The labourers who had lied about the tomato trick fled from the farm.

"They returned to work for me after the war," Jack said. "We bear them no grudge. They were terrified. As they say themselves, what could they do? If they had not obeyed the terrorists and had warned Roy, they and their families would have been killed."

Ambushes, attacks and incidents escalated throughout 1977, '78 and '79 in the Chipinga area. It is impossible to mention them all.

Grace and John, however, survived two attacks uninjured. "It wasn't that we were brave staying on," Grace said. "We couldn't leave. We had no other income and nowhere to go. The loneliness was the hardest to bear. We rarely saw anyone and could never have stuck it out without 'phone calls from friends and the *agric-alert*. Listening all the time for unusual sounds, we found the TV saved our lives. We would watch programmes and take it in turns to get some sleep. When we went to Chipinga I dreaded the journeys home. Our home, desecrated by the attacks, the protective walls and fences, was no longer the happy home where our children had grown up. I loved the troopies who came – black or white, whatever rank, I treated them all alike to a big stew and they'd help me wash up afterwards. We had no electricity, only gas and candles.

"We made friends with our Bright Lights and have kept in touch with five of them."

Many Chipinga residents and farmers had miraculous escapes and attributed their protection to the saving power of prayer.

Hendrik and his mother somehow managed to drive through an

ambush when attacked by 14 terrorists near their home. Louis and his wife were shot at in their home three times in three months; once 400 armour-piercing bullets hit the house – ten minutes of hell, they said, but neither was hurt.

Marius was driving to the milking shed when four blacks in blue denims rose up from behind stones in a small graveyard and wounded him in three places, shooting six metres from the truck, but Marius and his injured black workers ran to safety.

Phil and Lynn had 250 armour-piercing bullets riddle their house as well as rockets and grenades. Three bullets stopped short of the sleeping baby's cot.

Some families seemed to suffer a string of tragedies. Olive, who lived on a remote farm, lost her son, Ken, her husband who was ill and shocked, then her daughter, Rosemary, (at Odzi) by a landmine. Terrorist action killed eight of her relatives.

Cois and Ceylonia also suffered endless tragedy. It began in April 1978 when Ceylonia's sister, Elsabe, told them of her husband's death at Mutambara, attacked while driving his tractor on the lands. Cois had an escape during a landmine incident with the Police Reserve. Then in August the family went for a picnic, but only 400 metres from the house ran into an ambush – bullets, rockets, dust and incredible noise. Ceylonia's prayers to God to save them were answered.

Cois and Ceylonia carried on at their farm but Elsabe moved to Umtali. Later Elsabe was killed on holiday in a car accident and Ceylonia took over her sister's children.

January 1979 was the worst month of all when many terrible events happened in the district. Herman was killed taking milk to town. Two men in an Army reaction stick were killed the same day by a landmine.

Ceylonia was alone on the farm while Cois was out with the Police Reserve, and had to get the children to school in Umtali. She had an awful feeling of impending tragedy. Her father-in-law sent a mine-protected vehicle to fetch them but she kept thinking of landmines – and then they hit one! It was a miracle that anyone survived. The body of the vehicle was so crushed there was hardly any space left inside for a human being. Ceylonia and her young niece, Erina, were badly injured.

"I heard the explosion," Cois said, "and knew it was a landmine – and my family. 'No, it can't be, man. We'll find out just now on the radio,' said my PR mates to cheer me up. But I was certain.

"I thank God that the Army medic who went to the scene was a Christian. The children were trapped and it seemed impossible to extricate them but he prayed to God for help and miraculously he was able to get them out. Two medics, one Army doctor, Dr Bob and 50 people rushed to the scene. Three ambulances took them all to Chipinga and Ceylonia and Erina were flown to Salisbury.

"It was hours later that I was able to get to my family. Erina's head was badly injured and took a long time to heal. Ceylonia lost both her heels. She was in hospital for seven months and is still suffering. I had to make decisions – should we stay on the farm? Should we visit Ceylonia in hospital or not? This was made worse when we heard that a woman in her ward, injured in ambush, had just lost her husband, killed in a convoy on his way to visit her in hospital – but when Ceylonia came home we decided to stay and carry on."

The same gang which planted that landmine and killed Herman also ambushed and killed the Chipinga vet's wife and their daughter as well as Will, who was bringing milk to town.

Throughout all this Cois and Ceylonia said their black Guard Force men were 'tremendous'. "We could not have stayed without them."

Dr Bob, mentioned previously, was also wonderful, always willing to travel at a terrific pace when needed, whatever the risk, to save a life. He earned the MSM for bravery and devotion to duty. At Chipinga Hospital he and his staff cared for hundreds of wounded forces and civilians. Even terrorists passed through their healing hands.

The Dutch Reformed Church dominee travelled extensively over dangerous roads to cover his large parish. Once he came across five burnt-out lorries and a burning bus on one trip round Chipinga, Melsetter, Cashel and Umtali, and back. In January 1980 three ambushes occurred in one day on one road – and he missed all three. The dominee saw the Protected Villages as an opportunity to present Christianity to larger numbers of the rural population, now gathered together. He sent two black lay preachers to sell Bibles in the Protected Villages where they would be safe, guarded by District Security Assistants and Guard Force men. But they were confronted at a previous night's stop by 40 men armed with AK's and long knives, and kicked and beaten and warned not to try to promote Christianity.

Many Chipinga farmers are descendants of Pioneers who trekked up from the south to this area of beautiful mountainous land. Less than a century ago they came in a slow haul, dragging their wagons over uncharted rough terrain through rivers and over mountain passes to work in the heat and heavy rain to establish farms. There are still some living here who were born on the treks or who travelled as babes in arms.

Pat's mother was 12 when she walked beside an ox-wagon all the way to Rhodesia in 1893. Pat remembers it once took three months to get to Umtali for school – waiting for flooded rivers to subside. Chipinga folk are like the mountains, symbols of strength and steadfastness.

Pat's wife, Molly, was also born in Rhodesia. Hardworking and well-loved by the community, they are good Christian people, working quietly and devotedly in a dozen different ways, their hearts and the doors of their home open to all. Pat received two awards for his services, the Police Reserve Long Service Medal and the MSM for devotion to duty and exemplary conduct.

The Chipinga spirit also expressed itself in a light-hearted way with 'The Scaredy Cats' society, brainchild of Maureen.

"You can't 'phone folk to tell them how brave you think they are," she said. "The farmers were wonderful, and their wives especially so. While the men were away the women kept the places going, looked after the children, and drove to school over dangerous roads. They lived behind fences constantly wondering when the next attack would come, the next ambush or landmine, killing whom? They'd all been touched by tragedy."

To show their admiration the girls decided to offer them something to laugh about and their 'gaggle of hags' was born. They borrowed a five tonne truck and tied a piano on the back, stabilised with sandbags. With their piano, accordion, banjo, ukelele, guitar and drum tambourine for musical sound, Maureen made up words to fit well-known songs, making fun of all, including celebrities, in topical fashion.

"We even laughed at heads of states and the tunes were so well known that all could join in. Programmes and copies were provided and we took the shows to the farmers."

The first show was such a success they were joined by the farmer's wife who entertained the first crowd and then went on to visit other farms on subsequent Sundays.

"We packed into the truck and started playing right away. I wonder how many terrorists stood at the roadside to watch us go by? We were well known but never ambushed," said Maureen. "We refused escorts, took no collections or petrol coupons and our shows were free."

'The Scaredy Cats' called their Sunday entertainment 'Mad Hatters' Tea Parties' and each had a special name and matching hat. Kathleen, Tilly, Sarie, Yvonne, Maureen, Marion, Eve, Chris, Iris and Daphne, with their comical headgear, were irrepressible.

'Mabel' was a highlight, 'the semanjemanje' African woman who talked 'veree good English'. She blackened her skin, wore a wig and appeared unexpectedly, unrehearsed and unbeknown to the producer, in the middle of one of the shows – and brought the house down. Daphne became a permanent member of the cast and very few, if any, guessed that 'Mabel' was not really a black girl. In fact an African foreman watching the show lost his heart to 'Mabel' and wrote her a loveletter!

'The Scaredy Cats' were invited to Bikita, Enkeldoorn, Mid Sabi and Melsetter. They refused to appear on TV but went to Salisbury under the auspices of Rotary. They staged an ambitious 'Refugee Corral' at Chipinga Farmers' Hall which was the alleged venue for Rhodesian refugees, decorated with scenes depicting 'the Yellow Route' and 'The Owl and Chicken Runs'. It was obvious that Chipinga might be the refuge for all and guests were invited to arrive in what they were wearing when the emergency arose.

"The whole show was a laugh at the idea of Rhodesians ever becoming refugees." They collected $800 for St Giles Rehabilitation Centre.

Dave and Tilly were another couple who worked selflessly for the community. Dave received his MLM* as chairman of the Rural Council and Chipinga Area Co-ordinating Committee. "I received it on behalf of the people of Chipinga," he said. Dave did wonderful work on the School Advisory Board, the library, as president of Chipinga Rotary and as a member of the Police Reserve and Ground Coverage unit.

In 1979 the new Rural Council offices were built to show confidence in Chipinga progress. Dave also initiated an extensive security road system which contributed to the high morale maintained by farmers in the face of such adversity.

Michael, a Rural Council employee, was awarded an MSM for his courageous work on these roads, especially the reconstruction of the Jersey road to tarmacadam surface as protection against mines.

Tilly took Cubs throughout the war. "It was moving to teach these little ones whose news was so often of a bomb in their lounge or a relative killed or wounded. They were never able to enjoy camping or roaming in the bush like their elder brothers. Only once I risked a camp-fire at night, with three fathers guarding with guns."

Chipinga is a small centre and most people relied on Umtali for business, shopping and schooling, so the Chipinga convoy came into being. It was quite a social occasion. Anyone wanting a lift would be lucky at 07h00, when the cars gathered on the main road. It was the only occasion when villagers could meet the farmers because they no longer

---

*Member of the Legion of Merit.

244

travelled at night. Chipinga convoy linked up with Fort Victoria and Umtali convoys at Birchenough Bridge and people brought sandwiches and flasks to share while waiting.

The villagers opened their homes to farmers from the bush and people were drawn together with warm-hearted generosity.

The children of Chipinga were as courageous as their parents. They were on their way home from Umtali for the Christmas holidays in 1977 and the school bus, driven by Cois, was full of happy youngsters when a group of terrorists attacked.

The children were marvellous. They just baled out and lay in a ditch till it was all over. The convoy commander had asked for air cover so Police Reserve Air Wing planes soon arrived. They dropped rockets and a battle ensued. The parents were not told in case they worried unnecessarily at the time, so when the convoy arrived safely, astonished mothers accosted their mud-covered children angrily: "Why so dirty? What *have* you been doing?"

"We've been attacked! We've been in an ambush!" were the excited replies and the children were delighted to see parental anger swiftly replaced by loving concern.

Drivers in convoy had some nasty moments. Once a line of 16 cars was rounding a corner at Chipinga's 'ambush alley' when groups of terrorists lying hidden along a kilometre distance of road opened up. The last vehicle was the Police truck with revolving gun turret on the back. The young policeman was killed but a soldier, taking a lift in a private car, jumped out and ran back to take the dead man's place. Four people were wounded but no others were killed.

Fiona had the hair on top of her head parted with a bullet. Her scalp was grazed and blood poured down her face. Far from fainting or screaming and ducking, Fiona was angry and carried on firing her small pistol out of the car window.

Angela was hit in the leg but carried on driving the 34 km to Mid Sabi. Jane had a bullet hit her tyre but carried on for 2 km until she was out of the ambush area. She calmly changed her wheel, helped by an African lorry driver. Then she drove on to Chipinga without fuss.

Wendy was another brave girl attacked with her family in the Fort Victoria convoy. When they reached home there was no glass intact in their vehicle. They were quite calm, as were so many others over the years.

Perhaps the spirit of Chipinga can best be summed up by the man in a hurry to get on with his work who drove right through an ambush.

"Dammit," he thought. "I've driven through and quite forgotten to fire those new anti-ambush devices that I had fitted," so he turned round and drove straight back into the ambush area, let off his guns and grenades and killed five of his would-be murderers!

Whether this is a true story or not, it's typical of Chipinga to tell it.

25 Aftermath

A time to kill, and a time to heal;
A time to tear down, and a time to build up.
A time to weep, and a time to laugh;
A time to mourn, and a time to dance.
A time to throw stones, and a time to gather stones;
A time to embrace, and a time to shun embracing.
A time to search, and a time to give up as lost;
A time to keep, and a time to throw away.
A time to tear apart, and a time to sew together;
A time to be silent, and a time to speak.
A time to love, and a time to hate;
A time for war, and a time for peace.

ECCLESIASTES 3

Wars end but their effects linger on. Only time can erase the scars and dim the memories. The Rhodesian struggle is over, but the coming of peace did not bring a miraculous healing of the wounds of war. There are still people, broken in mind, body and spirit, needing rehabilitation.

Tsanga Lodge was a rehabilitation centre for wounded servicemen.

Situated 2 195 m up in the Inyanga mountains beyond Troutbeck, Tsanga, in the 1970's, was used to accommodate groups of school-children attending nature conservation courses. Then, when the war developed and it was no longer considered safe to continue the courses, it was decided to turn Tsanga Lodge into a convalescent centre for wounded servicemen sufficiently mended not to require further regular hospital treatment but unready physically or psychologically to be flung back into the full swing of society.

A retired Army Medical Corps man, Dick, was asked to run it and he and his wife, Anne, agreed.

Tsanga Lodge, in its new role, was officially opened in October 1976 and everyone, from generals to floorsweepers, was there. Although this was an Army establishment, Dick felt strongly that any regimented type of atmosphere would be detrimental to the recovery of an individual's self-confidence or self-motivation, so the official opening reflected the tone of Tsanga throughout the years. All ranks, ages and stages were subtly 'conned' into taking part in a not too strenuous cross-country run as the first item on the agenda. Each participant was handed a map of the route on which was marked 'watering holes'. These resuscitation points were considerately stocked with alcoholic as well as non-alcoholic refreshments to encourage the less dedicated ones. This innovation made some of the 'runners' take as long as three hours to complete the 2 km course!

The festivities over, Dick and Anne settled down to the task in hand – helping men and youths to recover not only their strength, but also to accept realistically their problems which, for some of the more seriously wounded, meant reconciling themselves to a radical change from their previous occupations or ways of life. Dick and Anne lavished parental care and concern on the endless variety of individuals sent to them.

Into the four little stone and wood chalets, taking a maximum of 16 patients at a time, were welcomed old and young, black and white, the rough with the smooth.

On arrival each patient was issued with a warm Tsanga track suit (a dull cherry colour with a gold stripe on sleeve and leg) and joined the motley family. Adding to the domestic atmosphere were Dick and Anne's four enormous Great Danes, who always gave the impression of being everywhere. One Sunday one of the dogs, aptly named Nuisance, ambled into the Recreation Hall where a church service was in progress. He silently padded up behind the unsuspecting visiting pianist and plonked his large head affectionately in her lap. To her eternal credit she carried on playing, hardly faltering, but the congregation did not take it so calmly.

The 'family' was further extended with the arrival of six former Grey Scouts' horses. When these animals were not being used to give patients rides around the countryside they wandered at random in the grounds. Anne's dulcet tones could frequently be heard as she bellowed at them to move off the flowerbeds she was battling to establish. On several occasions a grey, called Trigger, had to be firmly escorted from the Recreation Hall, where he was enjoying the cosy warmth of a crackling log fire.

The emphasis at Tsanga was on physical fitness. "Fitness may not add years to your life, but it definitely adds life to your years," it was said. Dick, with the loyal helpers he'd attracted, worked untiringly in the gym, encouraging patients to do far more than they ever believed was possible. And everything at Tsanga had its lighter moments, a fact that undoubtedly contributed extensively towards the phenomenal successes achieved. Typical was the time one of the shyer patients, studiously pulling himself up on the horizontal bar in the gym one morn-

248

ing, suddenly found himself hanging helpless with his shorts fallen down around his ankles.

The altitude of the place, with its invigorating effect, together with Dick's enthusiasm, pushed most mobile patients into taking part in a 06h00 walk, run or hobble – often a frosty or misty one at that hour – always on hilly, rough roads. Tales of resultant casualties were greeted not with sympathy but hilarity. Dick, with his outrageous sense of humour ("Do your big dogs like children?" "Oh yes, medium rare") and natural ability to entertain, could unmaliciously transform all potentially depressing or frustrating incidents into a comedy half-hour for all, including the patient concerned. In this way the patient learned to laugh at himself, thus taking a big first step towards acceptance of his often badly mutilated body.

Such an approach is infectious. This was shown when one of the patients went skinny dipping in the little dam just out of view of the lawn where all the patients relax. Some fellow patients whipped away the swimmer's clothes, then joined the others on the lawn to await their naked man. Soon his head and shoulders appeared over the slope – from the waist down he was modestly covered by an old cardboard box!

Another incident which amused everyone, though it could have had a nasty ending, was when some high-ranking officers were visiting Tsanga (they did this often) and joined the staff and patients for a meal. A colonel collected his plate of lunch (all officers graciously accepted that they were simply part of the family when they visited) and sat down at a table beside a patient with brain damage.

He introduced himself as Colonel, to which the patient replied: "As far as I'm concerned all colonels are bloody idiots." After a brief, stunned silence the dining room relaxed again as the colonel gallantly rallied and agreed that it was probably a fair comment. Apart from the entertainment in the dining room the meals were superb. None of your Army dishes at Tsanga, Anne and her kitchen staff produced sumptuous meals which tempted even the poorest of eaters to enjoy their food.

The most popular spot between 17h00 and 19h00 was the attractive little pub called, undeservedly, 'The Athlete's Foot'. It had a revolting-looking toeless "takkie", with a horrible-looking plaster cast of a foot inside, mounted outside the door. All the day's traumas and events were laughed about and discussed, constructively or otherwise, as patients and staff relaxed together over a beer.

Patients like 'The Incredible Hulk' added to the entertainment. He was so named because he weighed 113 kg. A man with brain damage and consequent loss of balance, he carried on undaunted, crashing about alarmingly. One evening, getting up to leave the pub, he nose-dived onto a seated patient, sheering off the body of his beer tankard and leaving a rather bewildered man holding only the handle of his glass.

It was also in the pub, once a week, that the National Fitness Awards were presented with due ceremony and acclamation. Achieving the required standards for this award invariably meant very strenuous training and practice, as all standards were implicitly adhered to, with no concession granted because of injuries.

Then the war came to an end but Tsanga Lodge injuries did not automatically heal at the signing of a peace treaty. Many patients were injured, both during and after the war, in very bad vehicle accidents. So Dick and Anne stayed on for a time – but now Tsanga Lodge is no longer a rehabilitation centre for Rhodesian Security Forces.

The very word 'Rhodesia' is being wiped from memory. Books with 'Rhodesia' in their titles are frowned upon. In the schools, socialist ideals are taught, and there are already new history books being used in various grades – all teaching the wickedness of the white settlers and the glory of the new Communist revolution.

Rhodesians, black and white, who suffered and fought for the ideals of Christianity, free enterprise and democracy, have scattered. Some, as Christians, could not live in a Marxist state. Others found they could not live under the arrogant domination of people who, only yesterday, had been the enemy. For some, who stayed on hopefully, falling health and education standards finally proved the breaking point. Others again found it impossible to carry on farming or in business with the economy running down, talk of 'collectives', a chronic shortage of foreign exchange and hordes of people moving in to squat on the land.

So Rhodesians left, broken-hearted, bewildered, to scatter across the world. Some went to Canada, Britain or Australia, others to South Africa, New Zealand and Europe.

Bemused, unable to comprehend the fact that a political agreement, contracted overseas, had so suddenly taken their country from under their very feet when they were still fighting, Rhodesians packed up and left to try to start life again. The young – with scars of war on body and mind, bitter, resentful, confused – were brash and often encountered hostility and hardship as a result.

Older Rhodesians tried to settle down and make new friends and a new life in new environments and new jobs. Some found it near impossible and returned to Zimbabwe, sometimes to leave again. All found their lives irreparably disrupted.

Many black Rhodesians fled over the borders from their former enemies now in seats of Government – but refugees don't live an easy life in any country, and many were repatriated to face possible imprisonment, torture and death.

Many white Rhodesians have had to stay in Zimbabwe and make the best of it. The old couldn't leave to start again in a new country – they're not allowed to take out their capital so how would they live? Over 50's don't easily find jobs in new countries. The courage needed to stay on is not always fully appreciated. To see your country taken over by Marxists, hurts. To live with businesses closing, family after family leaving, the number of friends dwindling; to face, day by day, crude insults about 'white racist colonial oppressors' in the media and to have to compete with 'the masses' crowding into public places, shops, hotels, schools, flats and suburban homes, takes a very special kind of courage. And many are not only taking all this but are also holding their heads high. They openly stand up for the old Rhodesian principles – in spite of the fact that it is possible now to be arrested for the slightest criticism of the Government of Robert Mugabe.

Meanwhile thousands of black Rhodesians are bitterly learning what their 'vote' brought them.

The records and history, statues and memorials of the pioneers and builders of Rhodesia are being destroyed. In these pages is set down the courage, steadfastness and persistence of people of a small nation which fought alone against Communist aggression, constantly criticised by the West and suffering the effects of 16 years of economic sanctions. Only what is true has been recorded in the hope that there are still people in this world who want to know the truth – and have the courage to recognise it amid the cacophony of lies, propaganda and indoctrination that passes for news and history in the 1980's.

So where is Rhodesia now? Forgotten? Dead and buried like the many brave black and white soldiers, farmers, housewives and businessmen whose stories are told in these pages? No! Rhodesians will never forget those who died for their ideals and the spirit of Rhodesia, too, will live on – not in the laughable 'when-we' clubs – but in the hearts of the young. They will remember with pride the work that was done, the achievements which made a lovely, civilised, happy country rise out of wild bush in the heart of Africa.